Initially published in French as *Jeune Fille en Dior*
© Dargaud, 2013
All rights reserved
© 2015 NBM for the English translation
ISBN 978-1-56163-914-4
LC control number 2014956278
Translation by Joe Johnson
Lettering by Ortho
Book design by Philippe Ravon
Printed in China
Second printing May 2015
This book is also available digitally wherever e-books are sold.

Annie Goetzinger

Girl in
Dior

NANTIER • BEALL • MINOUSTCHINE
Publishing inc.
new york

Annie, without damaging anything.

La Demoiselle de la Légion d'honneur, Aurore, Casque d'or, La Diva et Le Kriegspiel, you can't imagine, Annie Goetzinger, to what extent those lives, those destinies, those novels that you told in images, which I discovered at a very young age, marked me.

You can't imagine and will never know, because I'm way too bashful to ever say so, but I know exactly how much I'm indebted to them. I owe to them my desire to tell my own stories.

Keeping quiet about it is proof of my debt.

I'm not losing sight of the story-writers of these works (Pierre Christin, Adela Turin), but without your talent, without your intelligence, without your artful attention to detail, to details, to the slightest details, without your lines, your faces, your shapes, your bodies, your dresses, your outfits, your hairdos, your scenes, your skies, your landscapes, without your love for your characters, without your high standards, without your generosity, without your femininity, your toughness, your lucidity, your rage, your elegance and your violence, without your calligraphy, without your layouts and your ever-sumptuous staging, I'd perhaps have long since forgotten all those stories... I've read so many.

I haven't forgotten them...and I just reread them now with the same passion. *La Demoiselle de la Légion d'honneur* in particular. It lays me bare each time...

One day, a long time ago, I said in an interview to what extent that "souvenir portrait" had counted for me, and on another day, much later, I received a letter.

Already, the writing on the envelope impressed me, and I went to look for a kitchen knife to open it without damaging anything. Inside, there was a page in the A4 paper format folded in three and, on that letter, was standing the young woman, that young woman, my young woman with her sad uniform, her white collar and her colored ribbon looking me squarely in the eyes and daring me: "Well, when I grow up, I'll read your books!"

Whoa.

No pressure.

But, you know, Annie, it wasn't the tribute paid or your sensitivity that so moved me that day, it was seeing my heroine smiling. That was the first time. The first time she'd shown a happy, cheerful, mischievous face. So different from the one I'd known at her age, dressed like that.

It was the only smile of her entire youth, and it was for me.

It was like she was alive. It was proof she was alive, proof that I was right to believe in the strength of fiction, of stories, of characters, to believe that characters invented by others can be, are, as strong, as real, as true and as present to our minds as those close to you.

It was proof I'd not been mistaken. Neither about life, nor belief, nor a role model.

What a lovely gift you gave to me.

For you know like me the price to pay for being able to offer oneself such convictions, don't you? Yes, you know. We've never met one another, or barely, a few minutes a few years ago in a gallery doing an exhibition of your work, but I'm guessing you know that price, too. And by heart. The doubts, the solitude, that kind of gentle schizophrenia that always keeps us a little too distant from others and too near to ourselves. That exhaustion.

I can never thank you enough for reminding me that day and in a single drawing that I'd not deceived myself about solitude, and I don't have anything else that's important to tell you today.

Sorry?

The preface?

Oh yeah, that's right. The preface…

Well uh…so that I could write it under the best possible conditions, your publisher (the same one as for *La Demoiselle*, moreover) sent me a set of this *Girl in Dior*, but…uh..I didn't read it. I couldn't. I didn't want to discover your work on photocopies, whether or not they were in color and printed front and back on an acceptable paper. I couldn't do that to you.

Or rather, I couldn't do that to myself.

So there, you'll discover this text at the same time as I discover your drawings, meaning, once the publisher has prettied us up, too, cinched us, bound us, made patterns of us, and dressed us to measure.

I hope you won't be mad at me.

Don't be mad at me. Annie, don't be mad at me. It's better this way.

Writing the preface to a story you've not read keeps you from saying stupid things about it and from risking spoiling the reader's pleasure.

And then, I don't like prefaces.

I never read them.

I accepted this one because it was the dreamt-of occasion to finally thank you. To thank you and to keep myself between you and the young, bashful, dreaming girl or the young, bashful, dreaming boy who, in a few years and thanks, in part, to you, thanks to this volume here, will have made her or his career in design and high fashion.

It's not a preface, it's a round. I'm keeping myself between you and those whom your talent will yet inspire, the relay runners of the *New Look* of tomorrow, and we will pass the batons.
I'm here, I'm here in my life, in the life that you helped me to choose, and I'm smiling stupidly.
I'm telling myself I'm lucky.

ANNA GAVALDA
Bestselling French author *(Hunting and Gathering)*

In a machine age, dressmaking is one of the last refuges of the human, the personal, the inimitable.

CHRISTIAN DIOR

At the time, neither I, nor anyone else, had ever been to 30 Avenue MONTAIGNE. People said that CHRISTIAN DIOR had wanted something "Louis XVI-1900" for his fashion house. A style that didn't exist really, except in his childhood memories between GRANVILLE in NORMANDY and PASSY in PARIS.

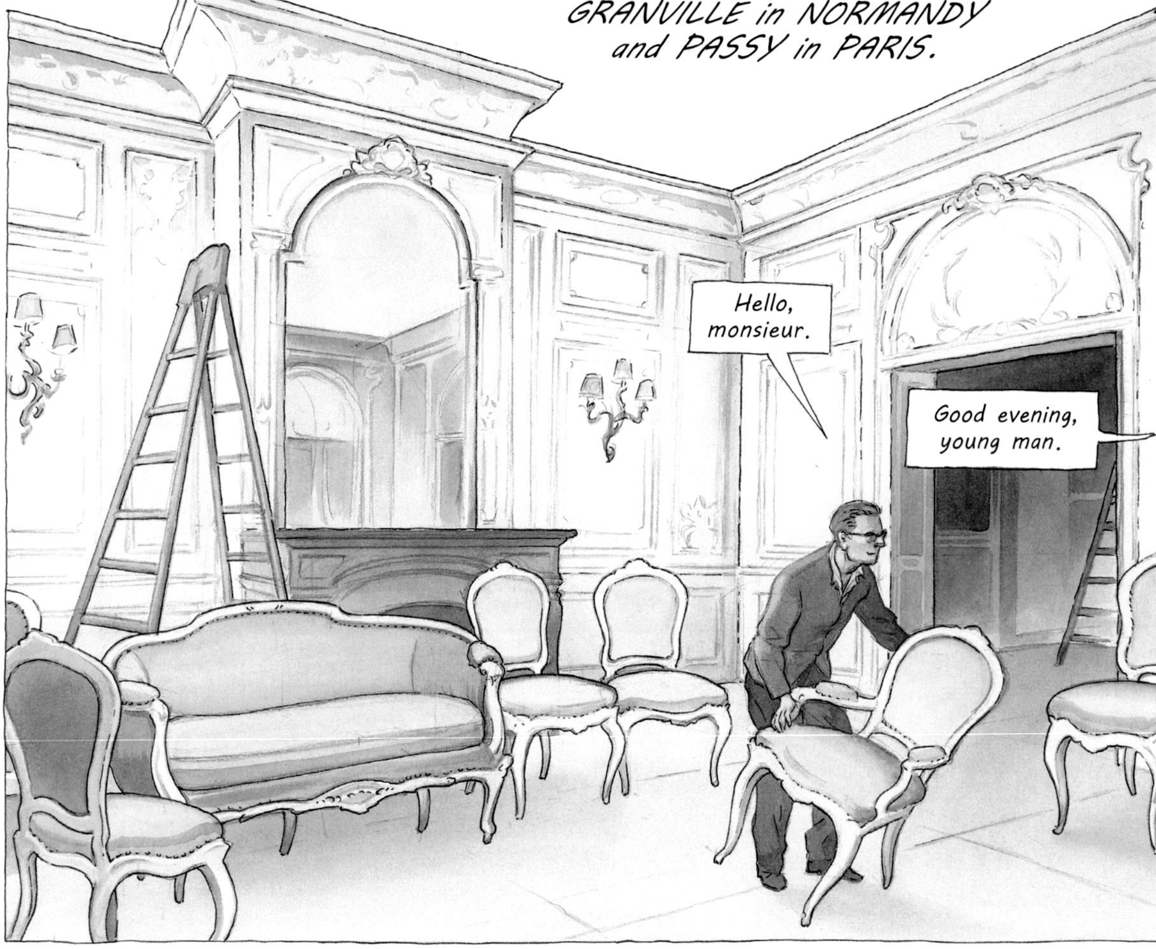
Hello, monsieur.
Good evening, young man.

White paneling, pearl gray satin, taffeta lampshades, and then some bouquets and kentia palms. I was expecting something chic and understated. I had no idea, as of yet, of the nocturnal effervescence on the eve of the very first fashion show.

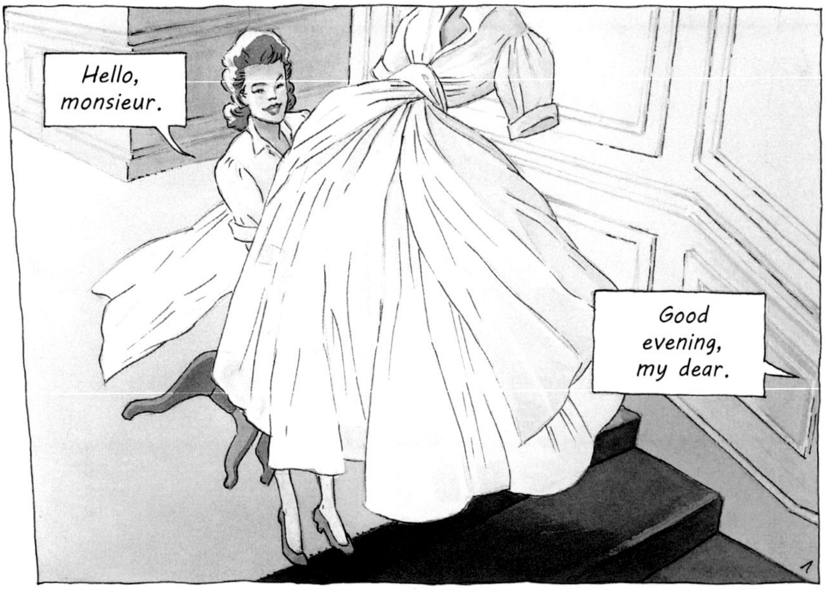
Hello, monsieur.
Good evening, my dear.

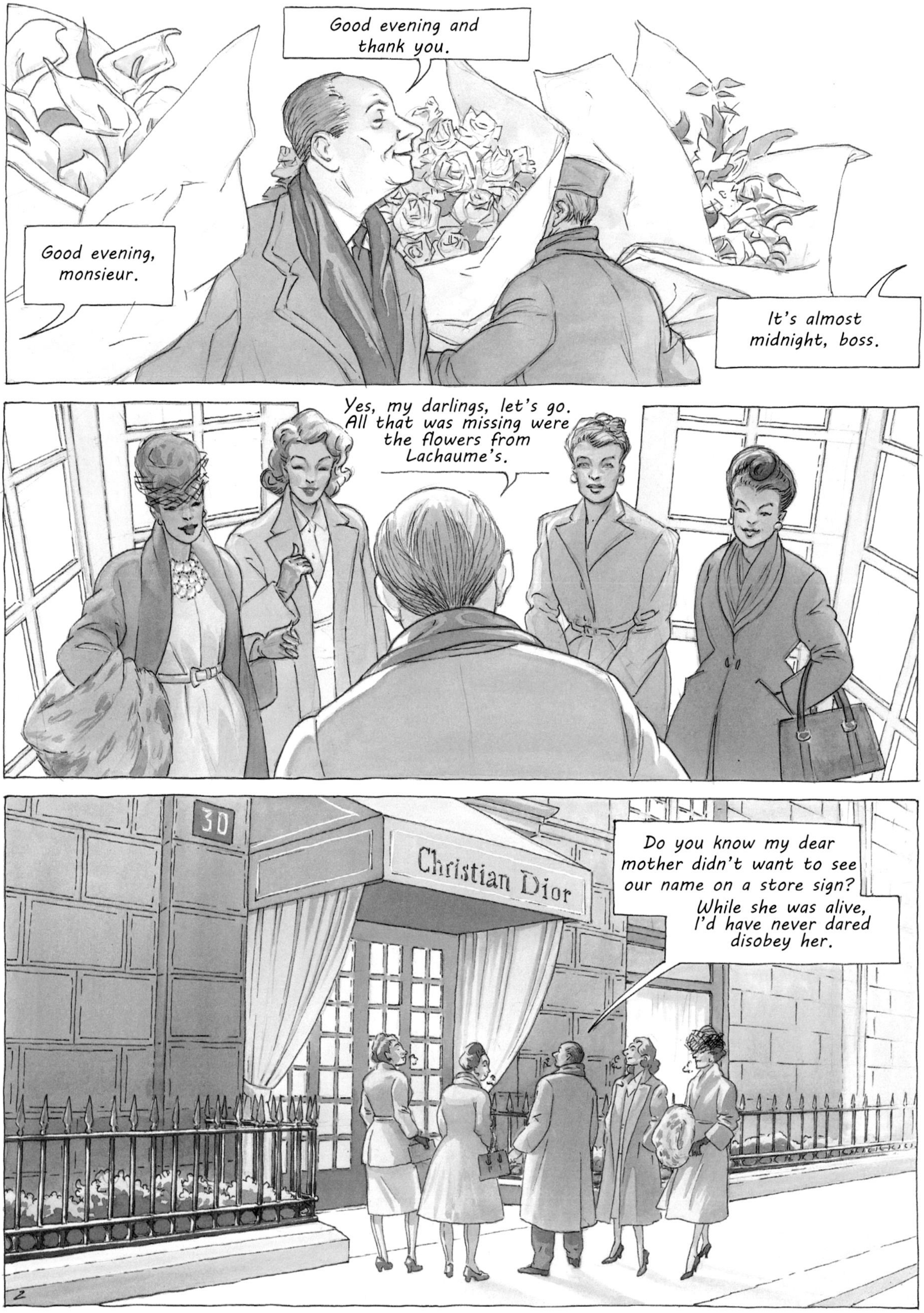
Good evening, monsieur.
Good evening and thank you.
It's almost midnight, boss.
Yes, my darlings, let's go. All that was missing were the flowers from Lachaume's.
30
Christian Dior
Do you know my dear mother didn't want to see our name on a store sign?
While she was alive, I'd have never dared disobey her.

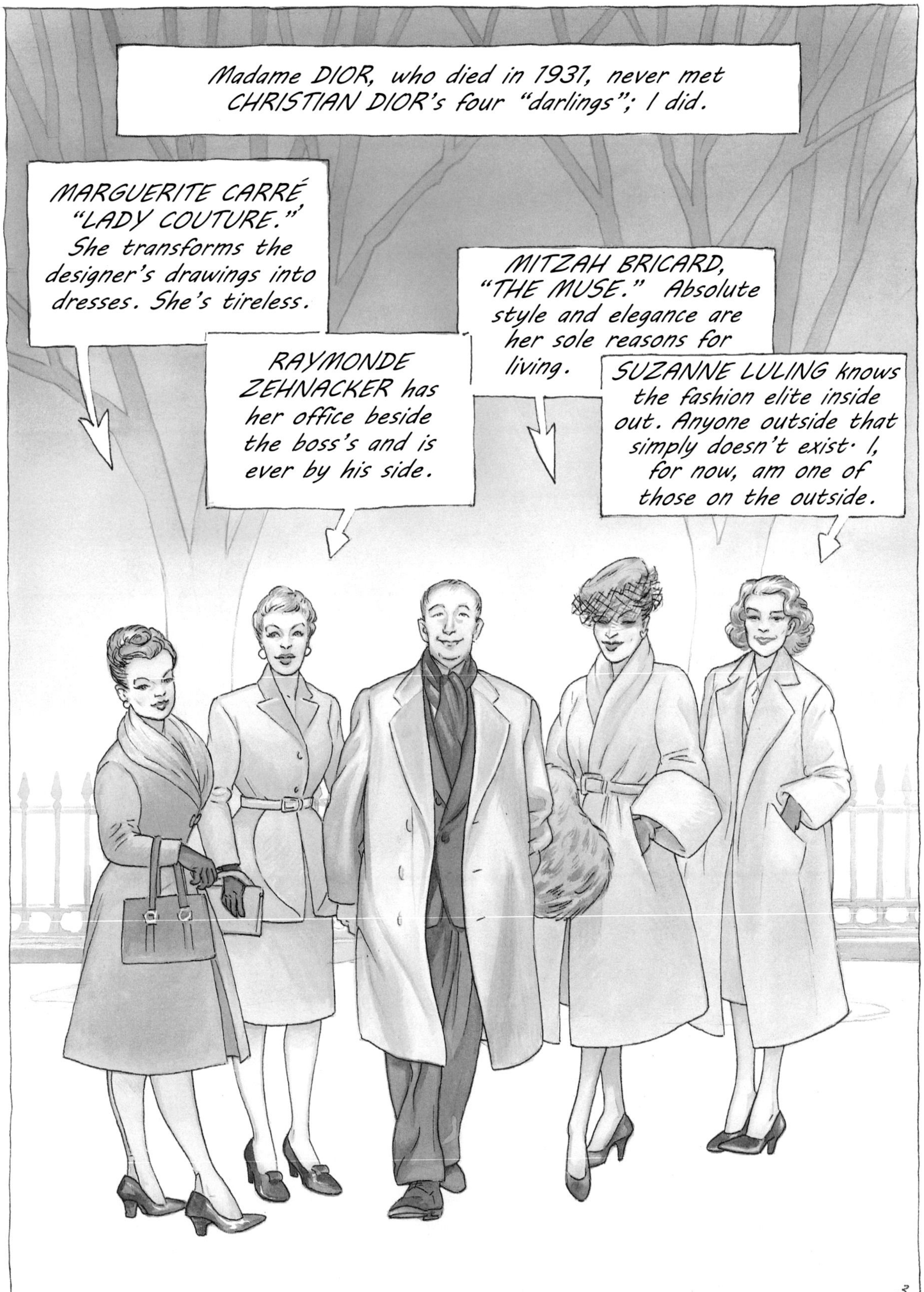
Madame DIOR, who died in 1931, never met CHRISTIAN DIOR's four "darlings"; I did.
MARGUERITE CARRÉ "LADY COUTURE." She transforms the designer's drawings into dresses. She's tireless.
RAYMONDE ZEHNACKER has her office beside the boss's and is ever by his side.
MITZAH BRICARD, "THE MUSE." Absolute style and elegance are her sole reasons for living.
SUZANNE LULING knows the fashion elite inside out. Anyone outside that simply doesn't exist. I, for now, am one of those on the outside.

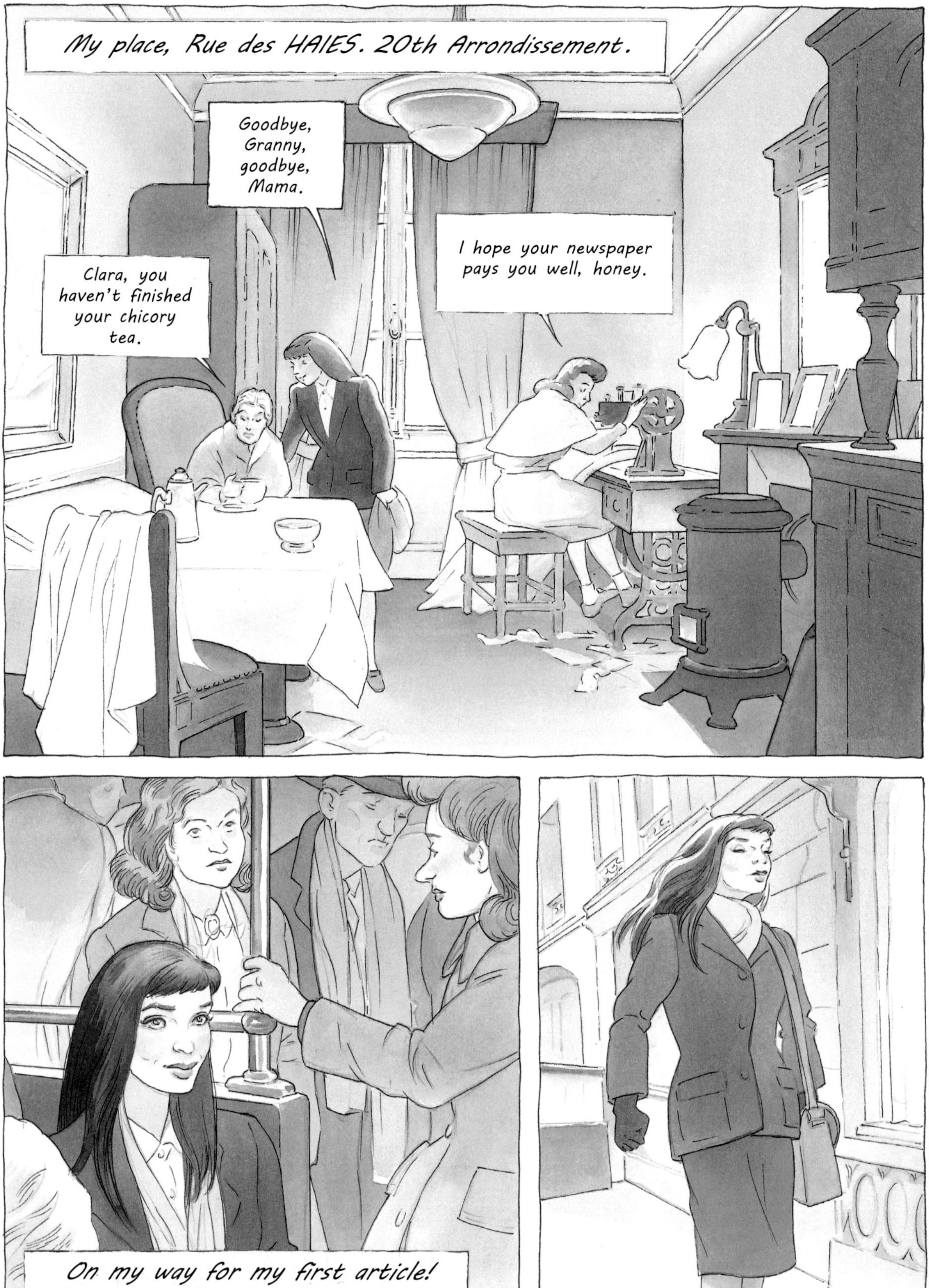
My place, Rue des HAIES. 20th Arrondissement.
Clara, you haven't finished your chicory tea.
Goodbye, Granny, goodbye, Mama.
I hope your newspaper pays you well, honey.
On my way for my first article!

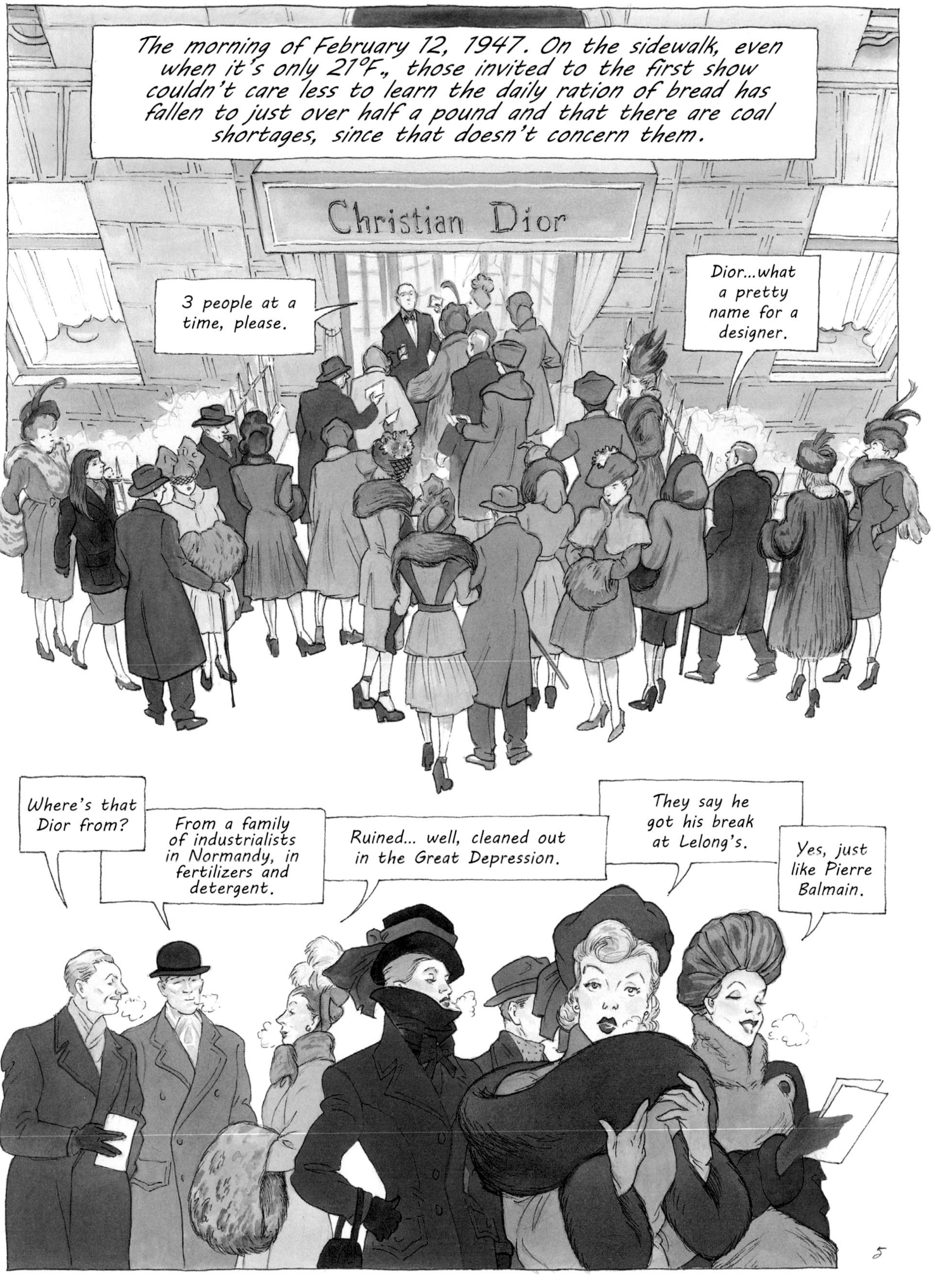
The morning of February 12, 1947. On the sidewalk, even when it's only 21°F., those invited to the first show couldn't care less to learn the daily ration of bread has fallen to just over half a pound and that there are coal shortages, since that doesn't concern them.
Christian Dior
3 people at a time, please.
Dior...what a pretty name for a designer.
Where's that Dior from?
From a family of industrialists in Normandy, in fertilizers and detergent.
Ruined... well, cleaned out in the Great Depression.
They say he got his break at Lelong's.
Yes, just like Pierre Balmain.

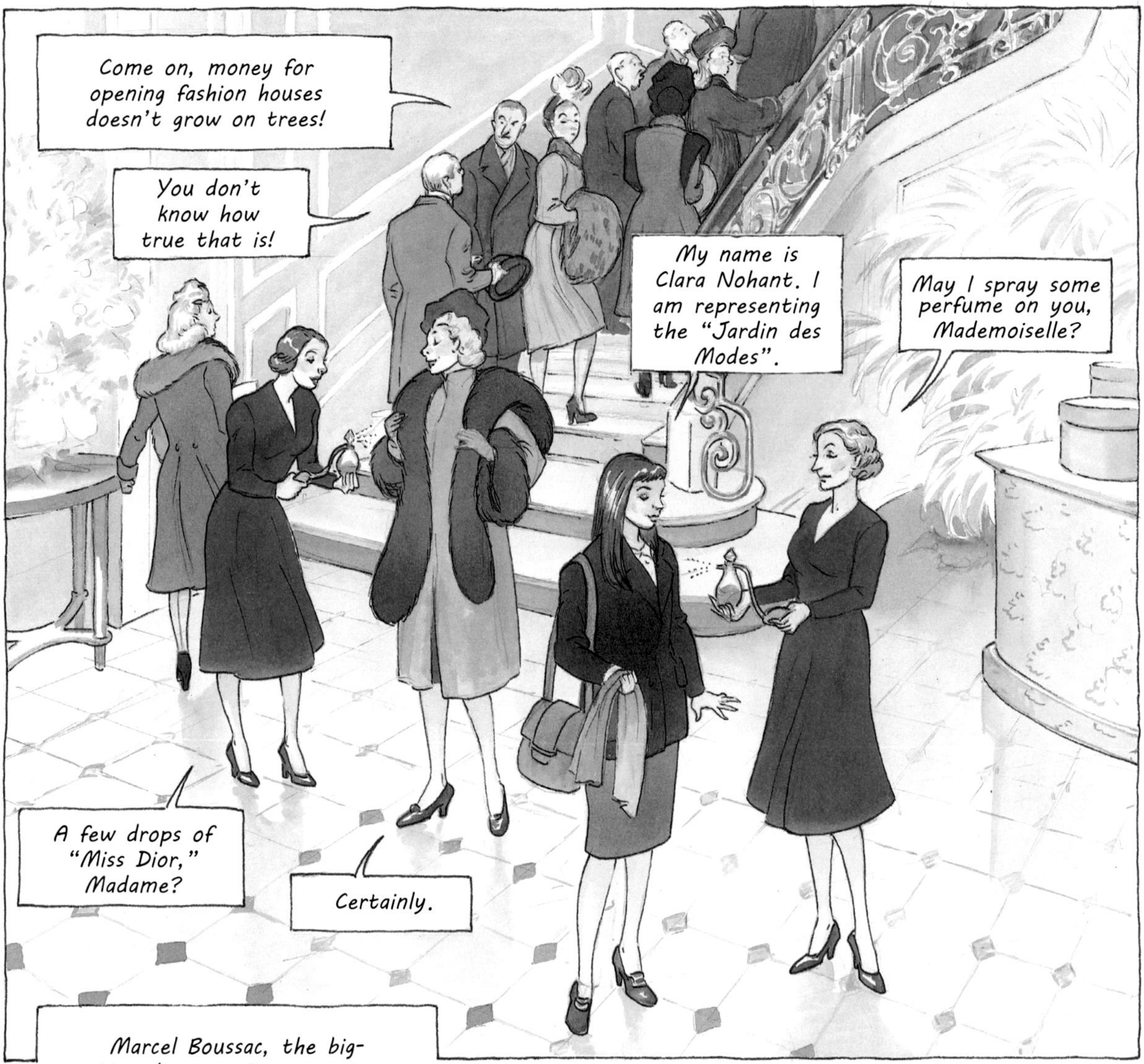
Come on, money for opening fashion houses doesn't grow on trees!
You don't know how true that is!
My name is Clara Nohant. I am representing the "Jardin des Modes".
May I spray some perfume on you, Mademoiselle?
A few drops of "Miss Dior," Madame?
Certainly.

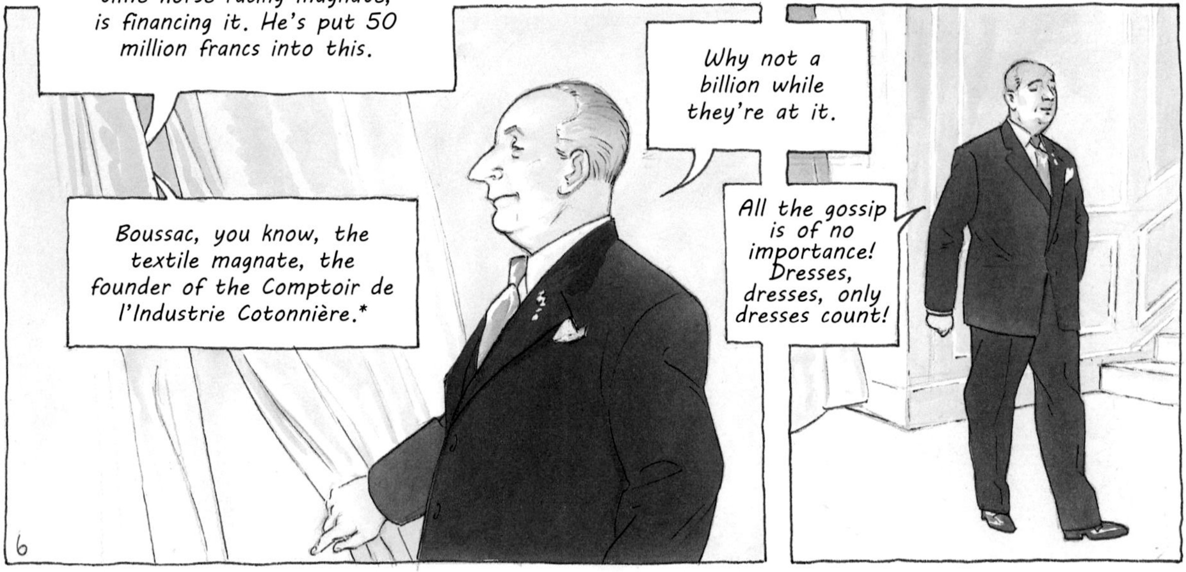
Marcel Boussac, the big-time horse-racing magnate, is financing it. He's put 50 million francs into this.
Why not a billion while they're at it.
Boussac, you know, the textile magnate, the founder of the Comptoir de l'Industrie Cotonnière.*
All the gossip is of no importance! Dresses, dresses, only dresses count!

*A French textile company dealing especially in cotton.

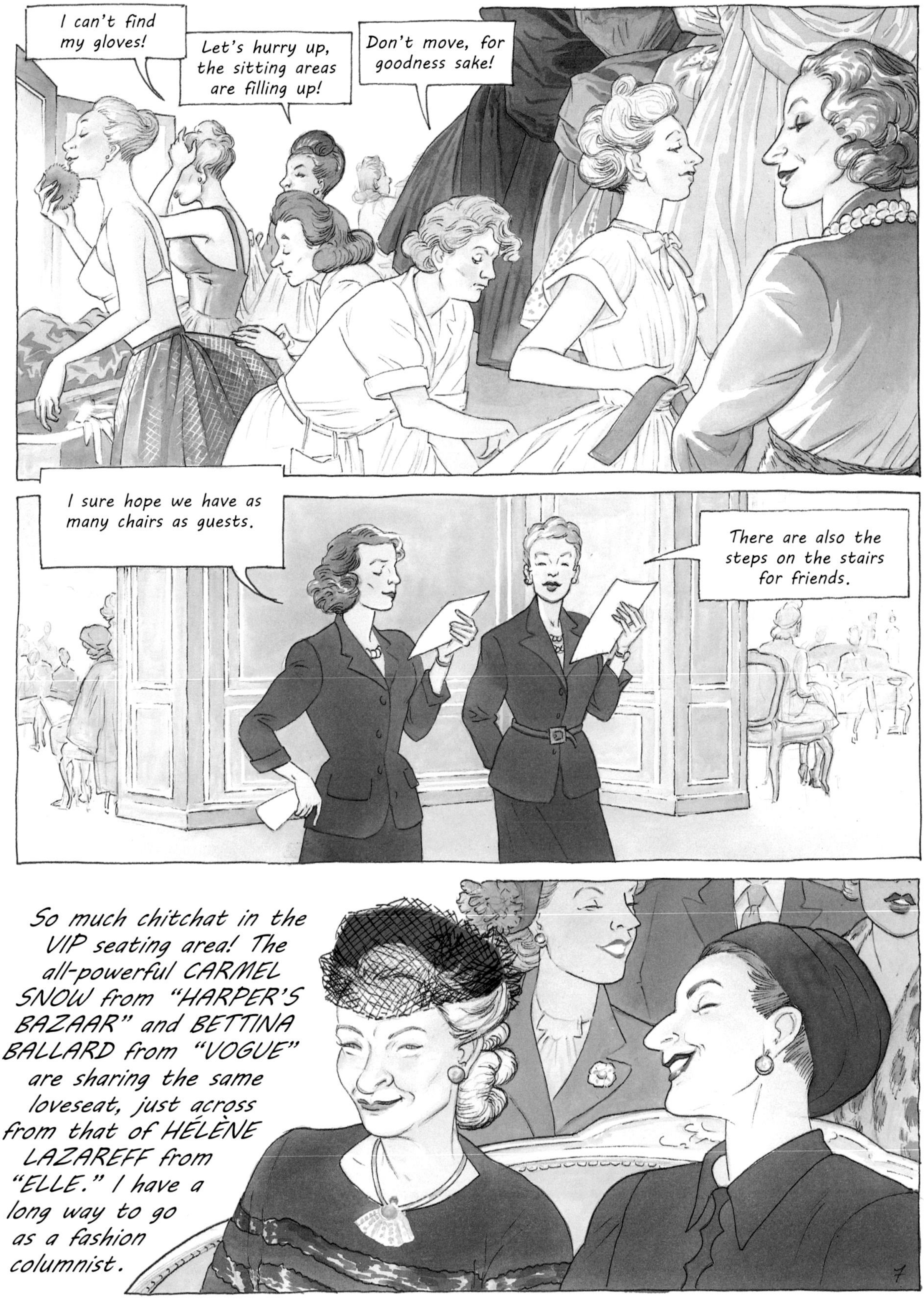
I can't find my gloves!
Let's hurry up, the sitting areas are filling up!
Don't move, for goodness sake!
I sure hope we have as many chairs as guests.
There are also the steps on the stairs for friends.
So much chitchat in the VIP seating area! The all-powerful CARMEL SNOW from "HARPER'S BAZAAR" and BETTINA BALLARD from "VOGUE" are sharing the same loveseat, just across from that of HÉLÈNE LAZAREFF from "ELLE." I have a long way to go as a fashion columnist.

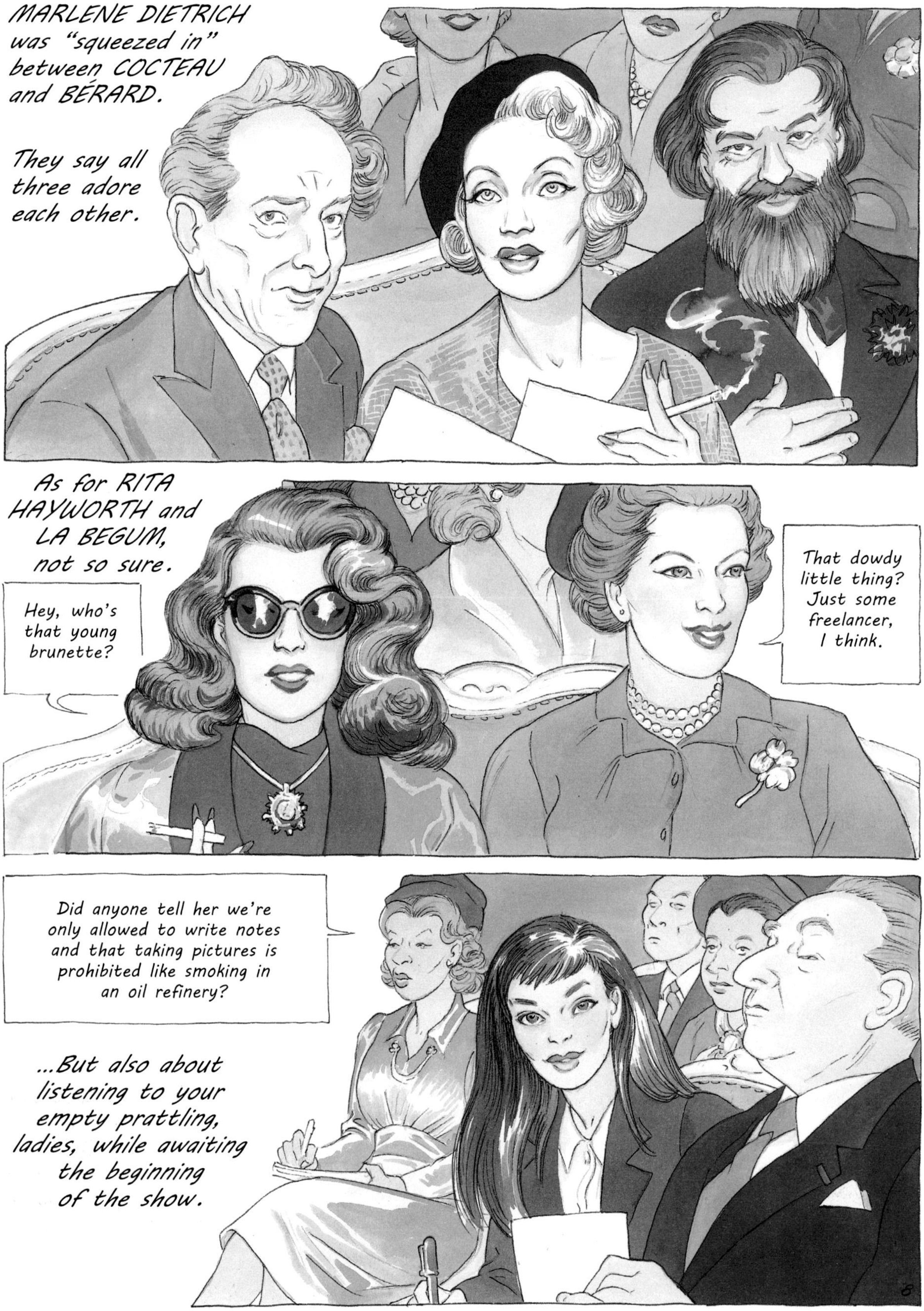
MARLENE DIETRICH was "squeezed in" between COCTEAU and BÉRARD.
They say all three adore each other.
As for RITA HAYWORTH and LA BEGUM, not so sure.
Hey, who's that young brunette?
That dowdy little thing? Just some freelancer, I think.
Did anyone tell her we're only allowed to write notes and that taking pictures is prohibited like smoking in an oil refinery?
...But also about listening to your empty prattling, ladies, while awaiting the beginning of the show.

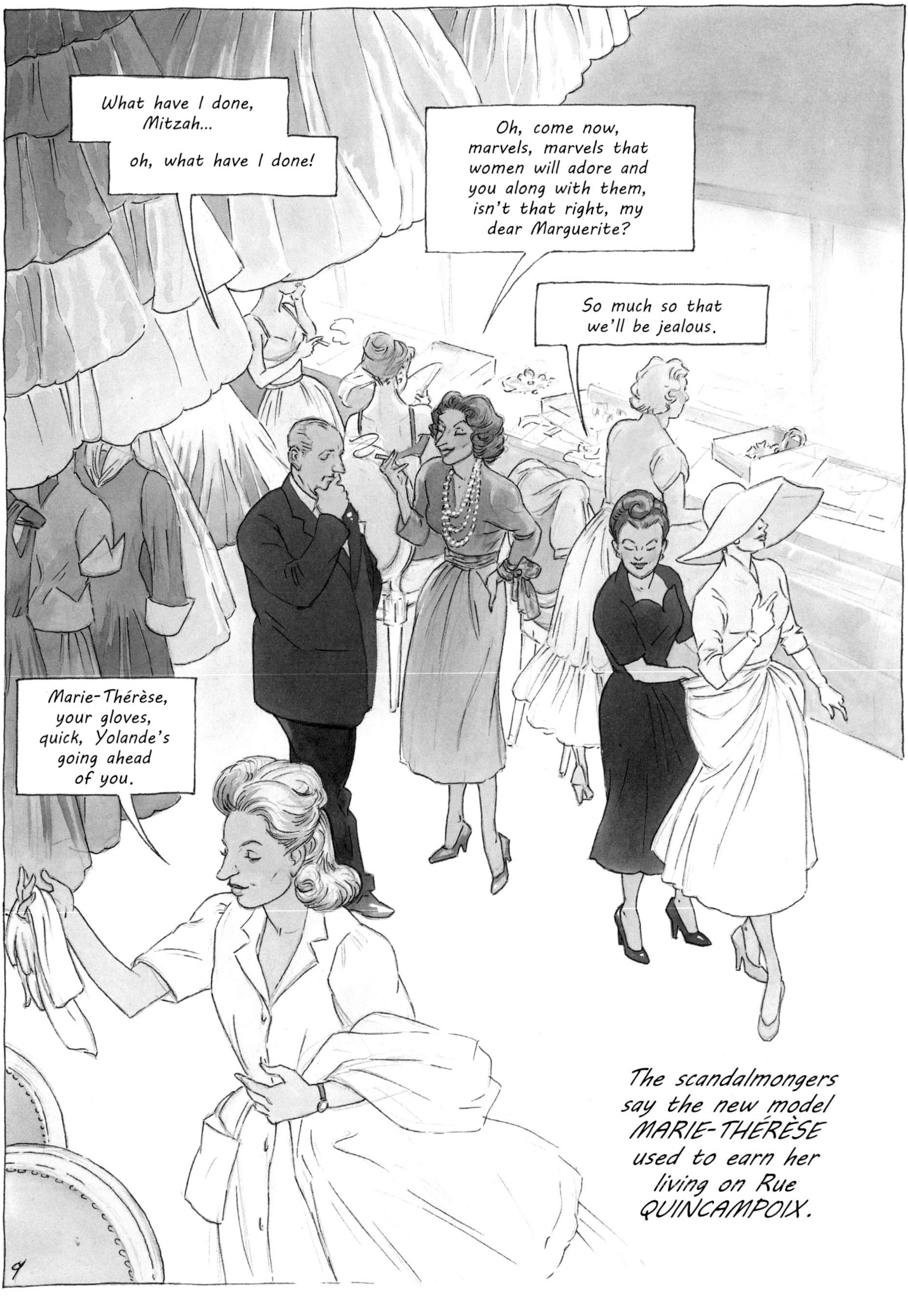
What have I done, Mitzah...
oh, what have I done!
Oh, come now, marvels, marvels that women will adore and you along with them, isn't that right, my dear Marguerite?
So much so that we'll be jealous.
Marie-Thérèse, your gloves, quick, Yolande's going ahead of you.
The scandalmongers say the new model MARIE-THÉRÈSE used to earn her living on Rue QUINCAMPOIX.

It's a fact that the brothels were closed right as CHRISTIAN DIOR was opening his doors. And since he was seeking young women to introduce his dresses, NÉNETTE, LUCIE-the-TROTTER, and PONETTE answered the ad that appeared in newspapers. They were not hired.

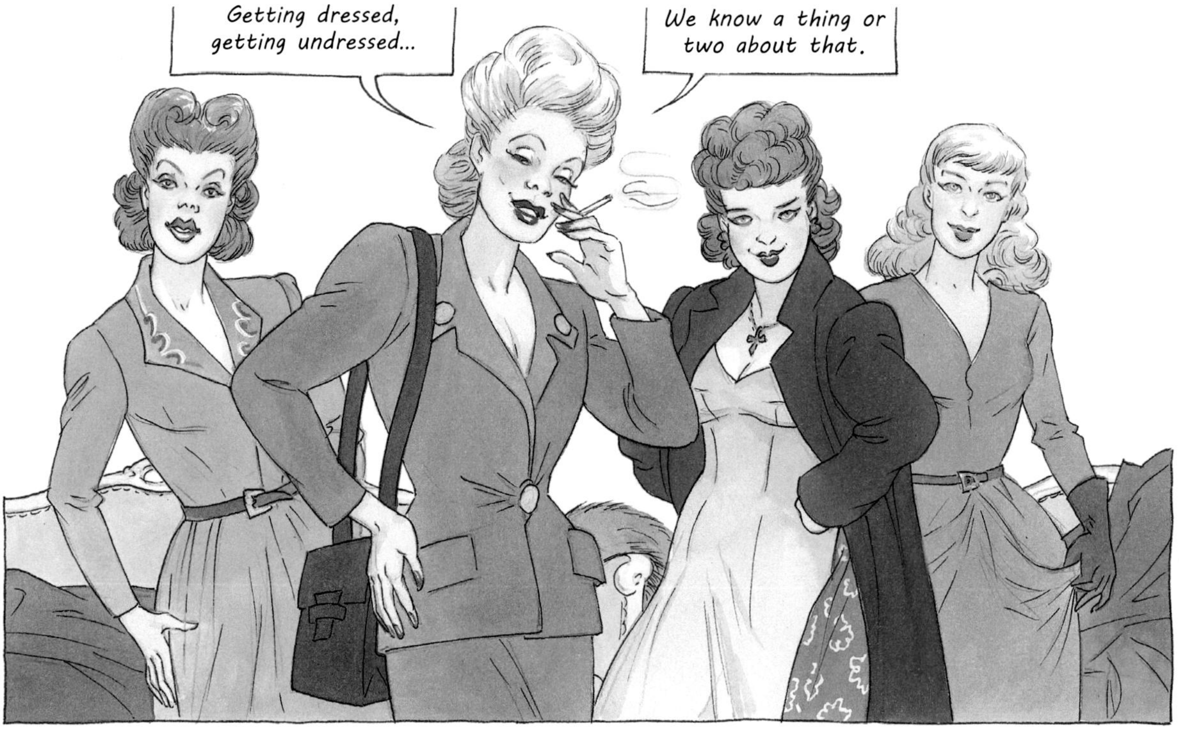

Getting dressed, getting undressed...
We know a thing or two about that.

That's not the case with MARIE-THÉRÈSE, a former shorthand typist, who joined YOLANDE, PAULE, LUCILE, NOËLLE, and TANIA, the five other "young ladies" (that's what the DIOR house calls its models), to introduce the 90 designs in his 1947 Spring-Summer collection.

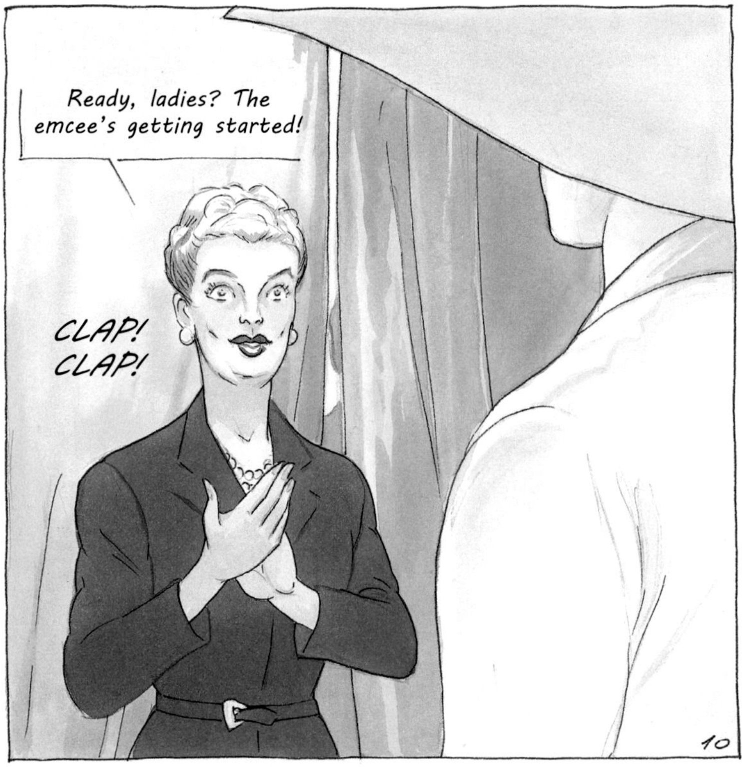

Ready, ladies? The emcee's getting started!
CLAP! CLAP!
10

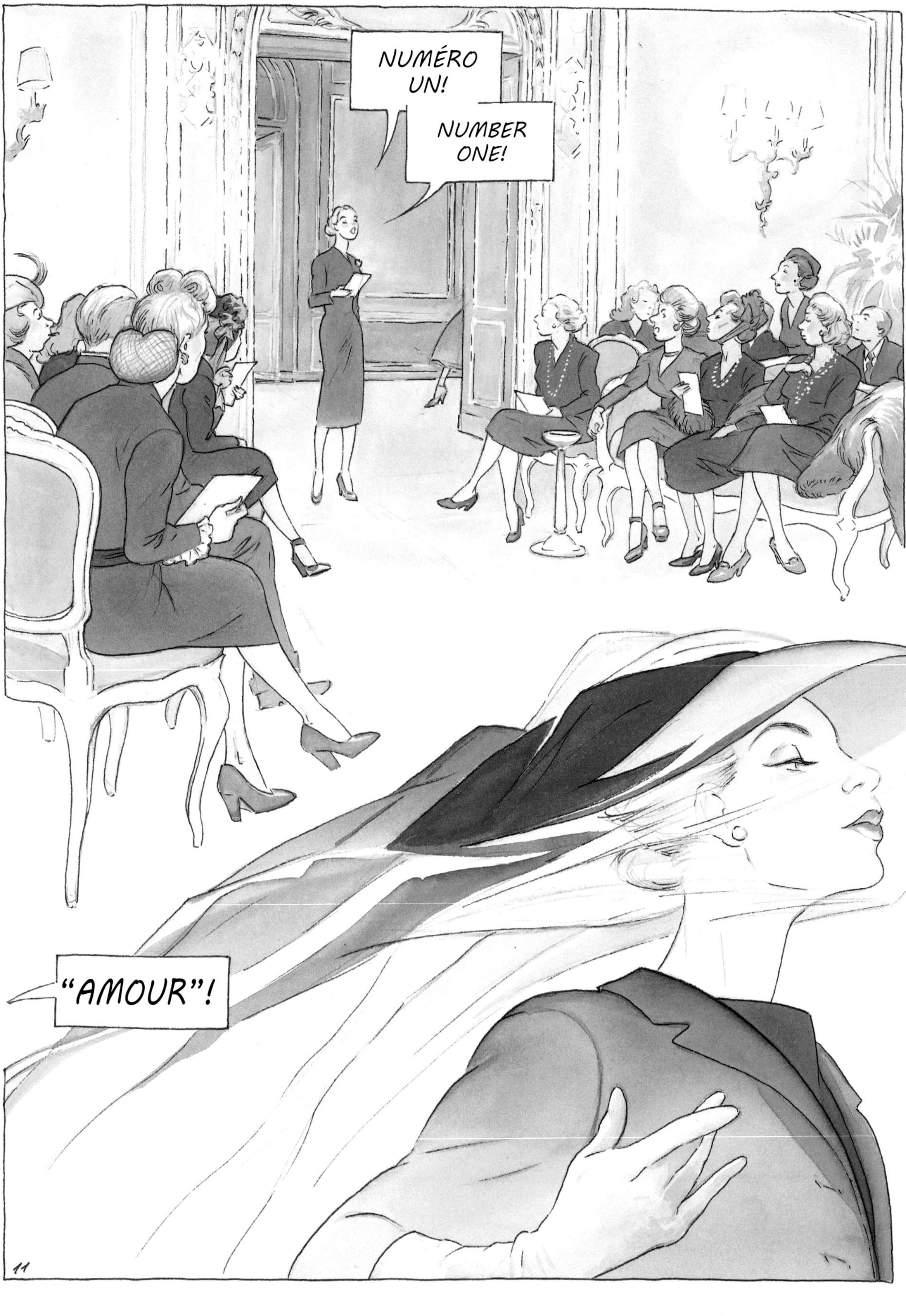
NUMÉRO UN!
NUMBER ONE!
"AMOUR"!
11

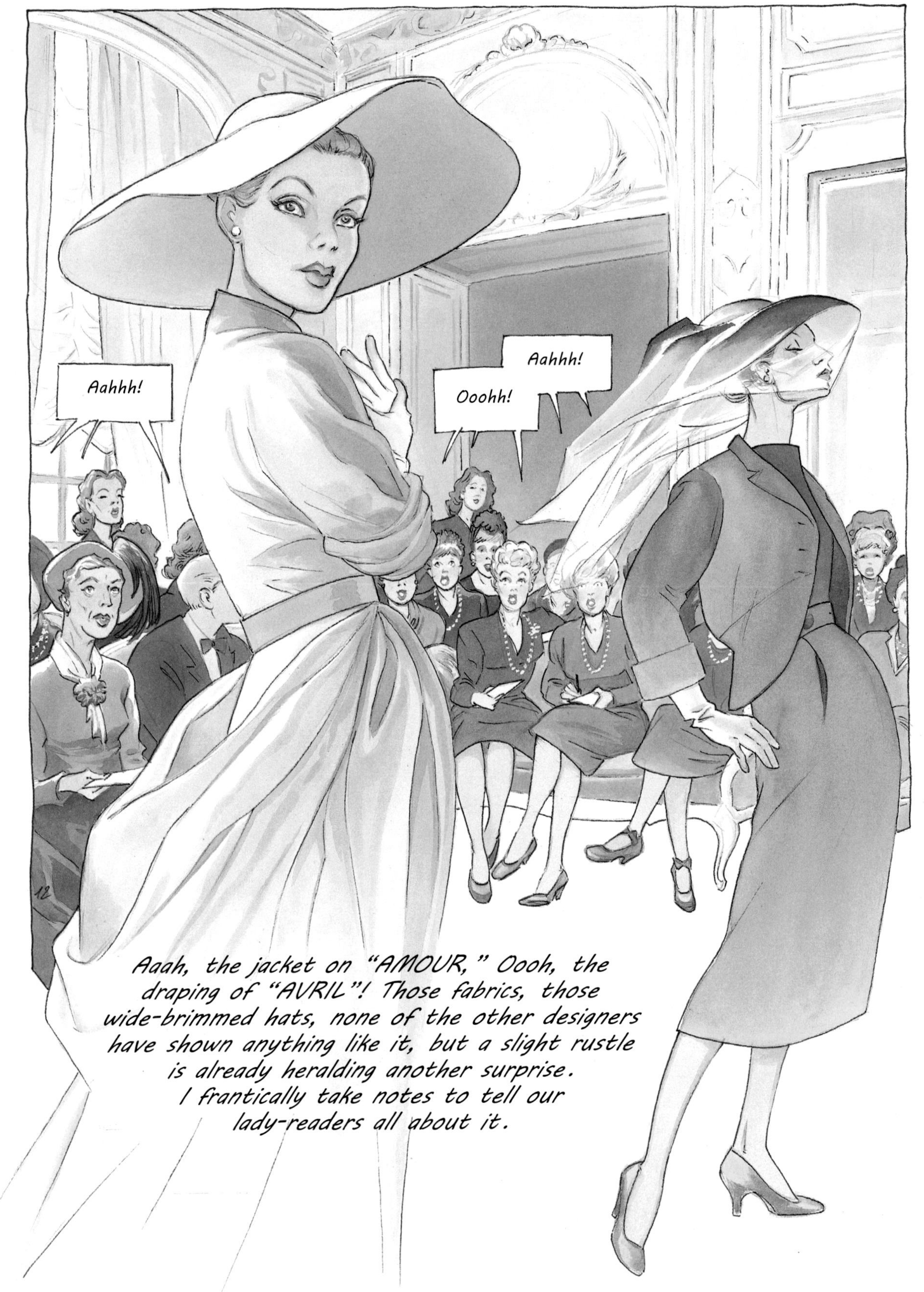
Aahhh!
Aahhh!
Ooohh!
Aaah, the jacket on "AMOUR," Oooh, the draping of "AVRIL"! Those fabrics, those wide-brimmed hats, none of the other designers have shown anything like it, but a slight rustle is already heralding another surprise. I frantically take notes to tell our lady-readers all about it.

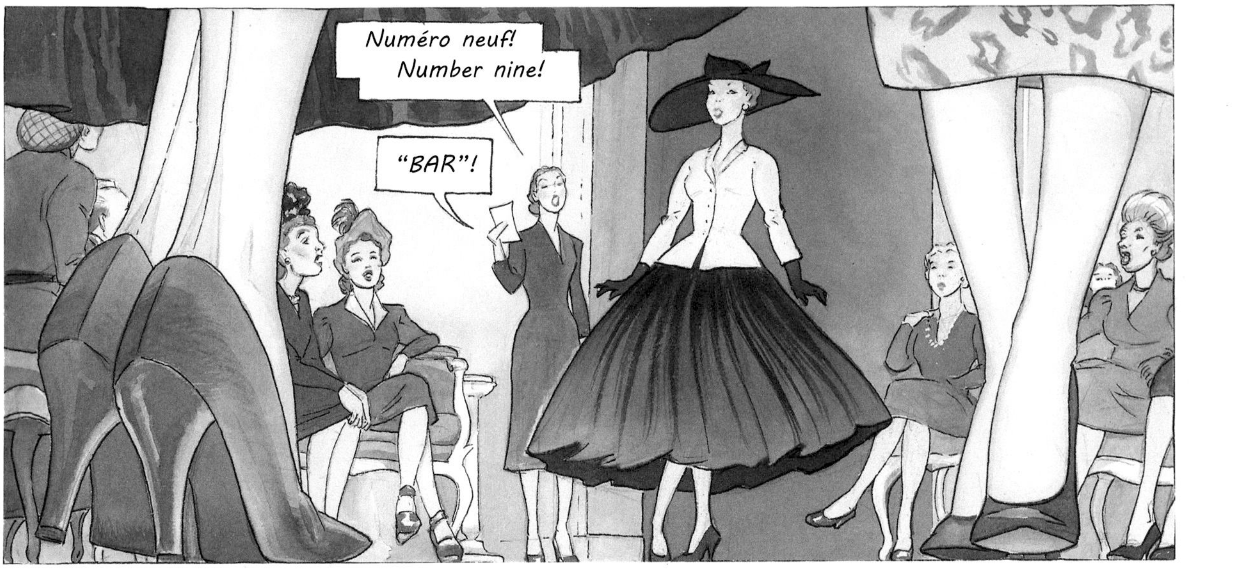
Numéro neuf!
Number nine!
"BAR"!

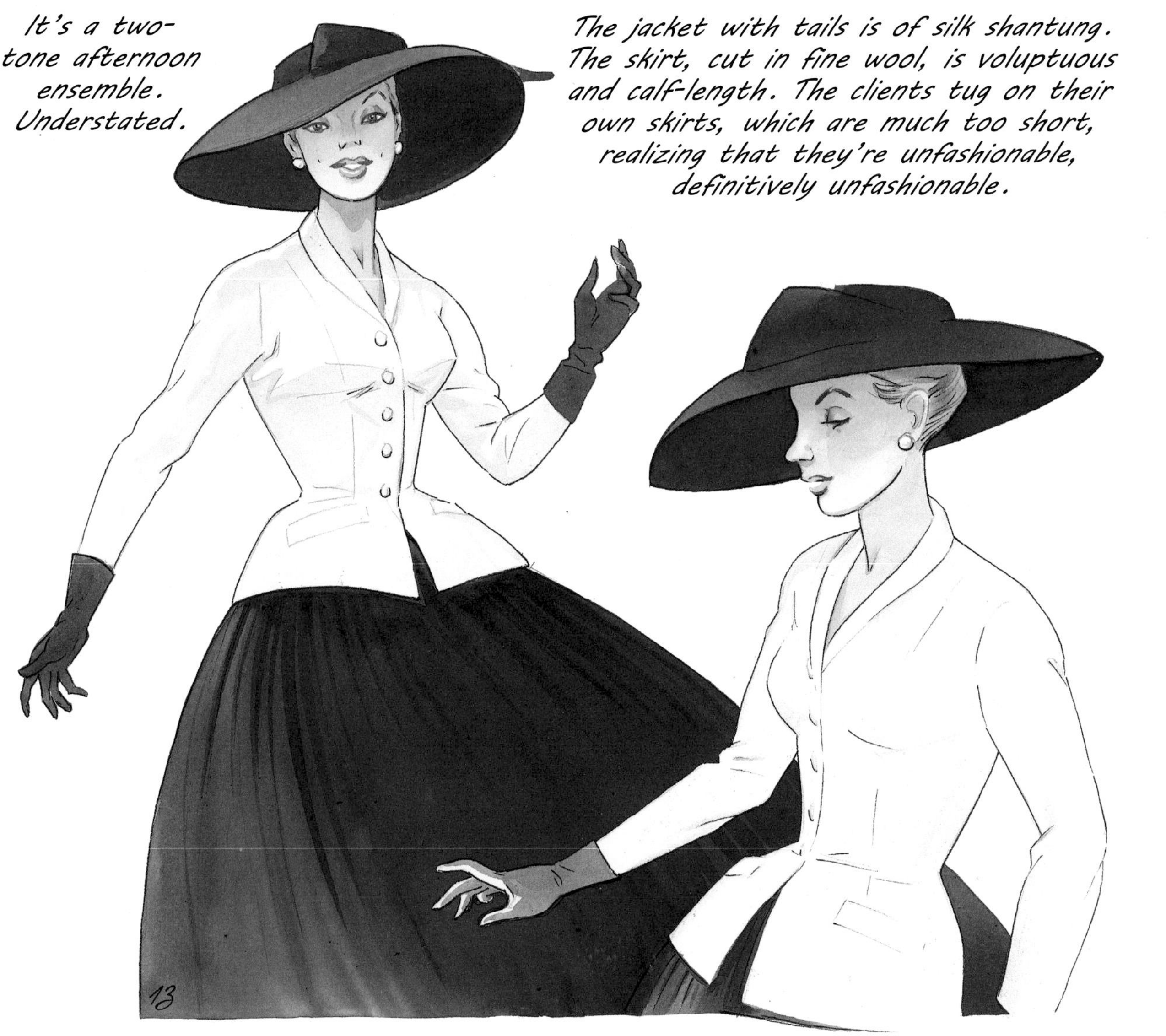
It's a two-tone afternoon ensemble. Understated.
The jacket with tails is of silk shantung. The skirt, cut in fine wool, is voluptuous and calf-length. The clients tug on their own skirts, which are much too short, realizing that they're unfashionable, definitively unfashionable.

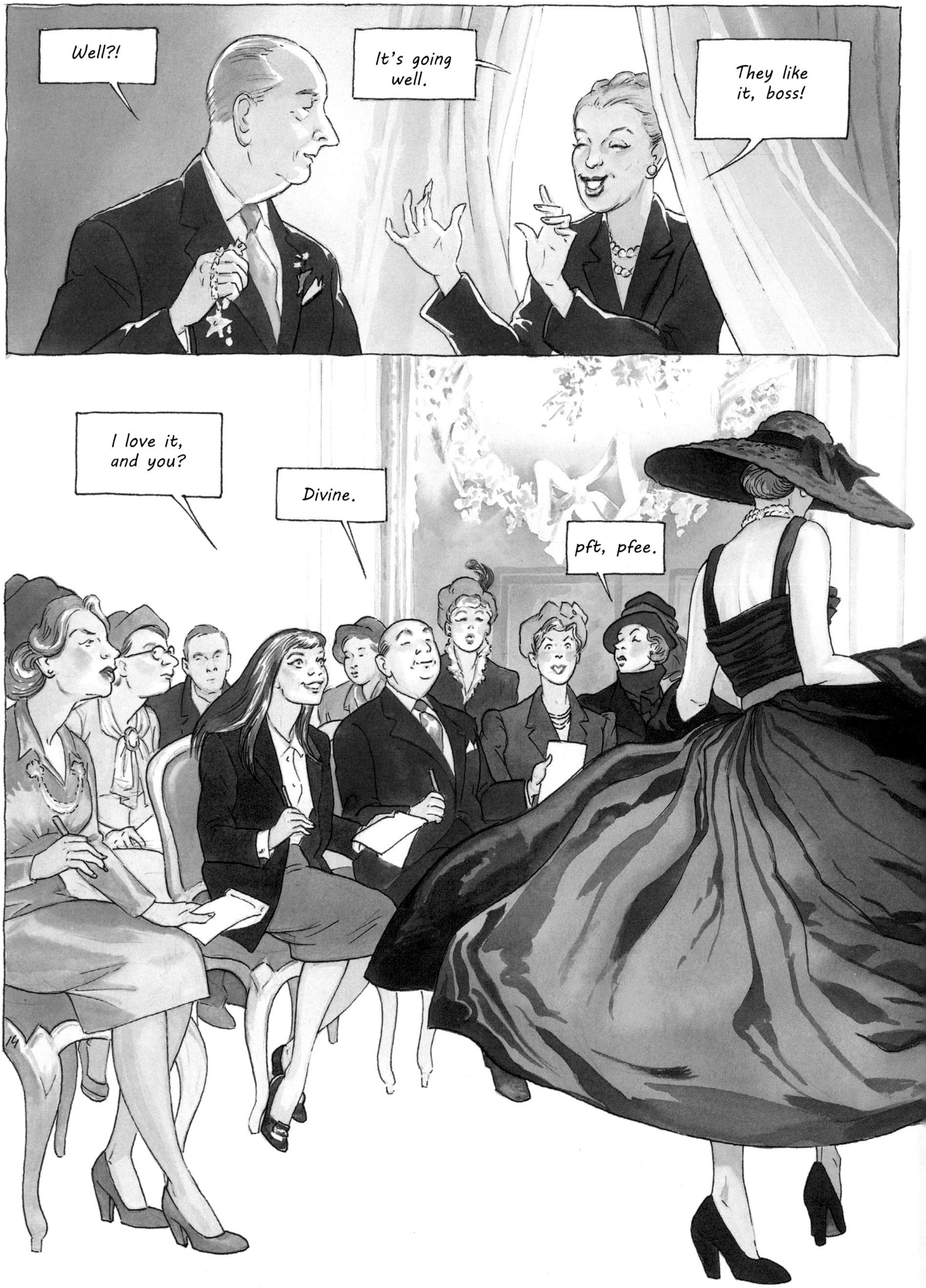
Well?!
It's going well.
They like it, boss!
I love it, and you?
Divine.
pft, pfee.

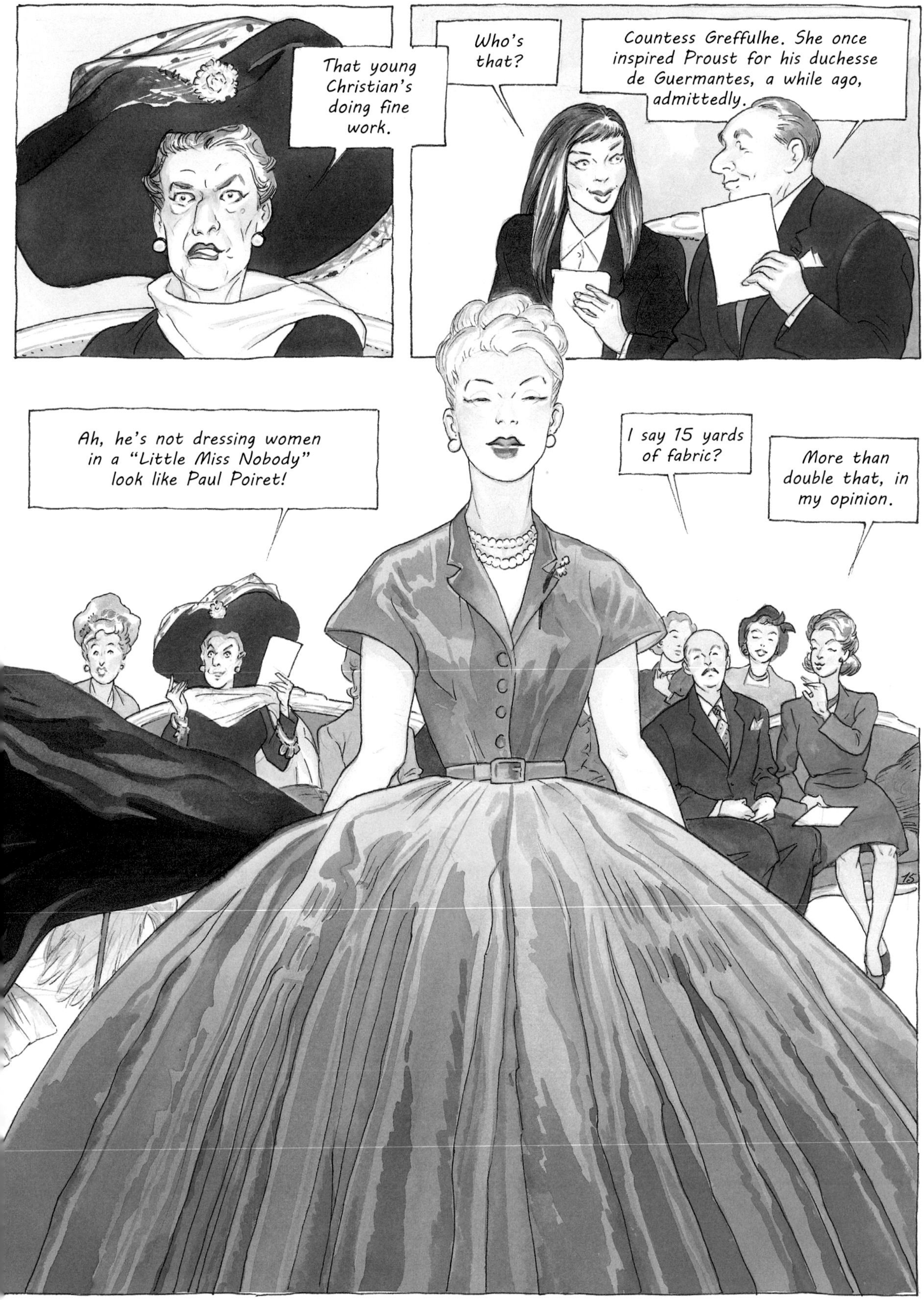
That young Christian's doing fine work.
Who's that?
Countess Greffulhe. She once inspired Proust for his duchesse de Guermantes, a while ago, admittedly.
Ah, he's not dressing women in a "Little Miss Nobody" look like Paul Poiret!
I say 15 yards of fabric?
More than double that, in my opinion.

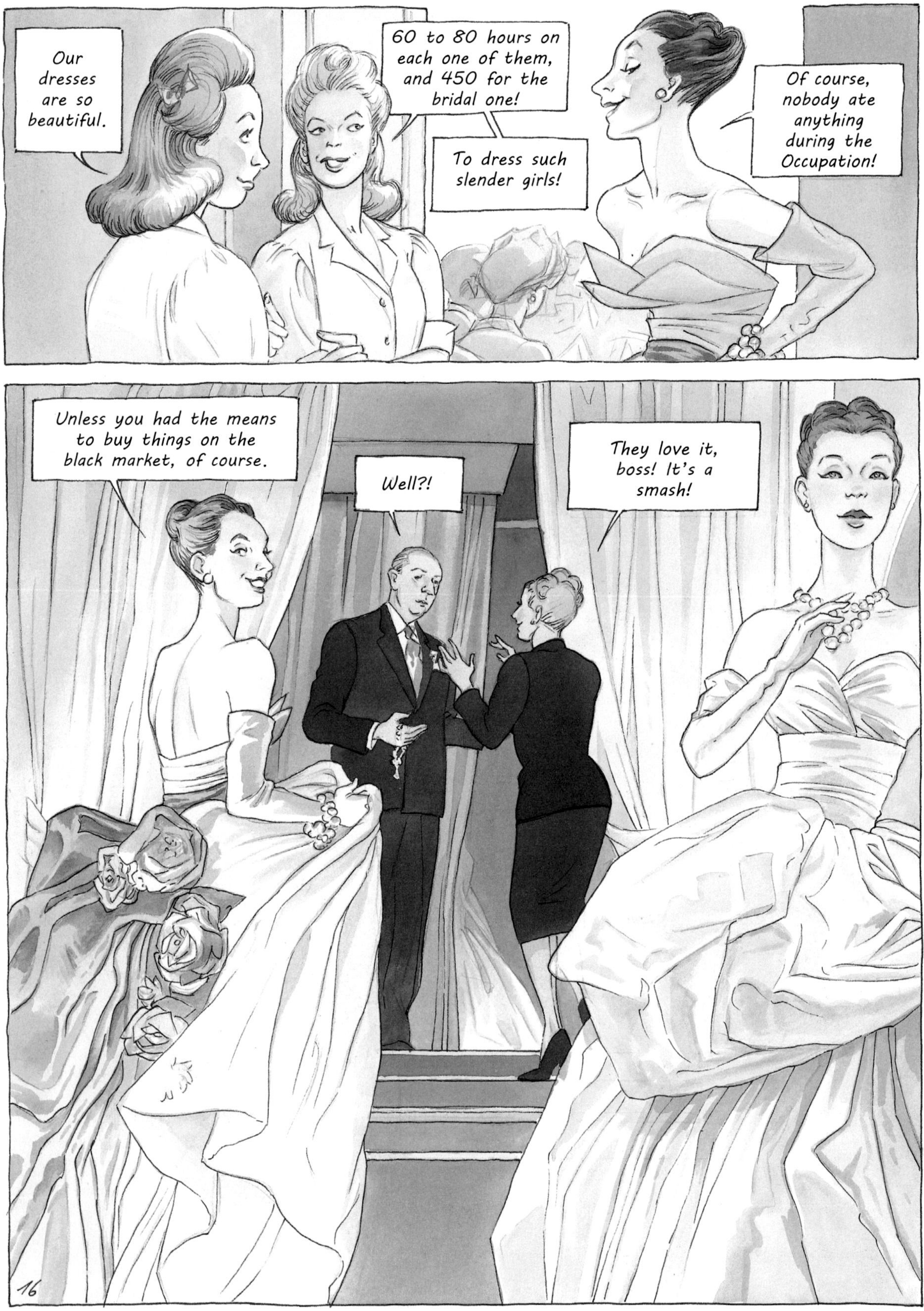
Our dresses are so beautiful.
60 to 80 hours on each one of them, and 450 for the bridal one!
To dress such slender girls!
Of course, nobody ate anything during the Occupation!
Unless you had the means to buy things on the black market, of course.
Well?!
They love it, boss! It's a smash!
16

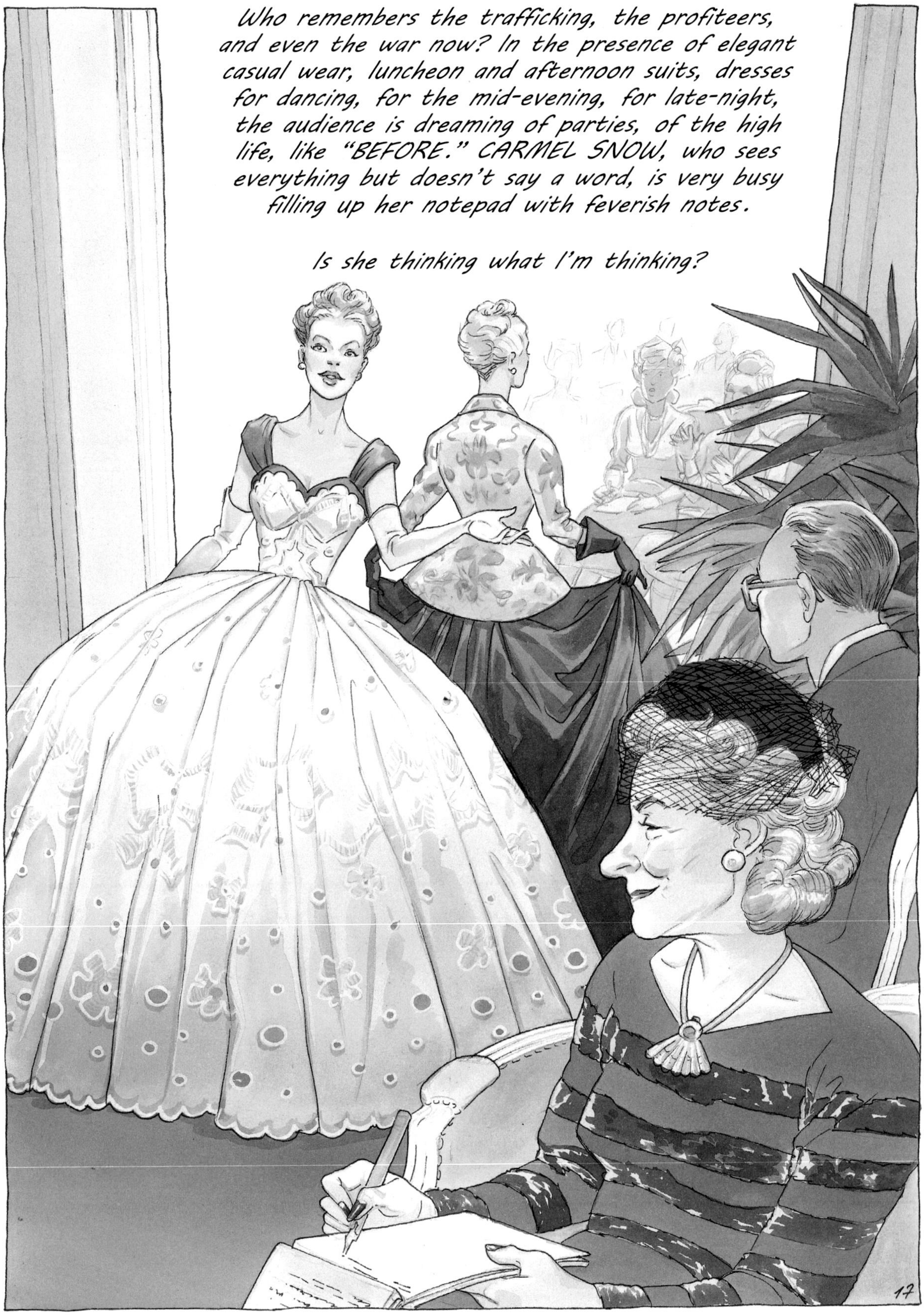
Who remembers the trafficking, the profiteers, and even the war now? In the presence of elegant casual wear, luncheon and afternoon suits, dresses for dancing, for the mid-evening, for late-night, the audience is dreaming of parties, of the high life, like "BEFORE." CARMEL SNOW, who sees everything but doesn't say a word, is very busy filling up her notepad with feverish notes.
Is she thinking what I'm thinking?
17

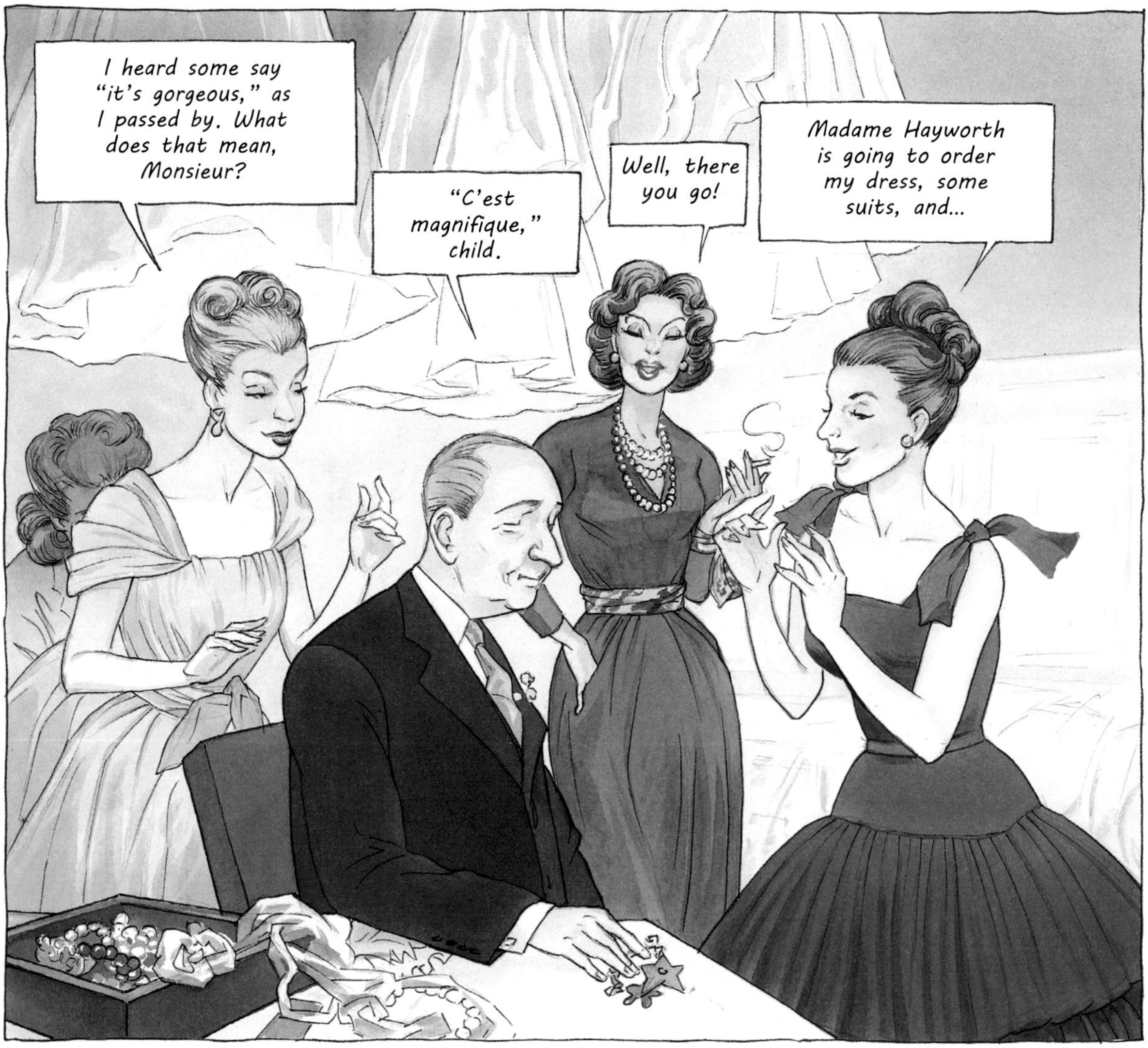
I heard some say "it's gorgeous," as I passed by. What does that mean, Monsieur?
"C'est magnifique," child.
Well, there you go!
Madame Hayworth is going to order my dress, some suits, and...

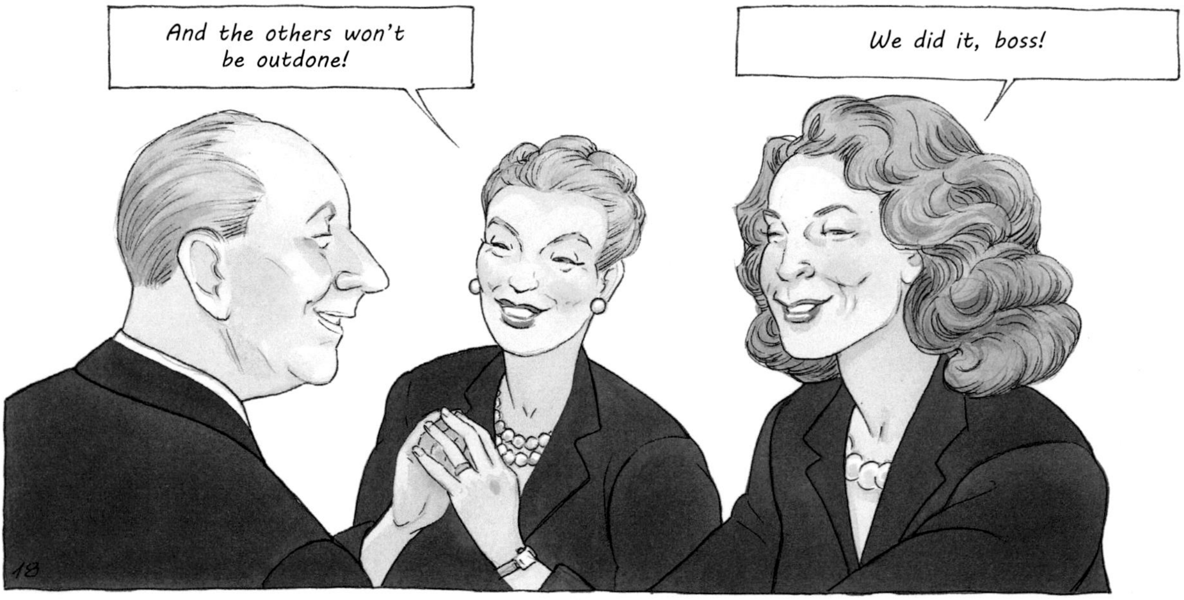
And the others won't be outdone!
We did it, boss!
18

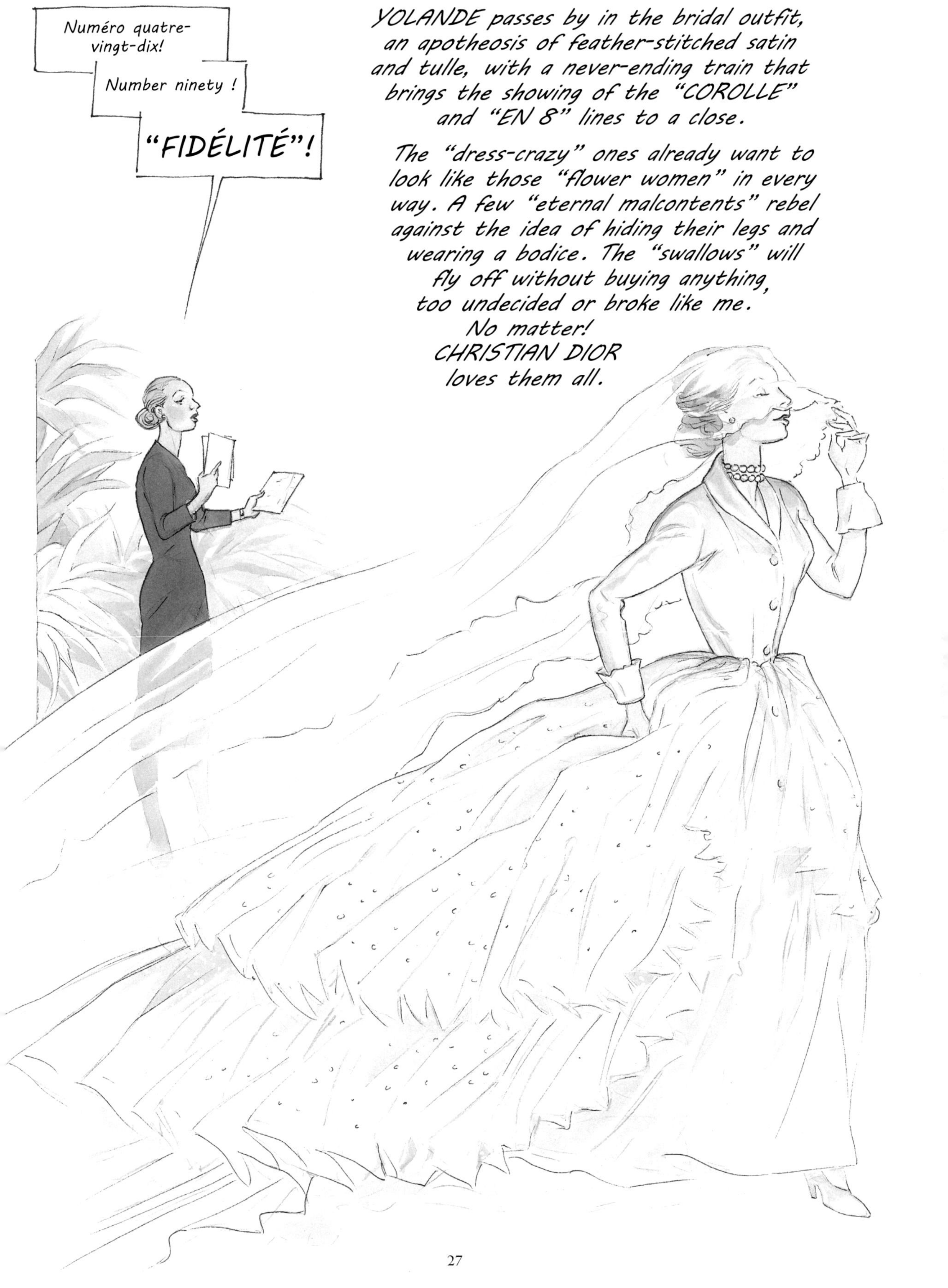

Numéro quatre-vingt-dix!
Number ninety !
"FIDÉLITÉ"!
YOLANDE passes by in the bridal outfit, an apotheosis of feather-stitched satin and tulle, with a never-ending train that brings the showing of the "COROLLE" and "EN 8" lines to a close.
The "dress-crazy" ones already want to look like those "flower women" in every way. A few "eternal malcontents" rebel against the idea of hiding their legs and wearing a bodice. The "swallows" will fly off without buying anything, too undecided or broke like me. No matter! CHRISTIAN DIOR loves them all.

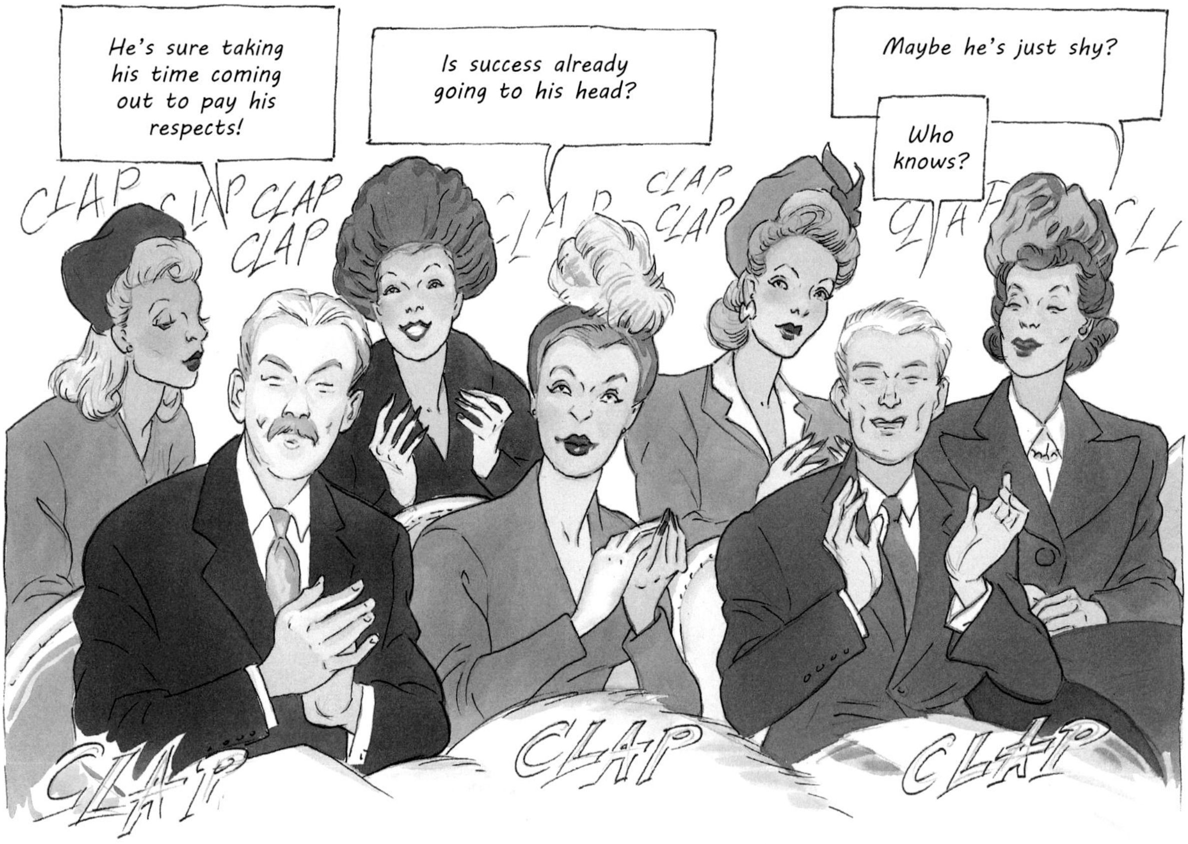
He's sure taking his time coming out to pay his respects!
Is success already going to his head?
Maybe he's just shy?
Who knows?
CLAP CLAP CLAP CLAP
CLAP
CLAP CLAP
CLAP
CLAP
CLAP
CLAP
CLAP

Behind the scenes, I imagine him being happy more than anything else, just like the fashion apprentices, dressmakers, certified seamstresses, shearers and crocheters.

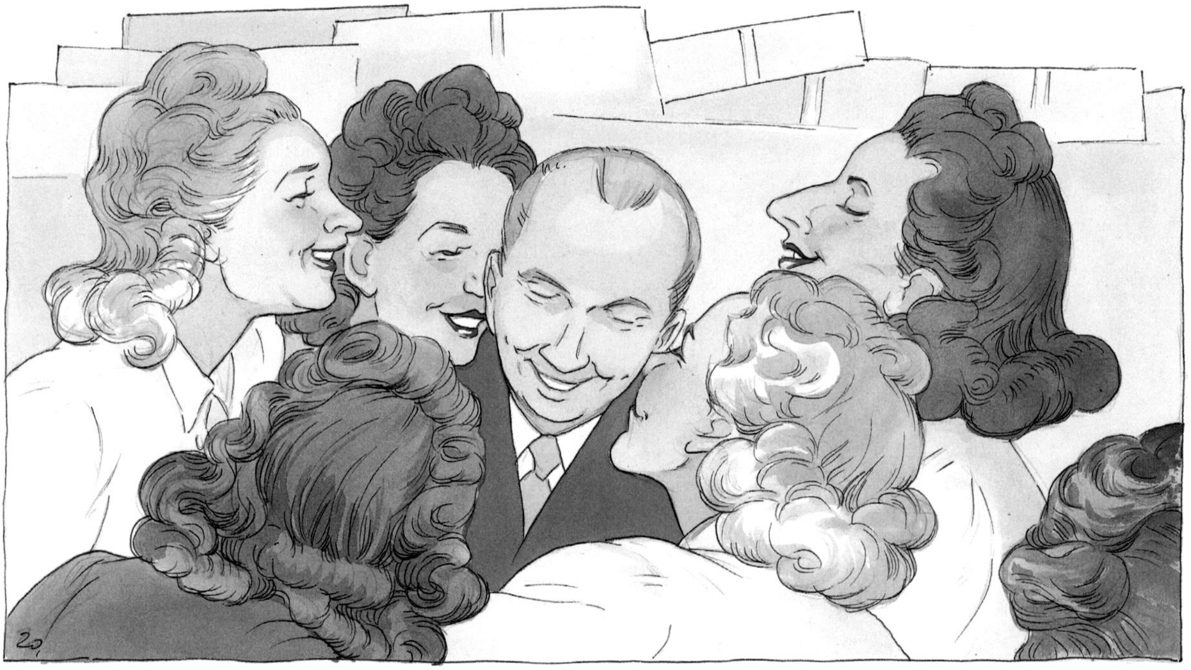

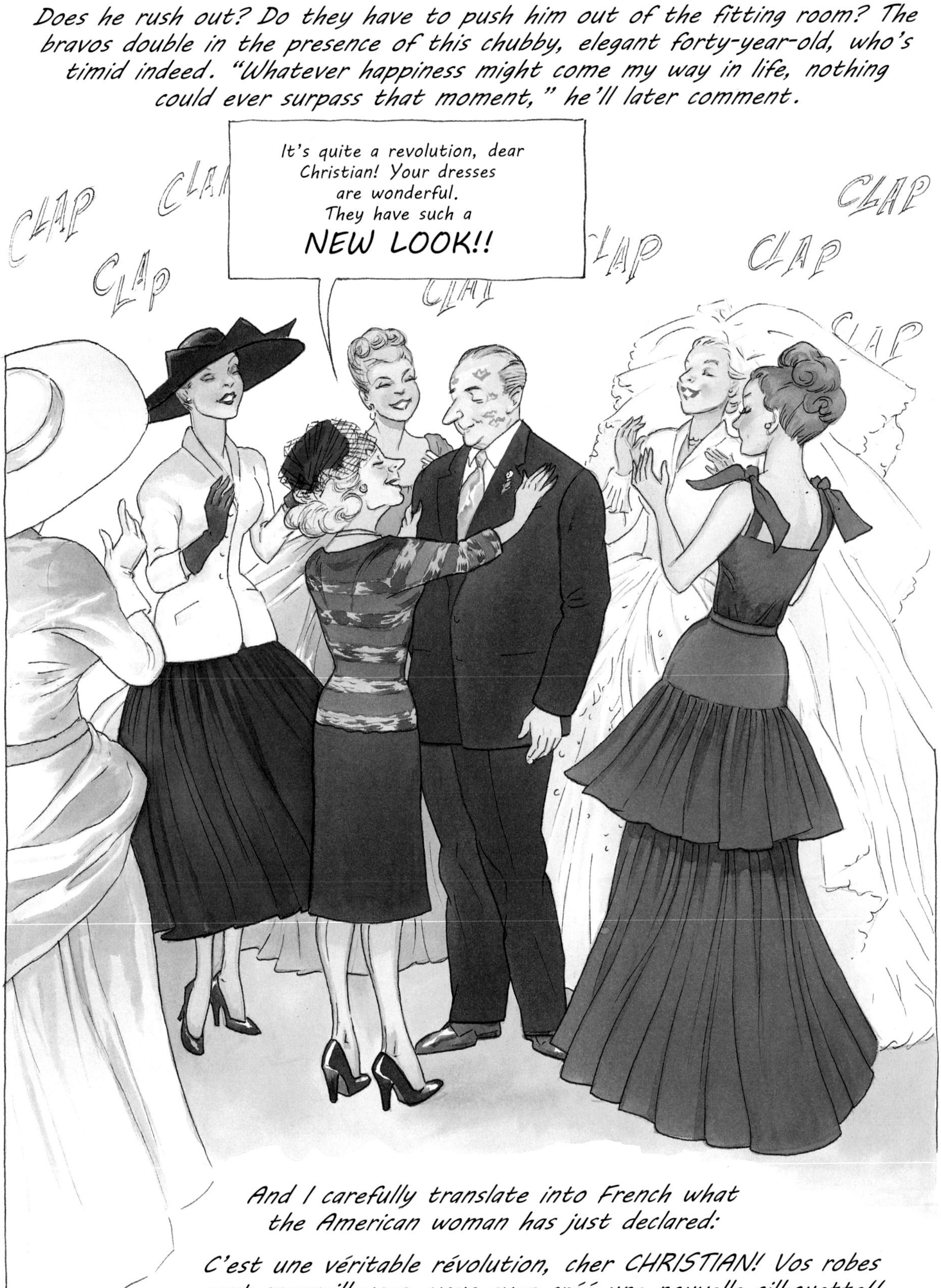
Does he rush out? Do they have to push him out of the fitting room? The bravos double in the presence of this chubby, elegant forty-year-old, who's timid indeed. "Whatever happiness might come my way in life, nothing could ever surpass that moment," he'll later comment.
CLAP
CLAP
CLAP
It's quite a revolution, dear Christian! Your dresses are wonderful. They have such a NEW LOOK!!
CLAP
CLAP
CLAP
And I carefully translate into French what the American woman has just declared:
C'est une véritable révolution, cher CHRISTIAN! Vos robes sont merveilleuses, vous avez créé une nouvelle silhouette!!
21

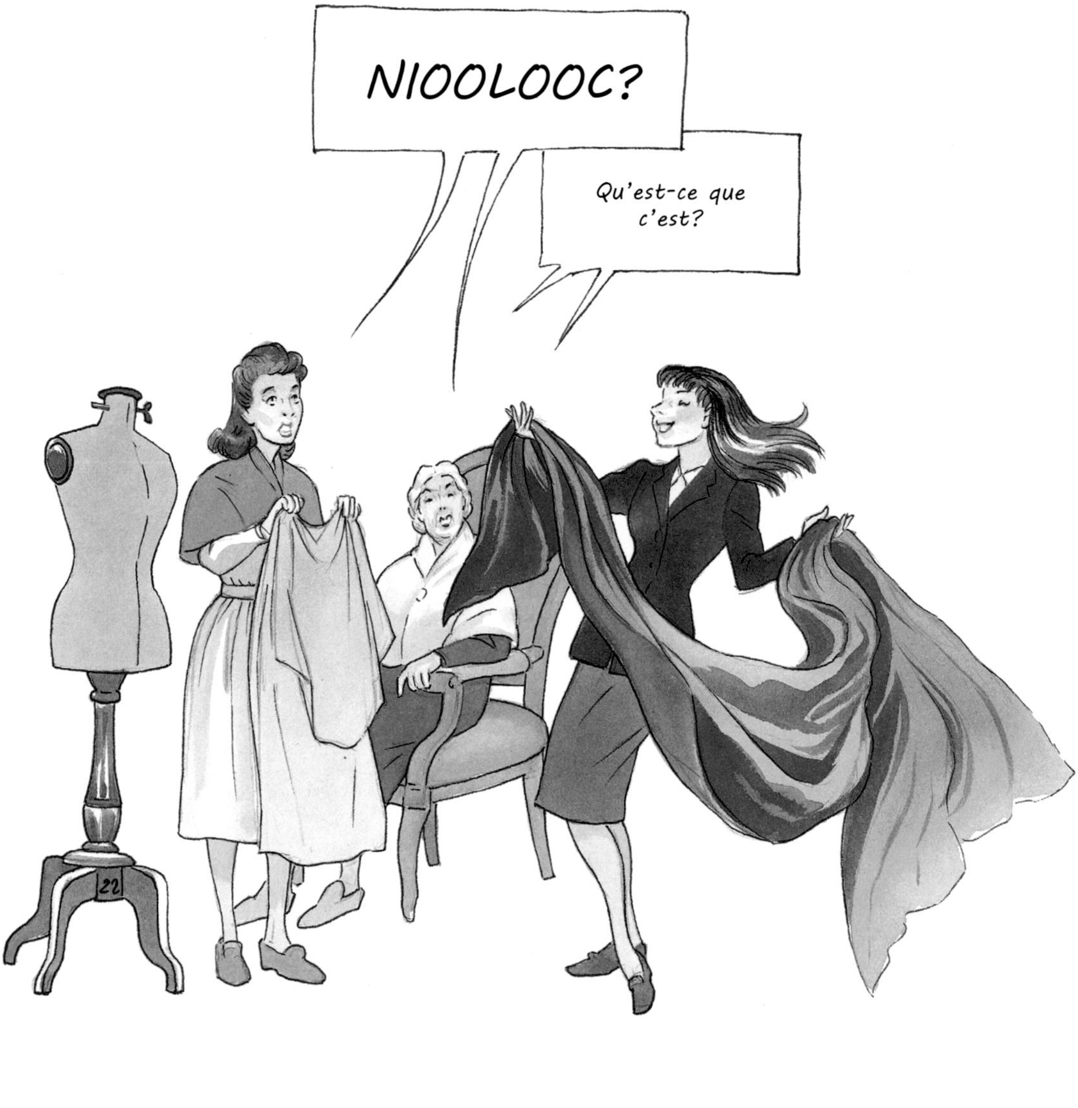
NIOOLOOC?
Qu'est-ce que c'est?

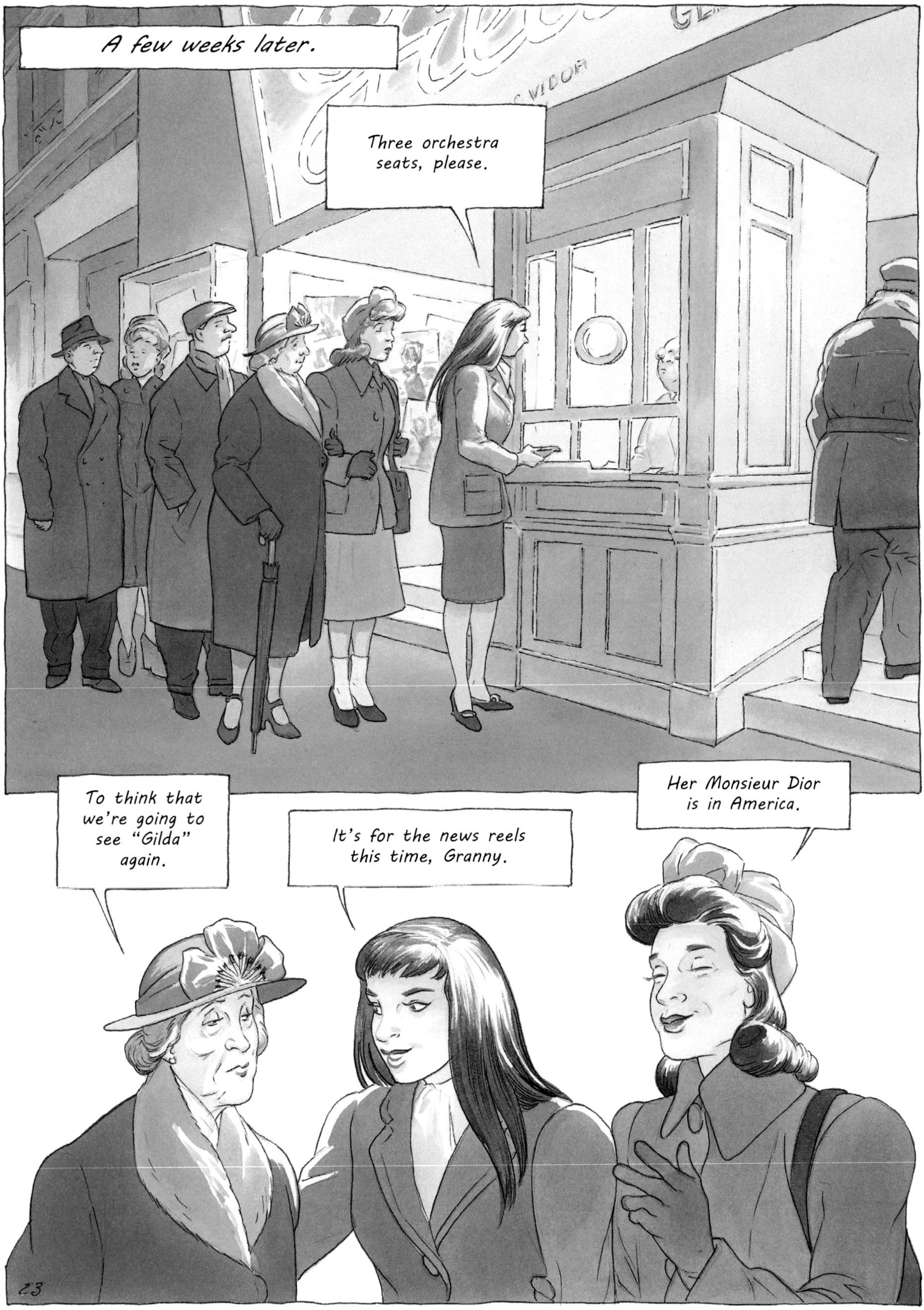
A few weeks later.
Three orchestra seats, please.
To think that we're going to see "Gilda" again.
It's for the news reels this time, Granny.
Her Monsieur Dior is in America.

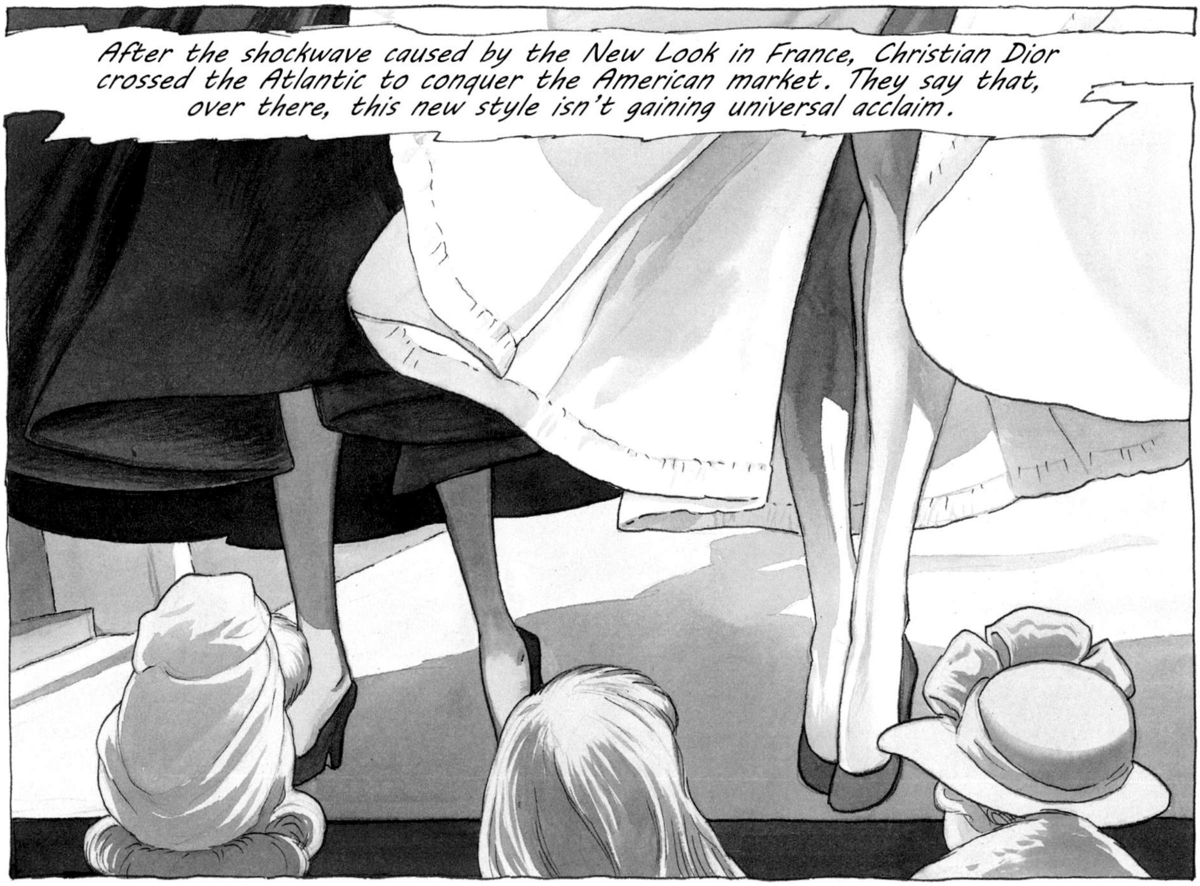
After the shockwave caused by the New Look in France, Christian Dior crossed the Atlantic to conquer the American market. They say that, over there, this new style isn't gaining universal acclaim.

He kindly responded to his detractors in a press conference on board the ocean liner "Queen Mary" after his arrival at the Port of New York.

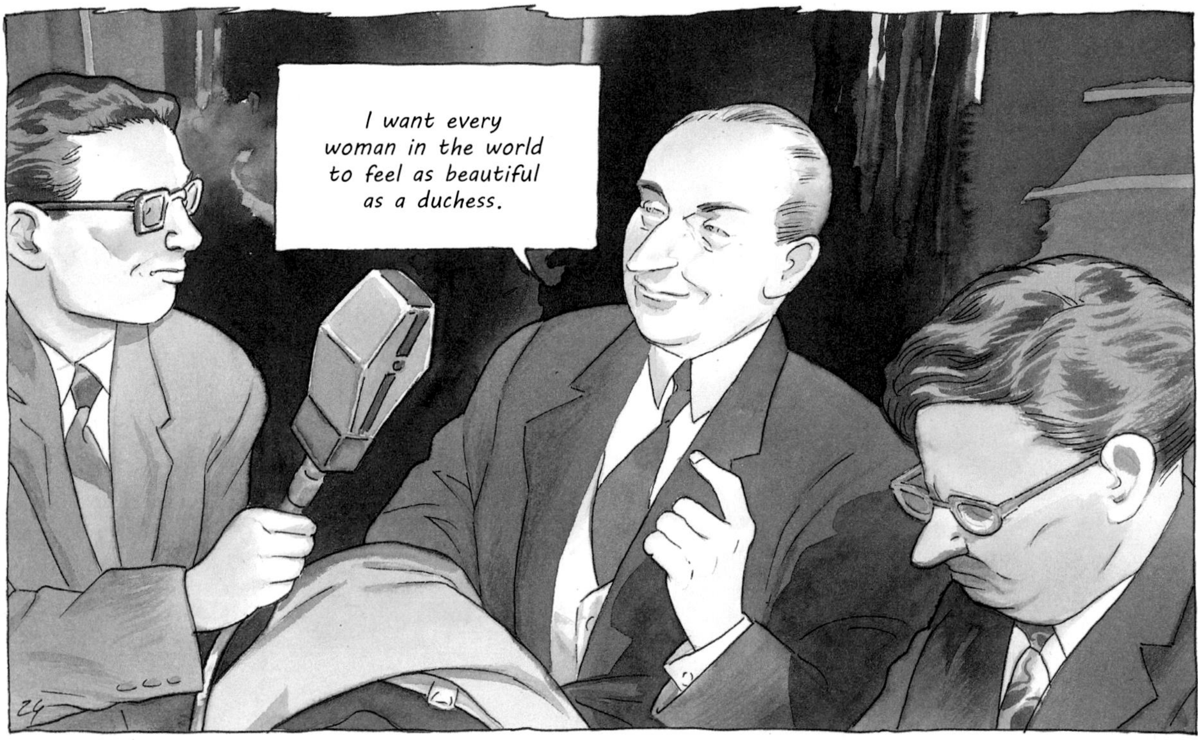
I want every woman in the world to feel as beautiful as a duchess.

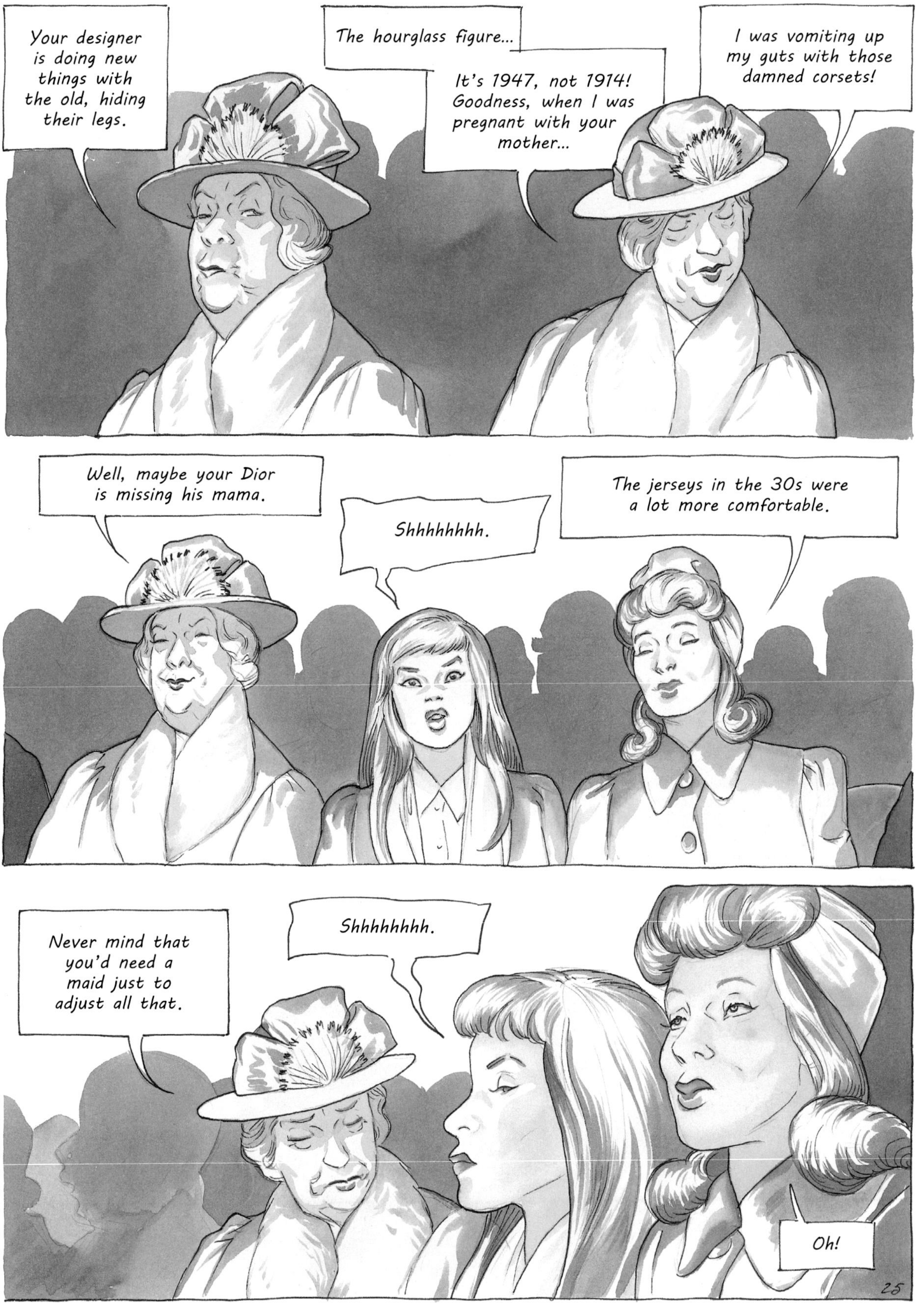
Your designer is doing new things with the old, hiding their legs.
The hourglass figure...
It's 1947, not 1914! Goodness, when I was pregnant with your mother...
I was vomiting up my guts with those damned corsets!
Well, maybe your Dior is missing his mama.
Shhhhhhhh.
The jerseys in the 30s were a lot more comfortable.
Never mind that you'd need a maid just to adjust all that.
Shhhhhhhh.
Oh!
25

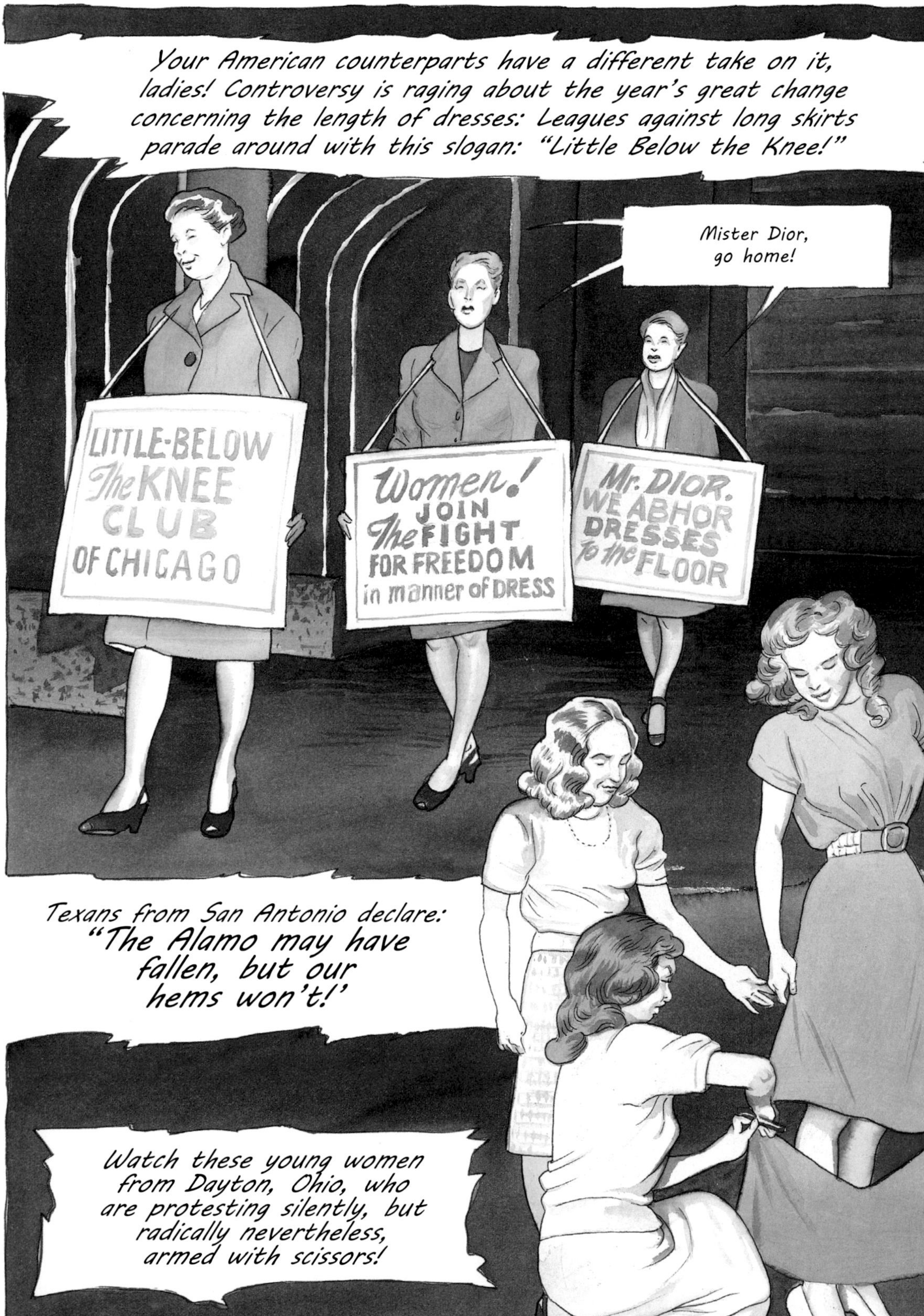
Your American counterparts have a different take on it, ladies! Controversy is raging about the year's great change concerning the length of dresses: Leagues against long skirts parade around with this slogan: "Little Below the Knee!"
Mister Dior, go home!
LITTLE-BELOW The KNEE CLUB OF CHICAGO
Women! JOIN The FIGHT FOR FREEDOM in manner of DRESS
Mr. DIOR. WE ABHOR DRESSES to the FLOOR
Texans from San Antonio declare: "The Alamo may have fallen, but our hems won't!'
Watch these young women from Dayton, Ohio, who are protesting silently, but radically nevertheless, armed with scissors!

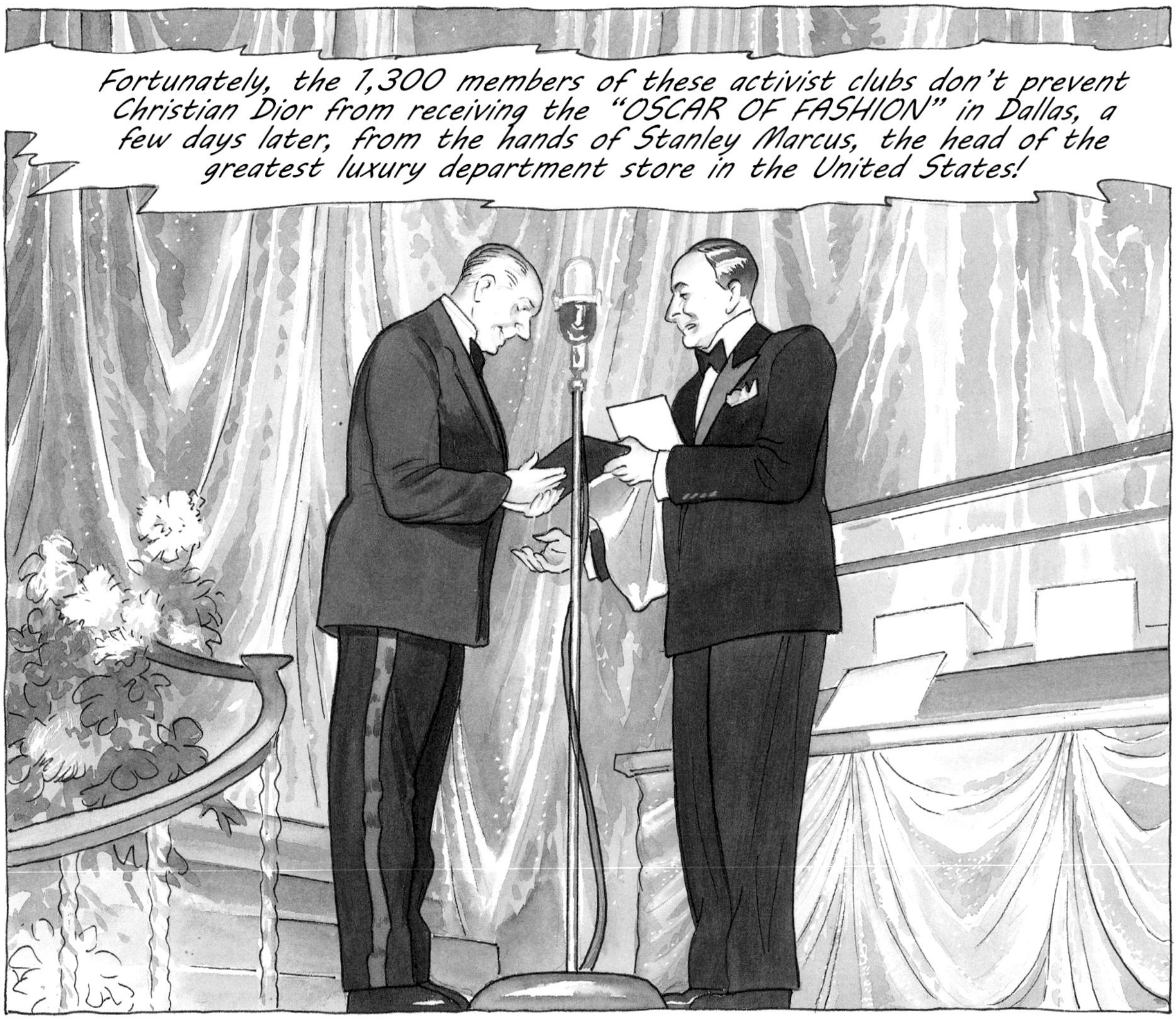

Fortunately, the 1,300 members of these activist clubs don't prevent Christian Dior from receiving the "OSCAR OF FASHION" in Dallas, a few days later, from the hands of Stanley Marcus, the head of the greatest luxury department store in the United States!

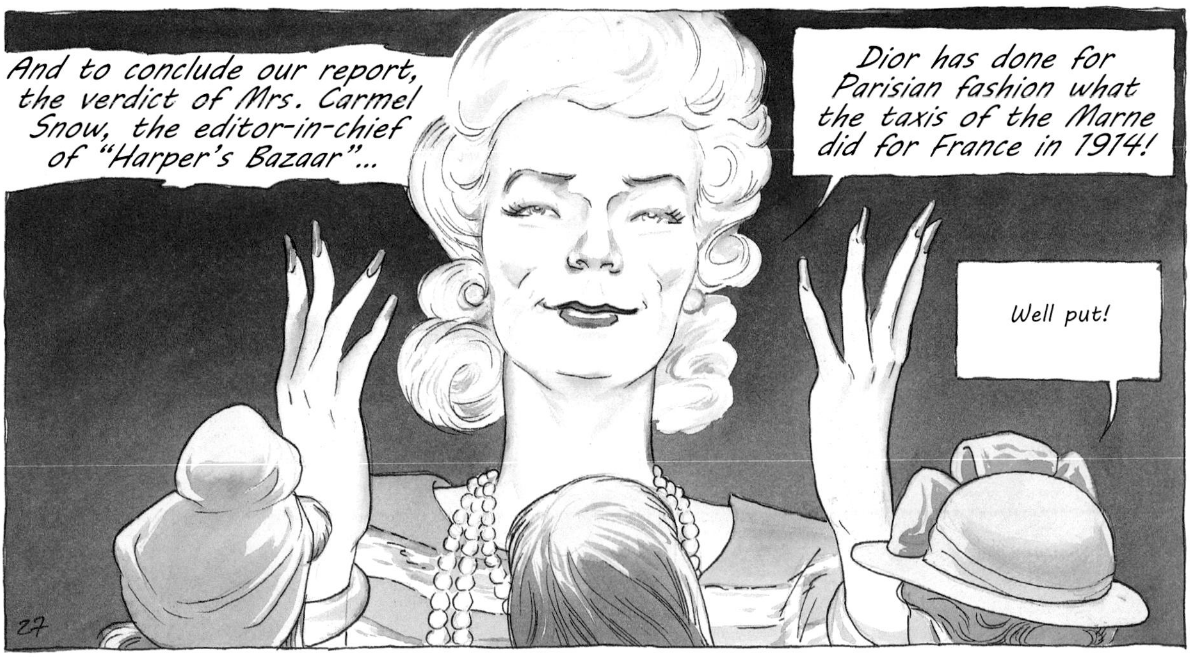

And to conclude our report, the verdict of Mrs. Carmel Snow, the editor-in-chief of "Harper's Bazaar"...
Dior has done for Parisian fashion what the taxis of the Marne did for France in 1914!
Well put!
27

My friends! Next year, we'll open a branch in New York!
What do you think of that, my dear Jacques?
Boss, as your administrative manager, I think it's bold. Let's go conquer the New World!

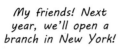

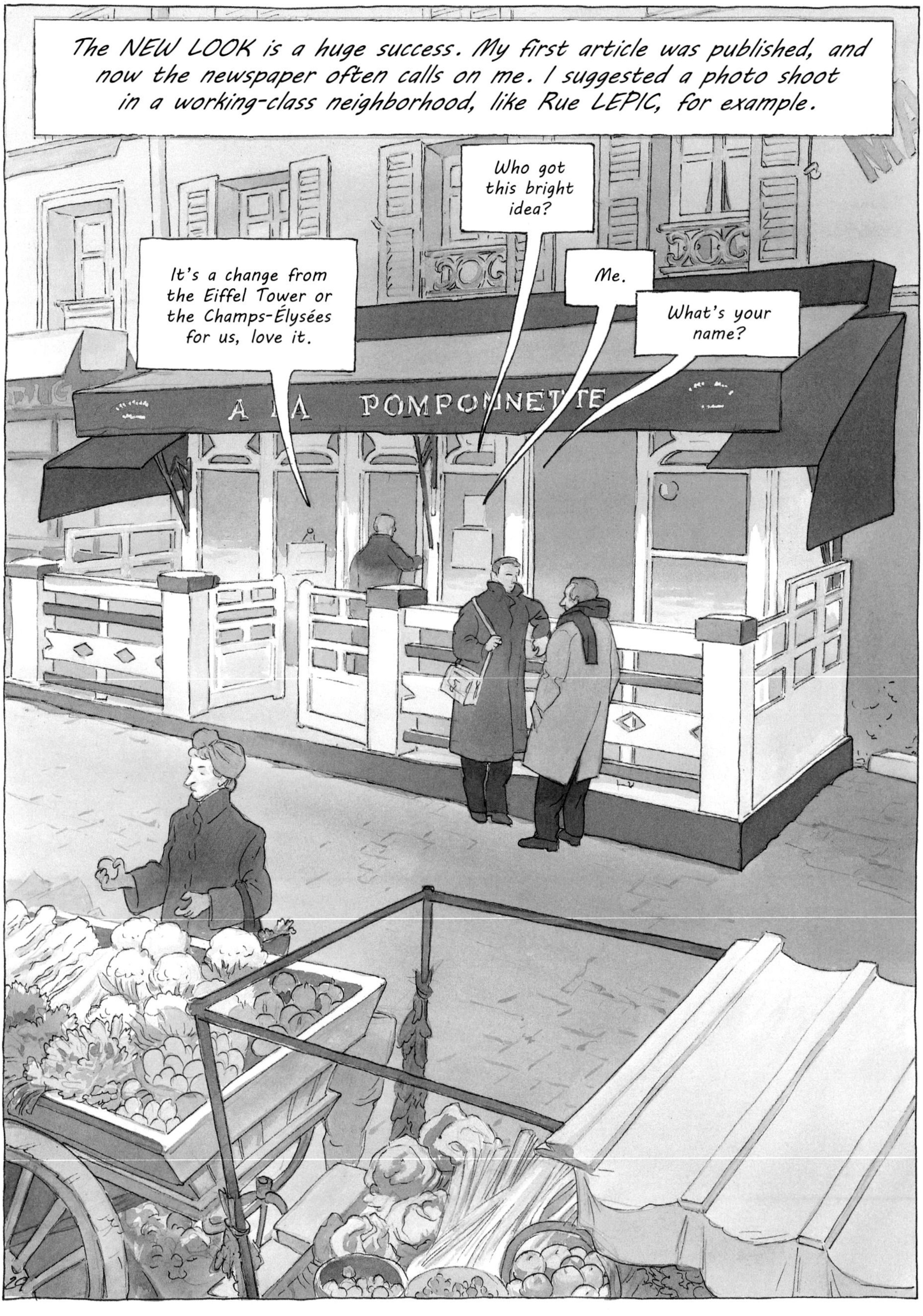
The NEW LOOK is a huge success. My first article was published, and now the newspaper often calls on me. I suggested a photo shoot in a working-class neighborhood, like Rue LEPIC, for example.
Who got this bright idea?
It's a change from the Eiffel Tower or the Champs-Élysées for us, love it.
Me.
What's your name?
A LA POMPONNETTE

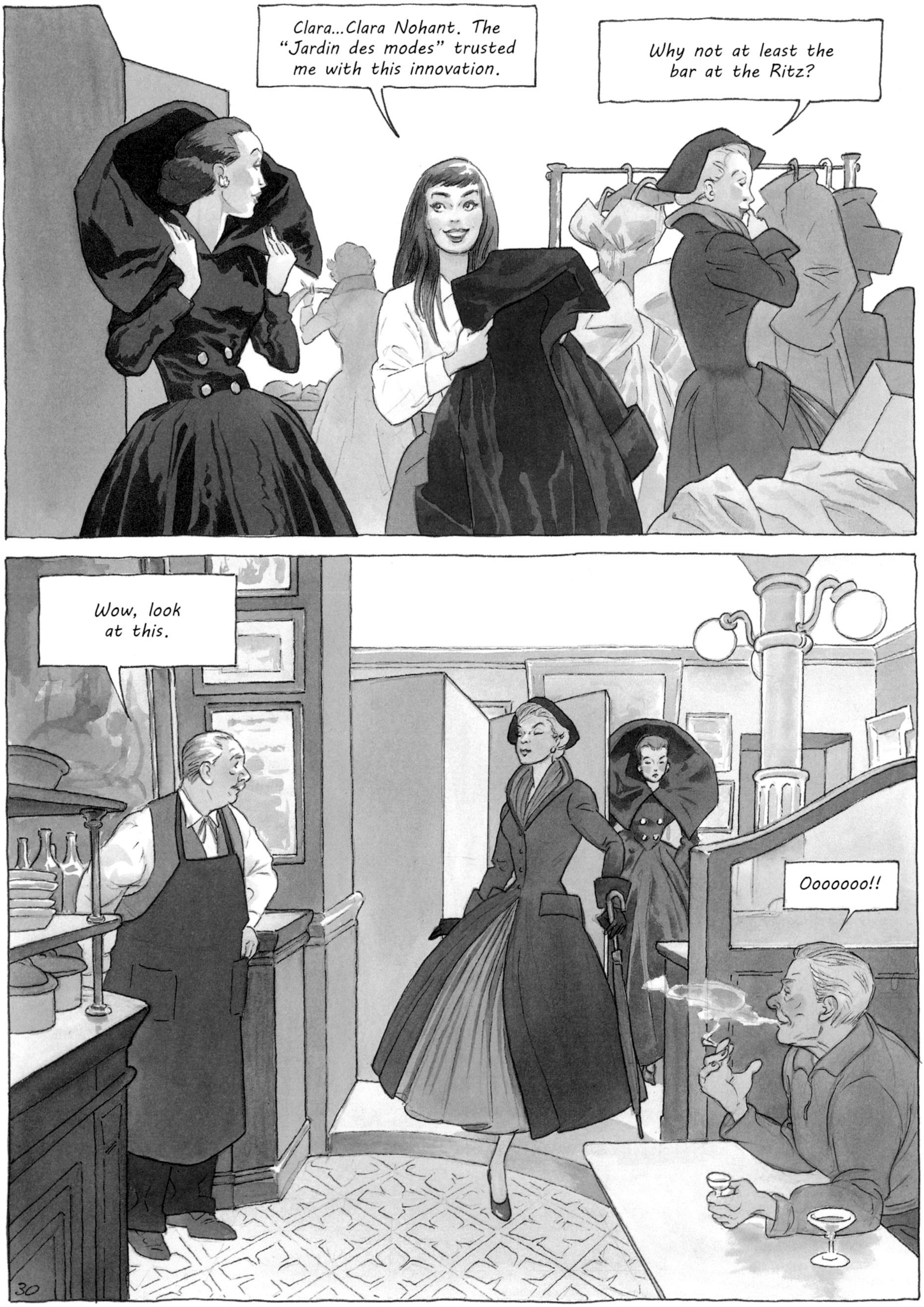
Clara...Clara Nohant. The "Jardin des modes" trusted me with this innovation.
Why not at least the bar at the Ritz?
Wow, look at this.
Ooooooo!!

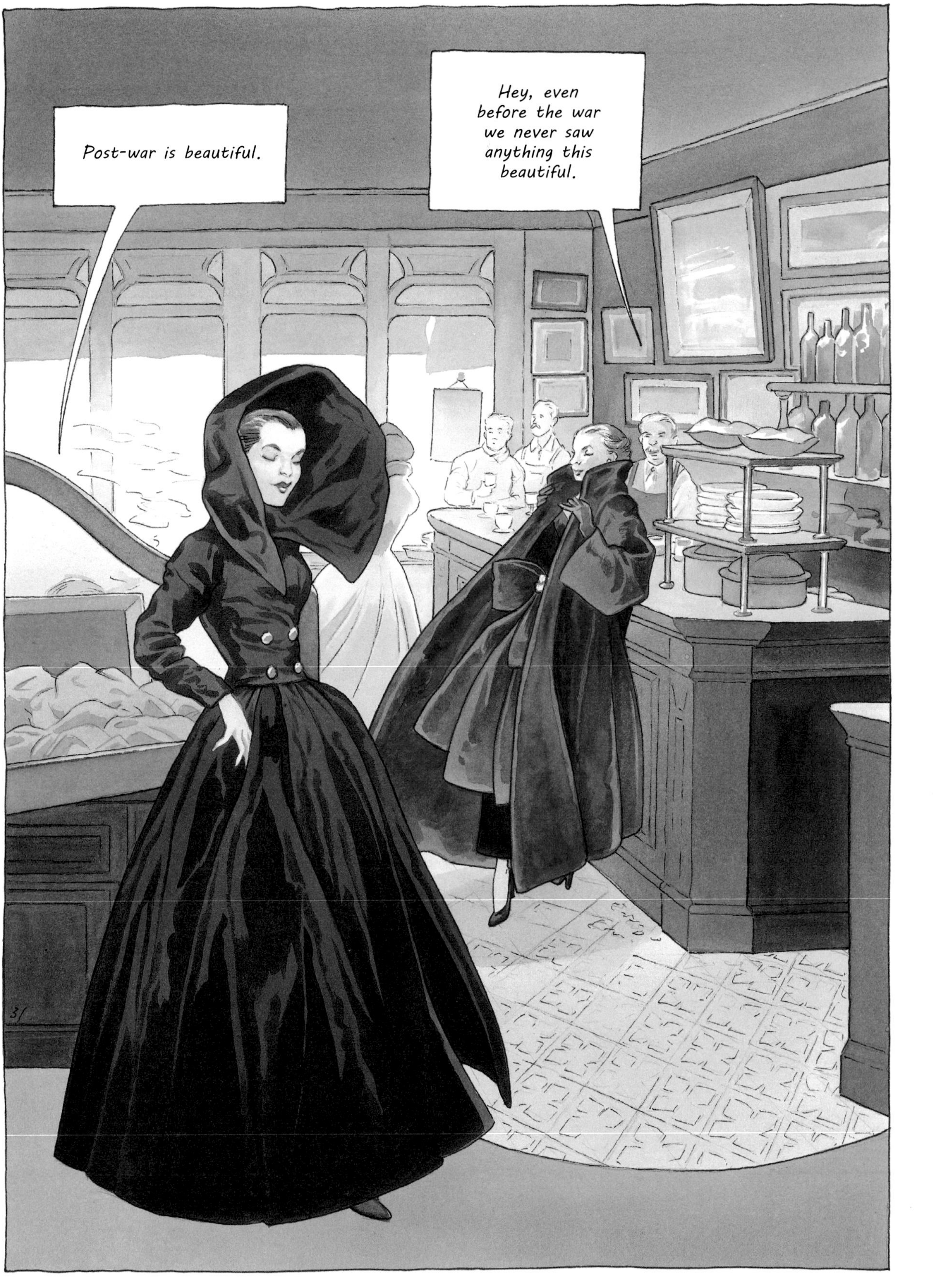
Post-war is beautiful.
Hey, even before the war we never saw anything this beautiful.

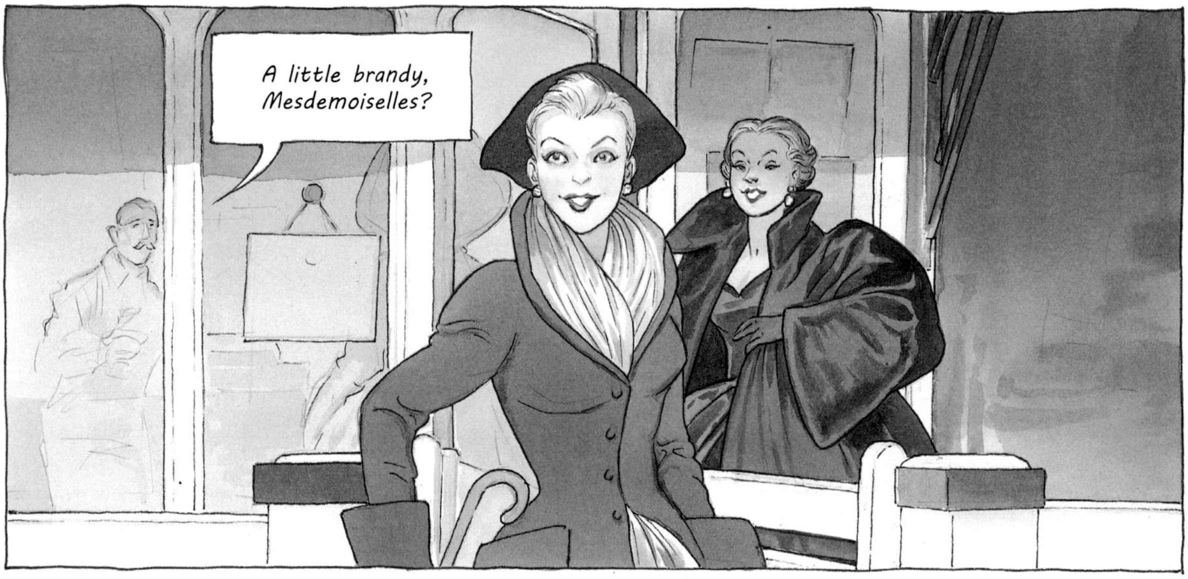
A little brandy, Mesdemoiselles?

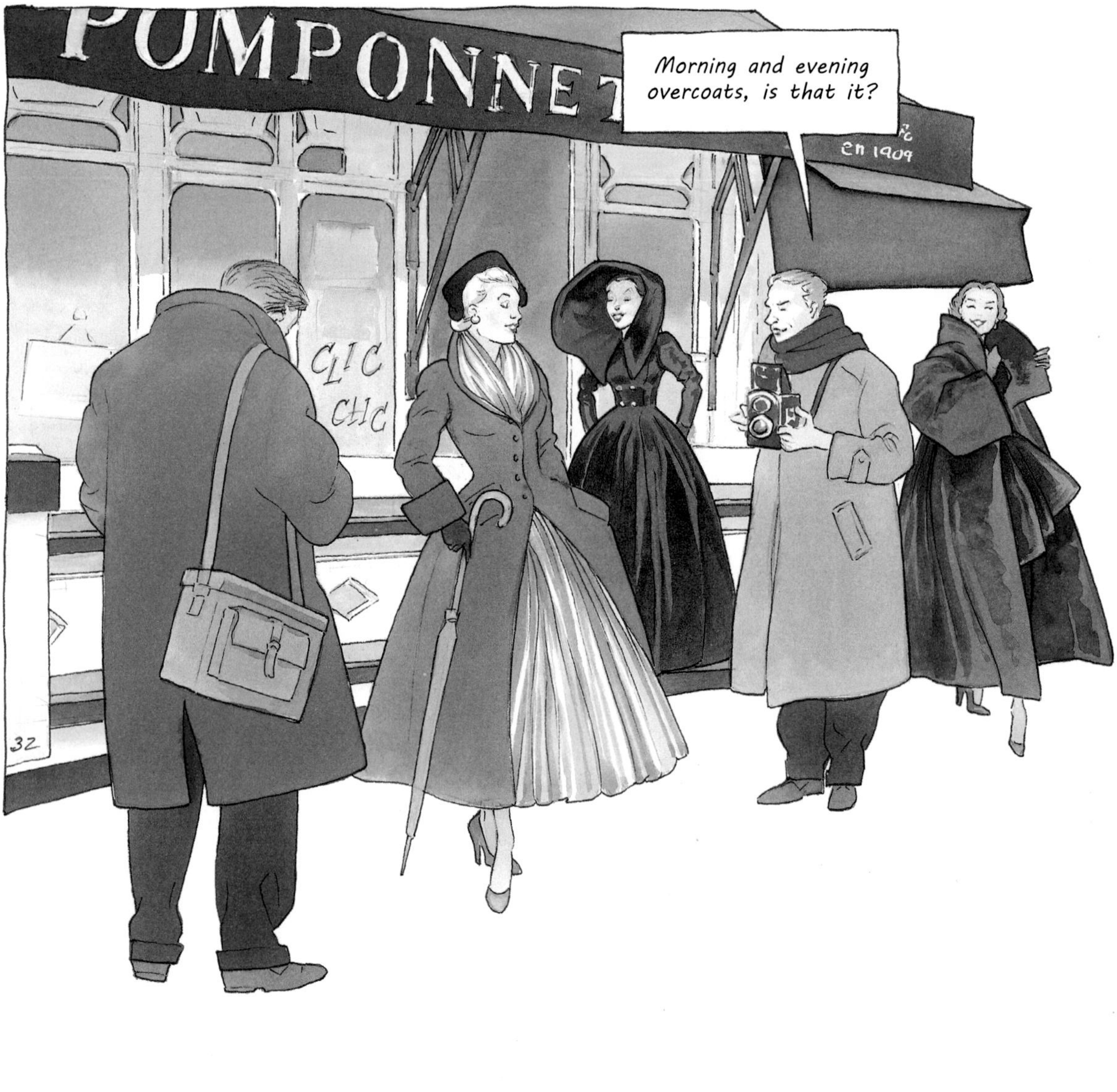
POMPONNET
Morning and evening overcoats, is that it?
en 1909
CLIC
CLIC
32

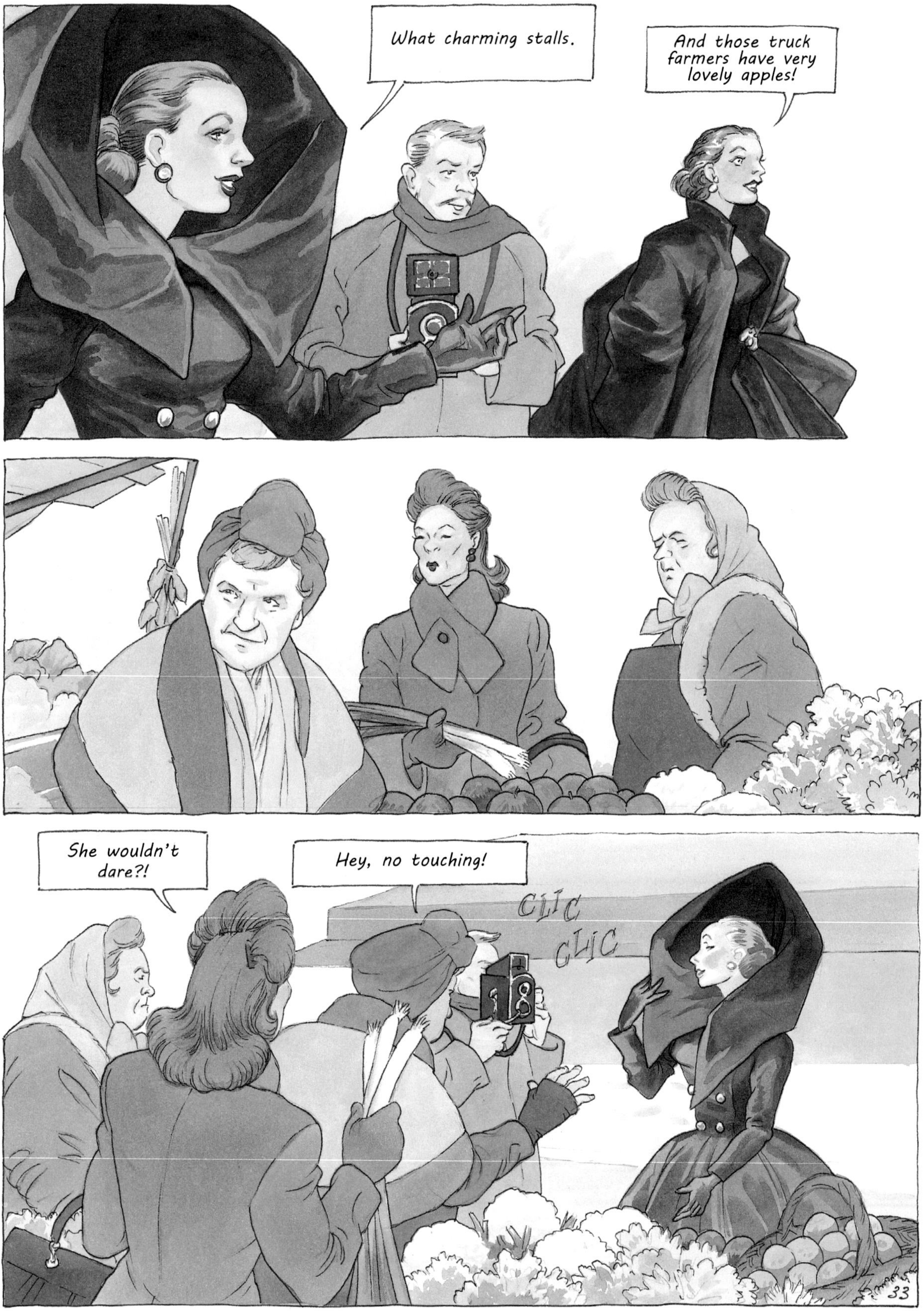
What charming stalls.
And those truck farmers have very lovely apples!
She wouldn't dare?!
Hey, no touching!
CLIC
CLIC

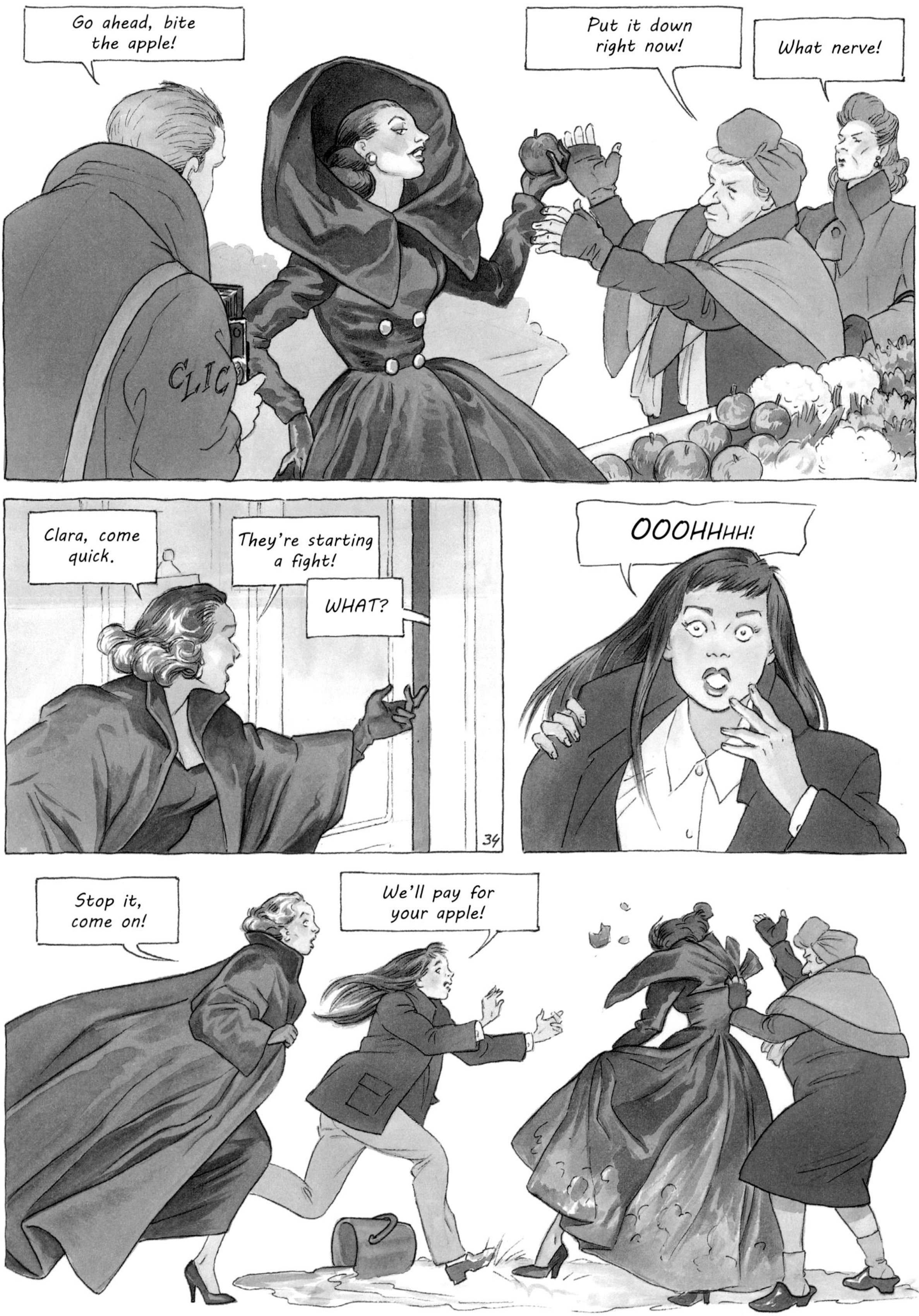

Go ahead, bite the apple!
CLIC
Put it down right now!
What nerve!
Clara, come quick.
They're starting a fight!
WHAT?
34
OOOHHHH!
Stop it, come on!
We'll pay for your apple!

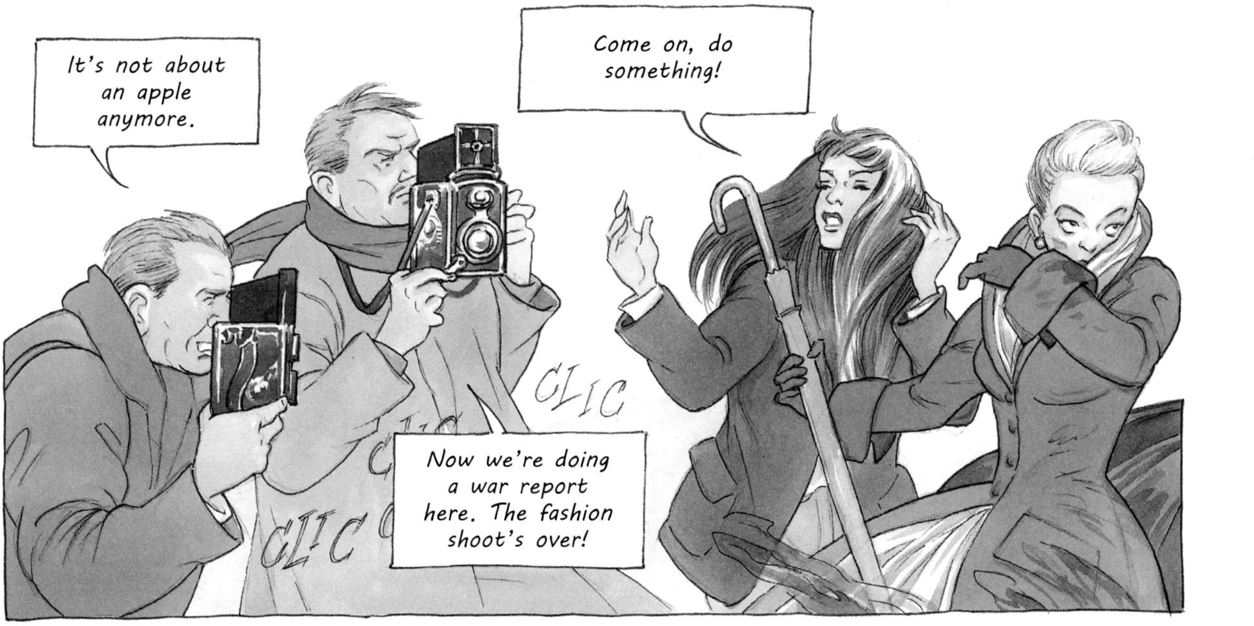
It's not about an apple anymore.
Come on, do something!
CLIC
CLIC
CLIC
Now we're doing a war report here. The fashion shoot's over!

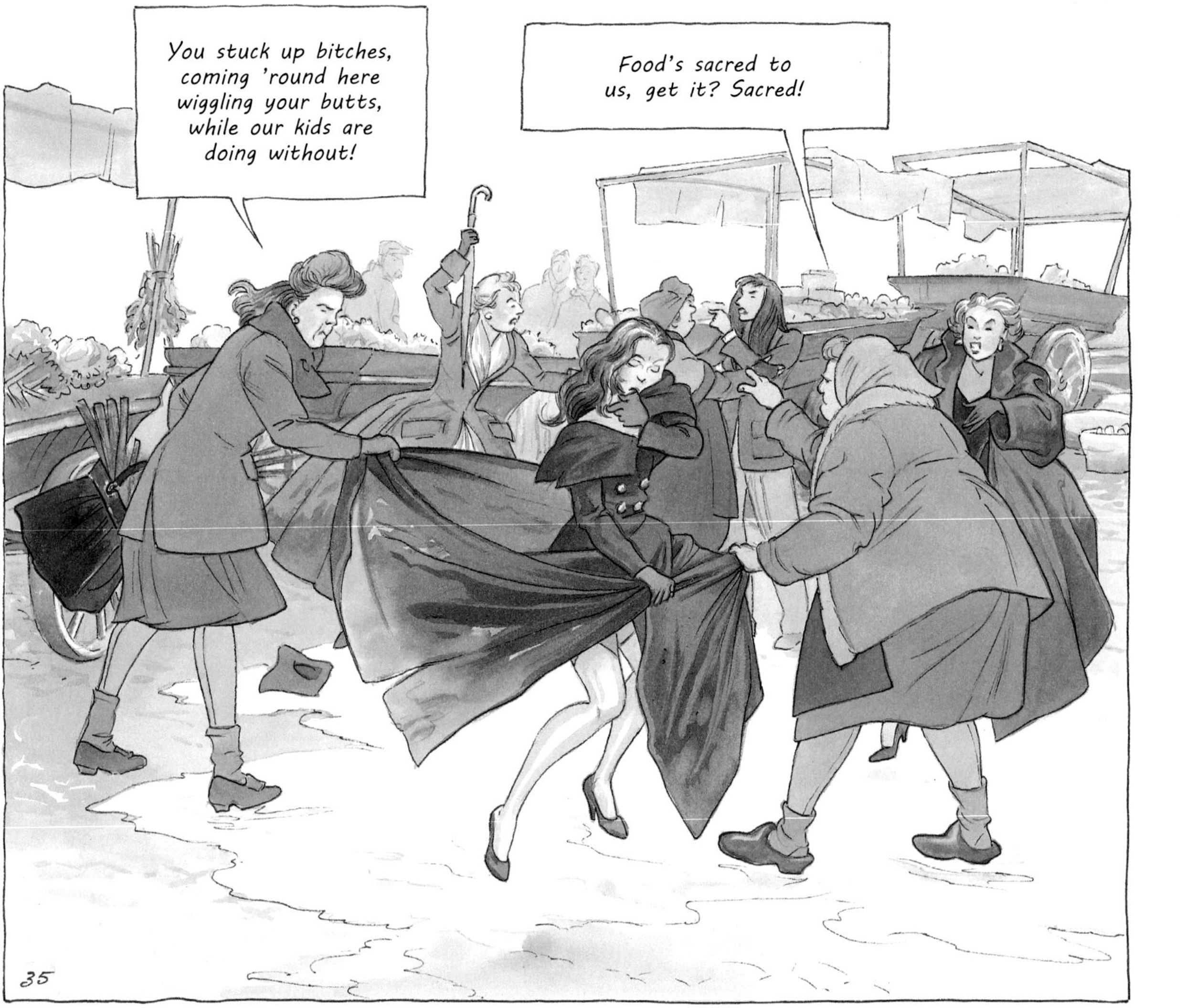
You stuck up bitches, coming 'round here wiggling your butts, while our kids are doing without!
Food's sacred to us, get it? Sacred!
35

RIDICULOUS, brutalizing my young women. Ah, they'll be hearing from me!
I know who had that ridiculous idea, Boss!

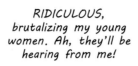

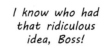

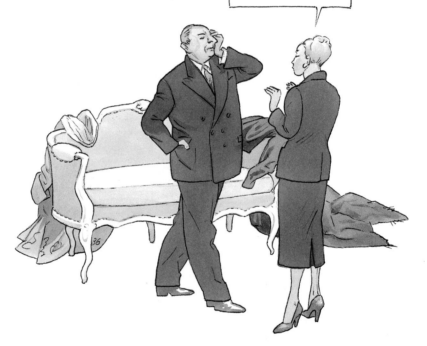

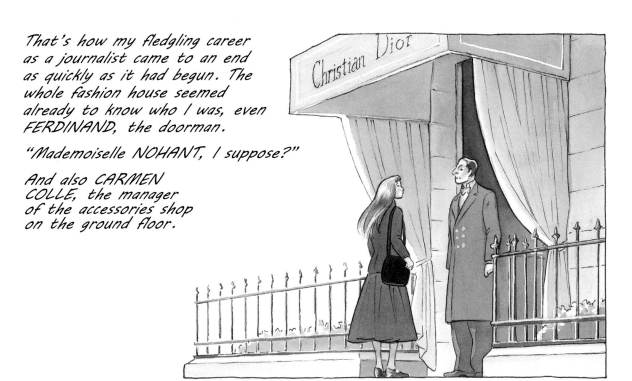

That's how my fledgling career as a journalist came to an end as quickly as it had begun. The whole fashion house seemed already to know who I was, even FERDINAND, the doorman.

"Mademoiselle NOHANT, I suppose?"

And also CARMEN COLLE, the manager of the accessories shop on the ground floor.

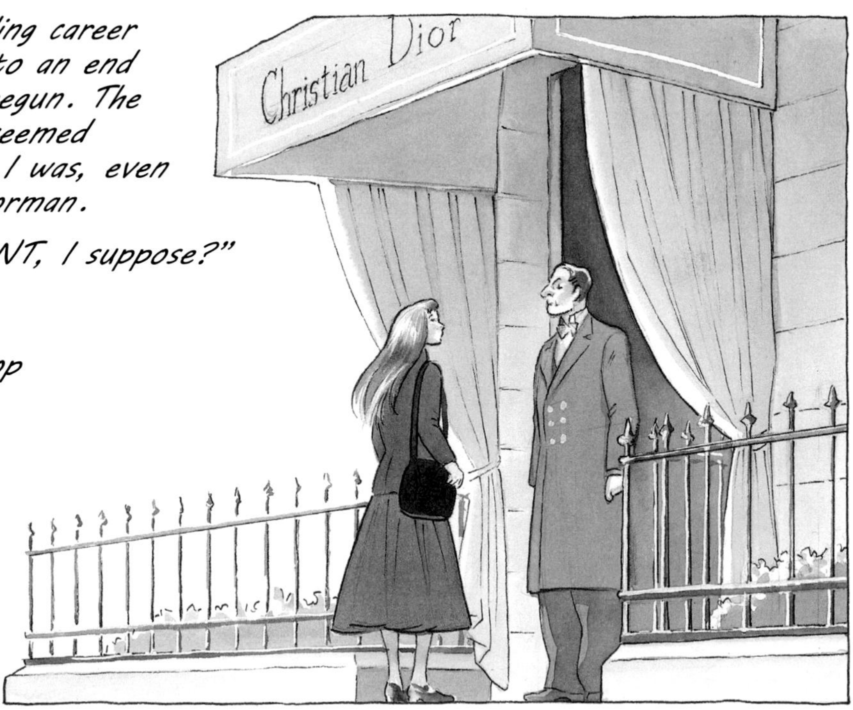
Christian Dior

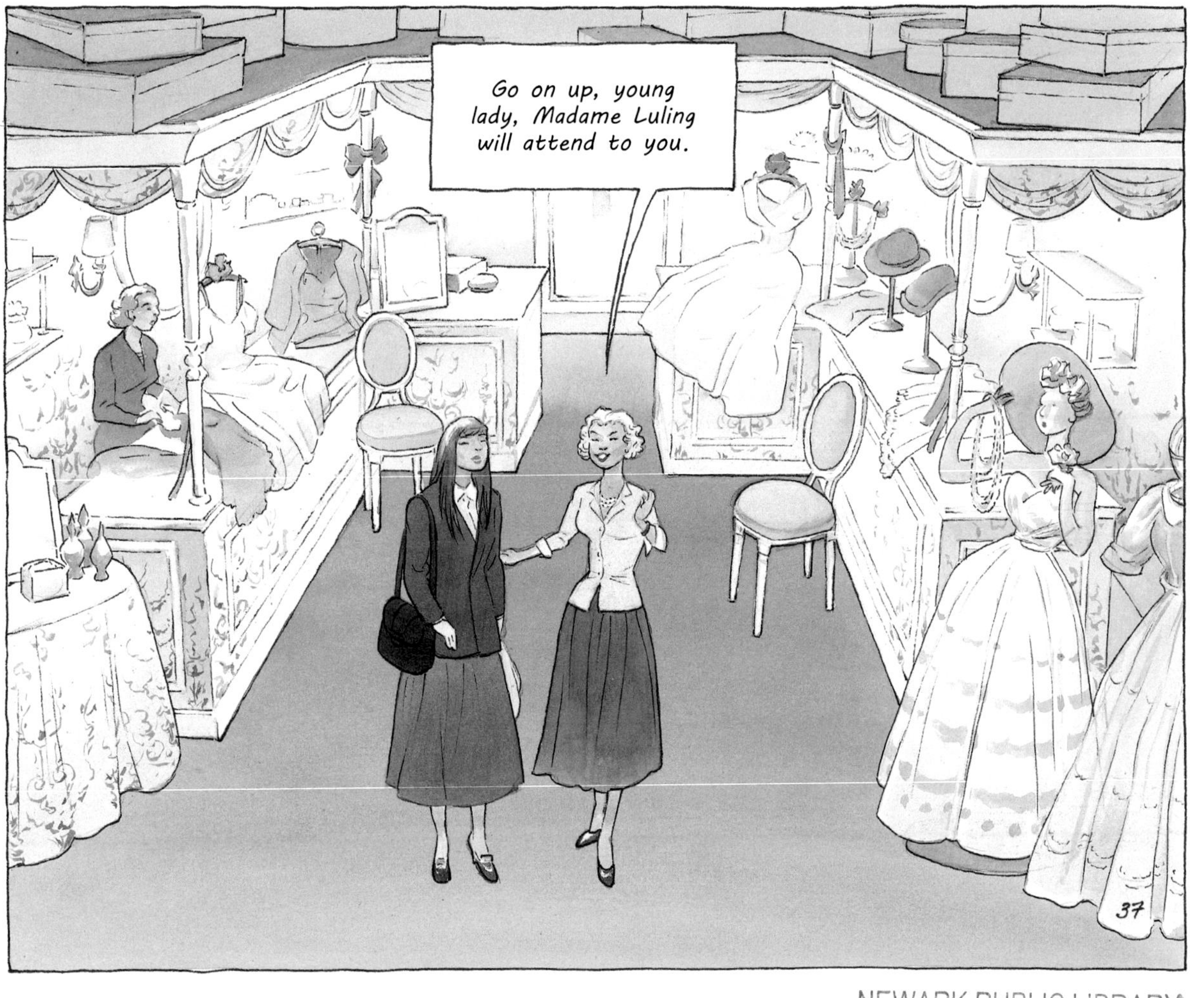
Go on up, young lady, Madame Luling will attend to you.
37

SUZANNE LULING, who's also CHRISTIAN DIOR's childhood friend. She makes no gesture of encouragement to me. My heart is pounding.

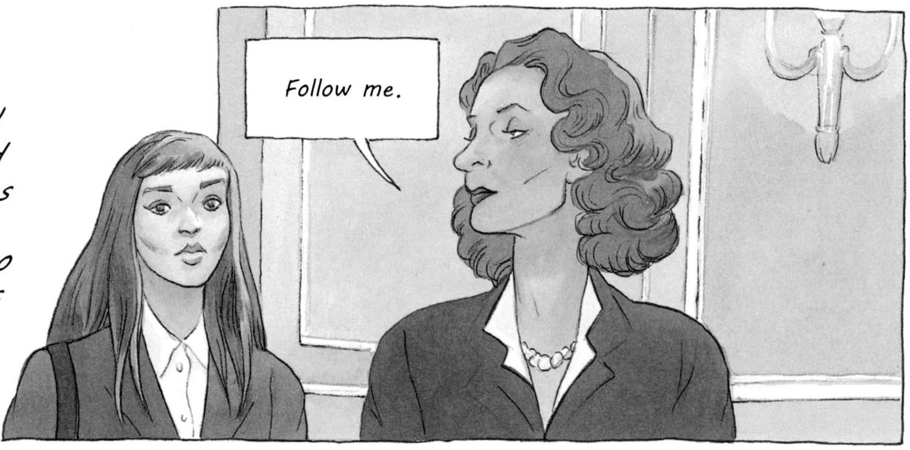
Follow me.

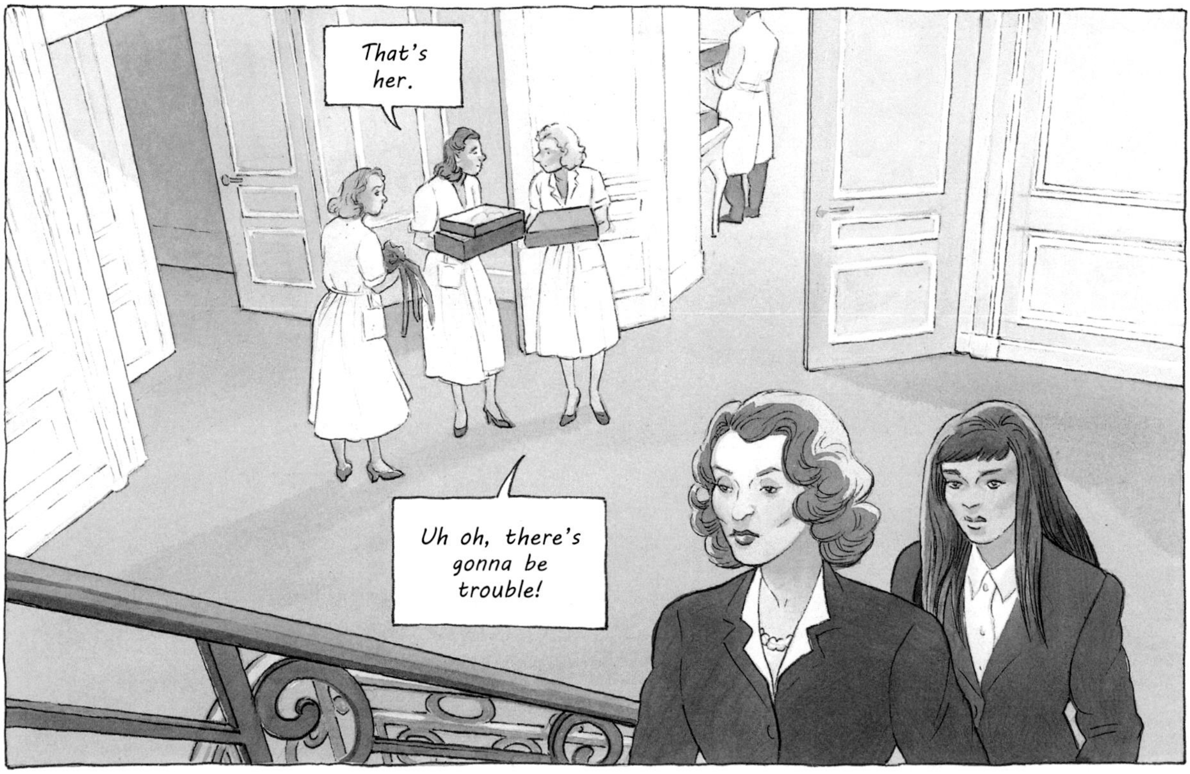
That's her.
Uh oh, there's gonna be trouble!

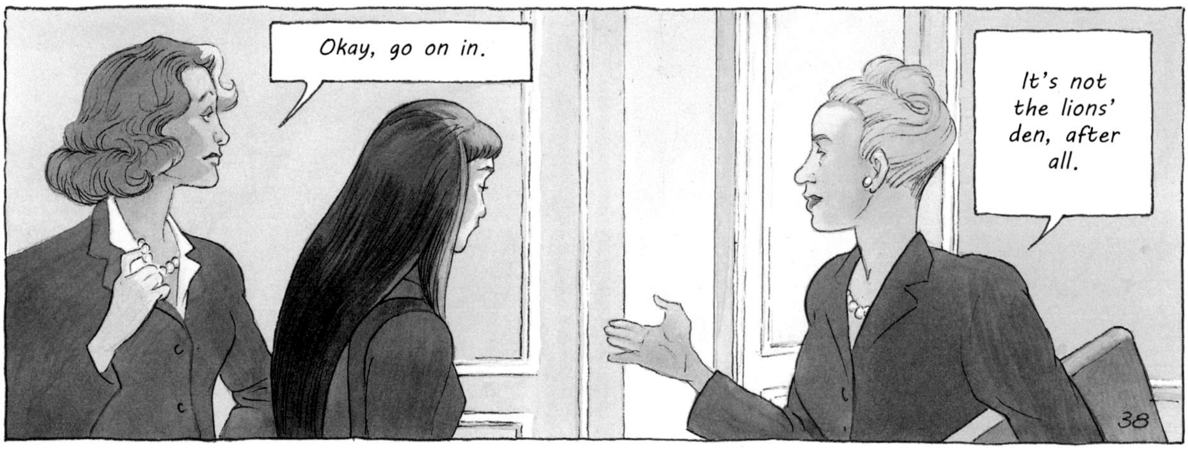
Okay, go on in.
It's not the lions' den, after all.
38

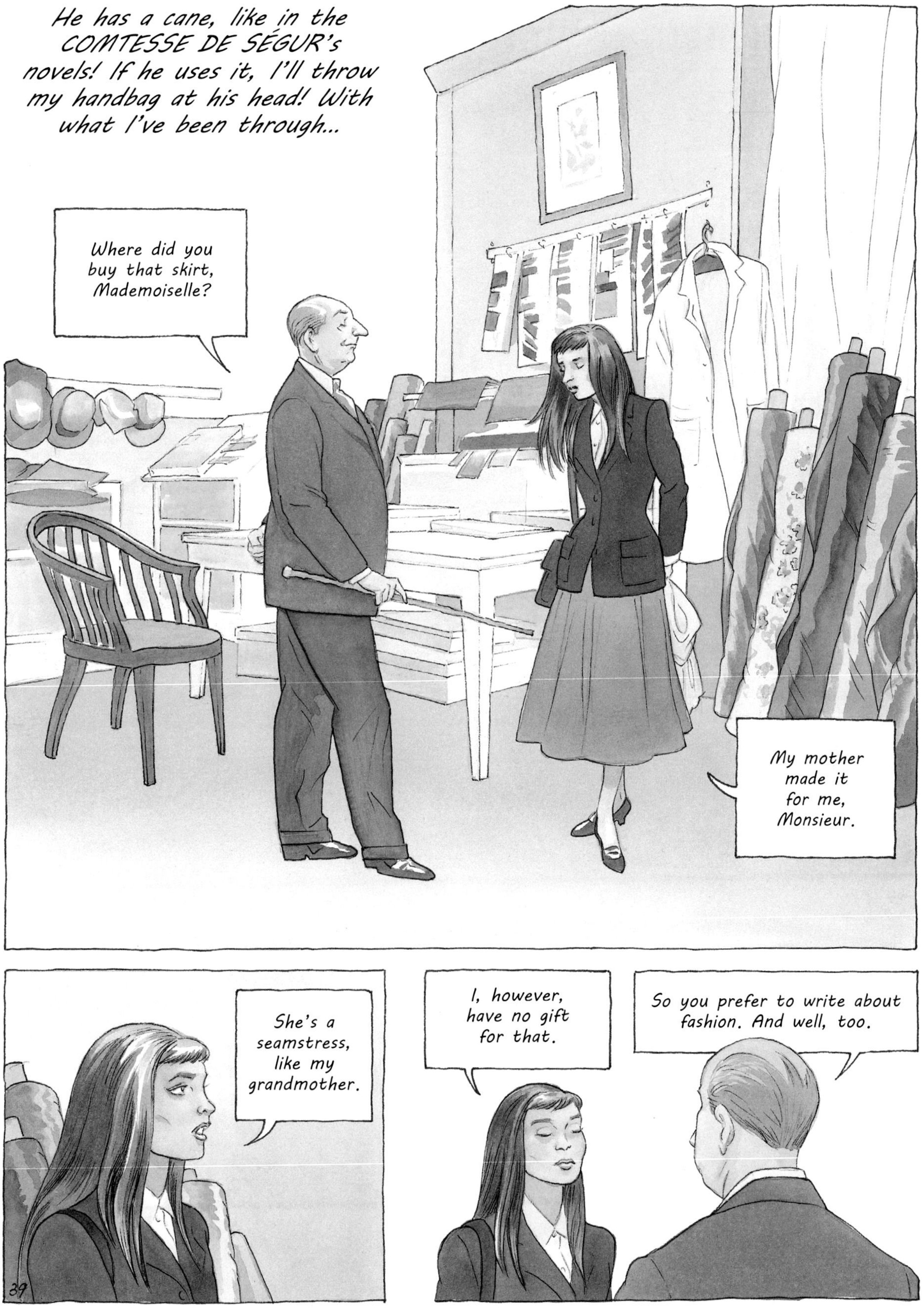
He has a cane, like in the COMTESSE DE SÉGUR's novels! If he uses it, I'll throw my handbag at his head! With what I've been through...
Where did you buy that skirt, Mademoiselle?
My mother made it for me, Monsieur.
She's a seamstress, like my grandmother.
I, however, have no gift for that.
So you prefer to write about fashion. And well, too.

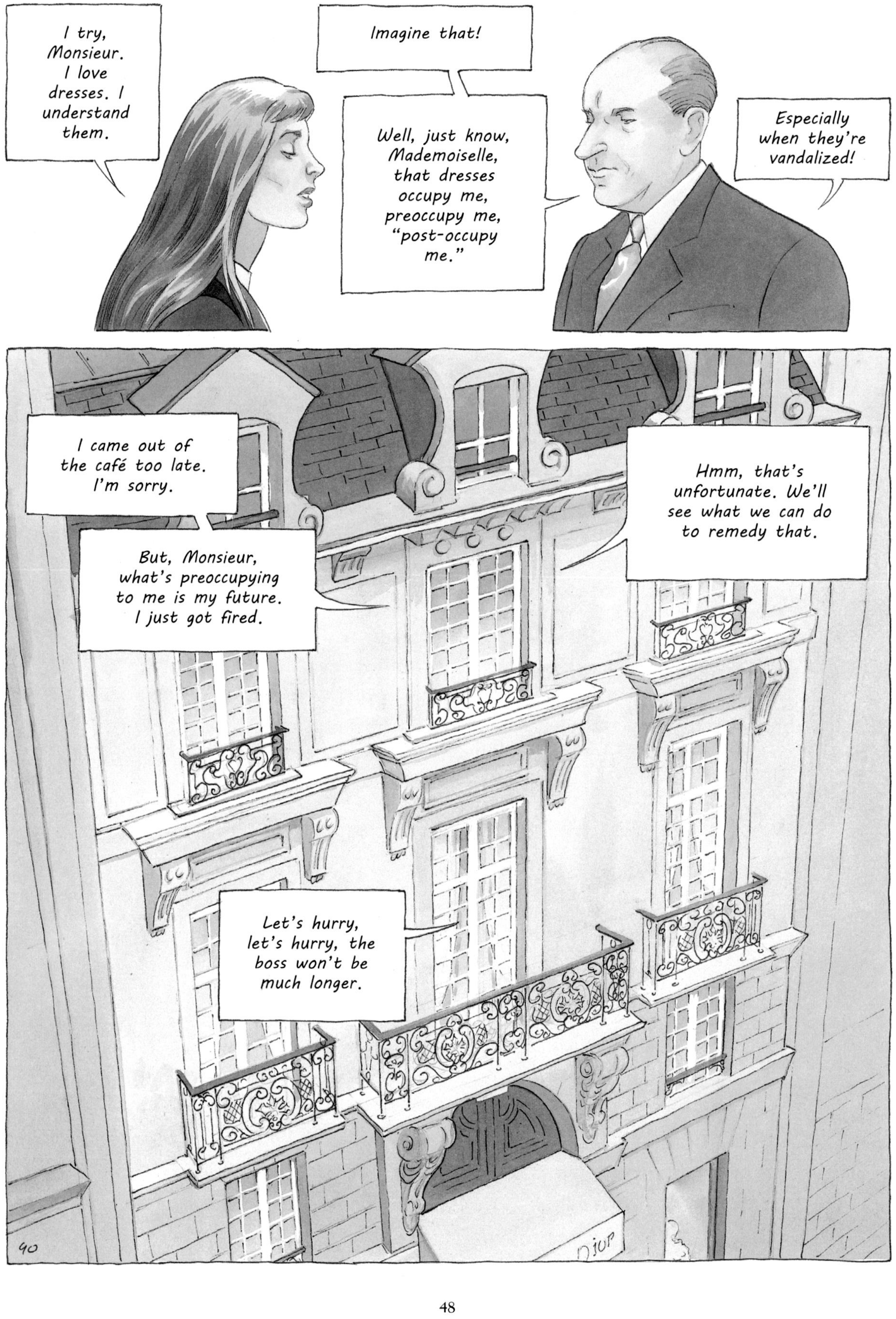
I try, Monsieur. I love dresses. I understand them.
Imagine that!
Well, just know, Mademoiselle, that dresses occupy me, preoccupy me, "post-occupy me."
Especially when they're vandalized!
I came out of the café too late. I'm sorry.
But, Monsieur, what's preoccupying to me is my future. I just got fired.
Hmm, that's unfortunate. We'll see what we can do to remedy that.
Let's hurry, let's hurry, the boss won't be much longer.

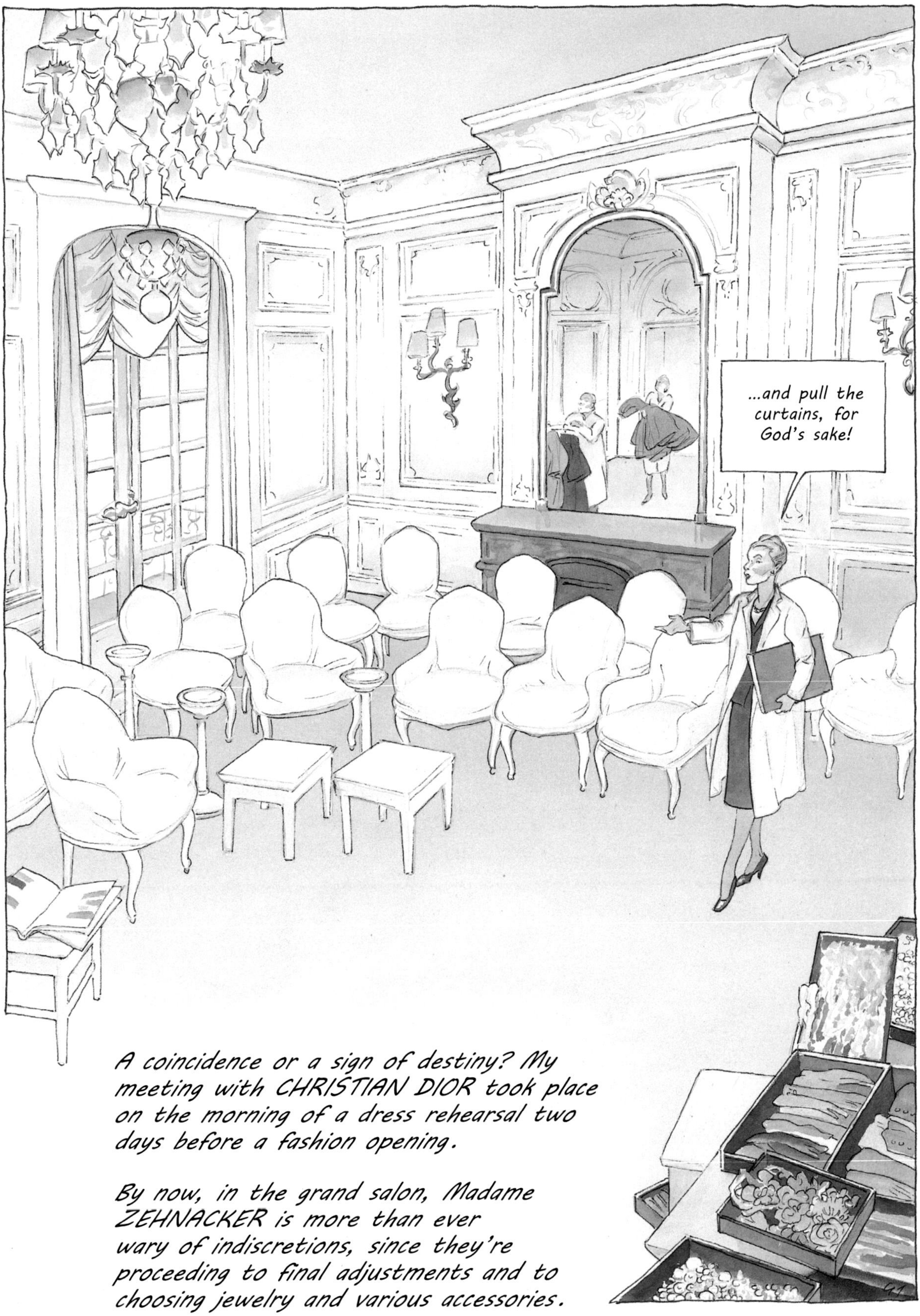
...and pull the curtains, for God's sake!
A coincidence or a sign of destiny? My meeting with CHRISTIAN DIOR took place on the morning of a dress rehearsal two days before a fashion opening.
By now, in the grand salon, Madame ZEHNACKER is more than ever wary of indiscretions, since they're proceeding to final adjustments and to choosing jewelry and various accessories.

Don't you know the photographers from the studio across the way are on the lookout for everything?!

Mitzah hasn't arrived?

Yeah, what about her?

Tsk, tsk, we'll get treated to her usual entrance.

Here I am!

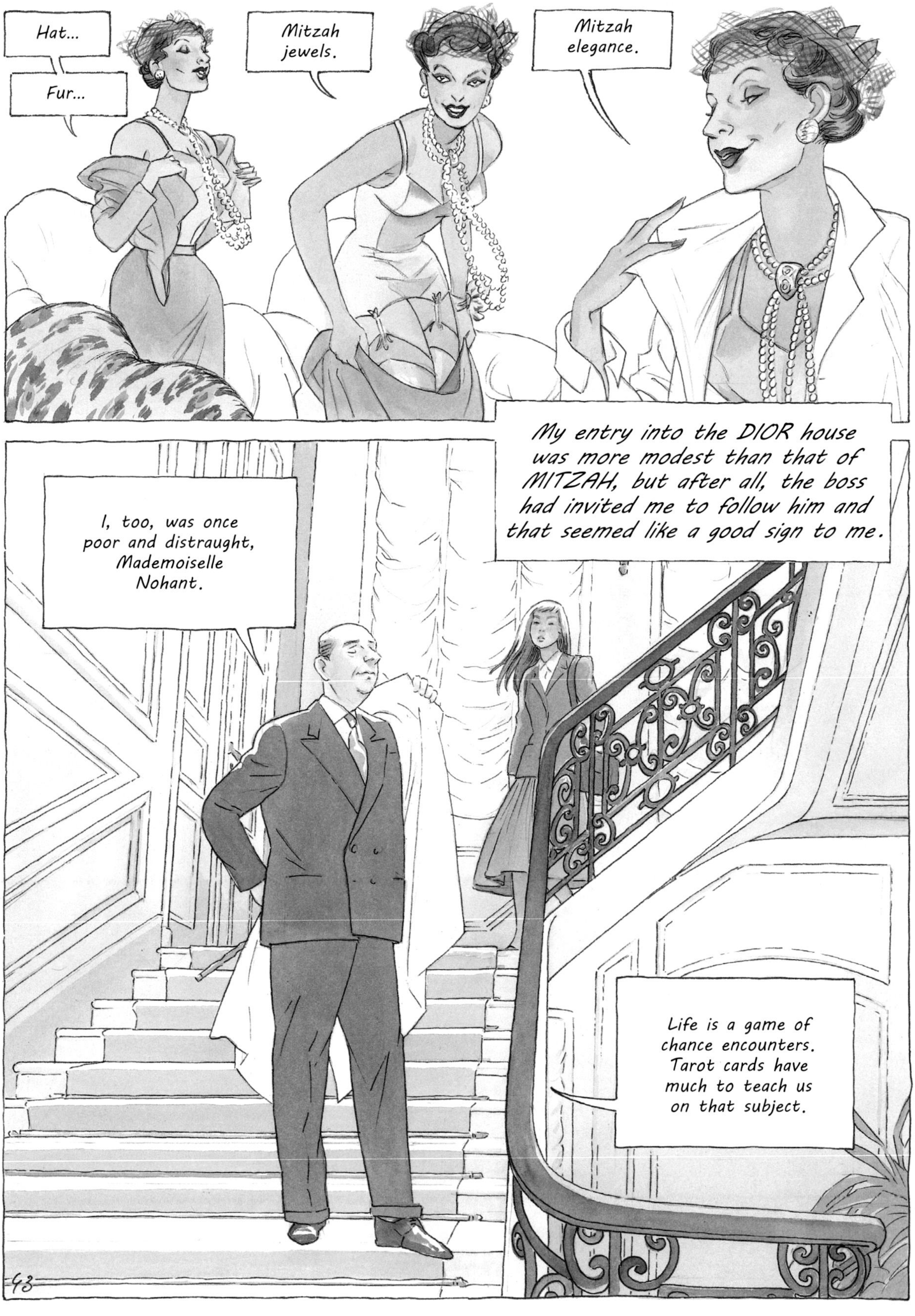
Hat...
Fur...
Mitzah jewels.
Mitzah elegance.
My entry into the DIOR house was more modest than that of MITZAH, but after all, the boss had invited me to follow him and that seemed like a good sign to me.
I, too, was once poor and distraught, Mademoiselle Nohant.
Life is a game of chance encounters. Tarot cards have much to teach us on that subject.

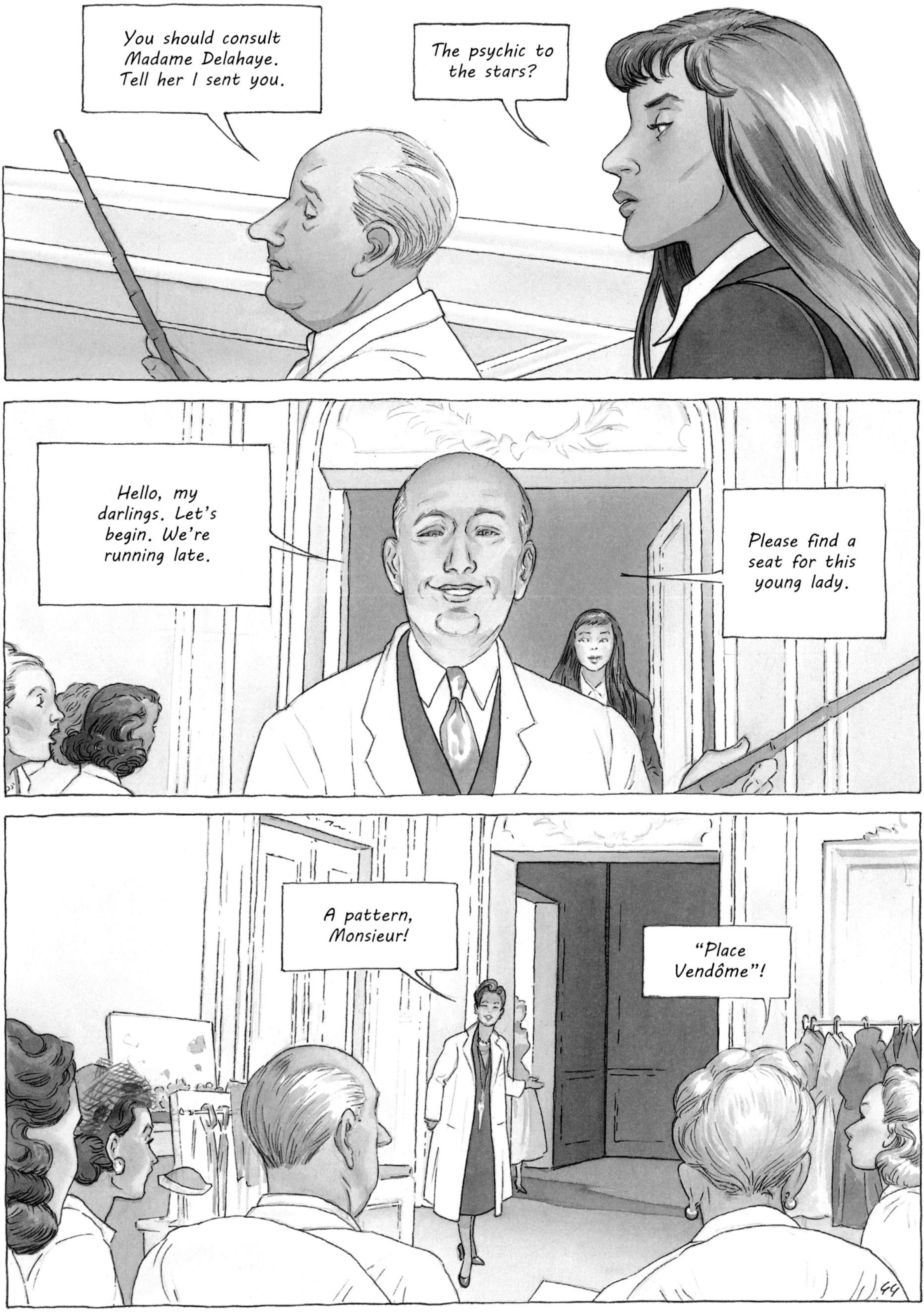
You should consult Madame Delahaye. Tell her I sent you.
The psychic to the stars?
Hello, my darlings. Let's begin. We're running late.
Please find a seat for this young lady.
A pattern, Monsieur!
"Place Vendôme"!

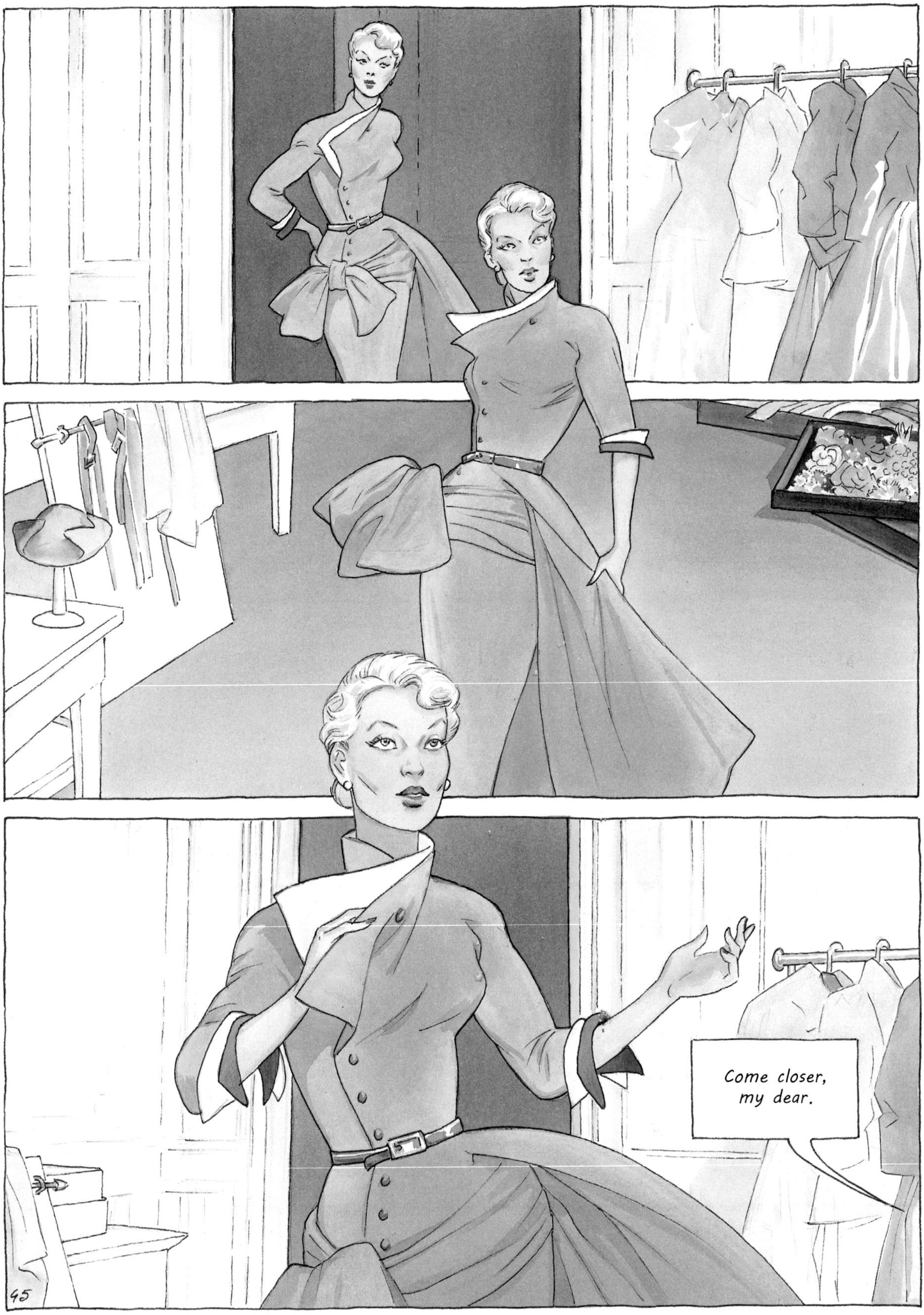
Come closer, my dear.

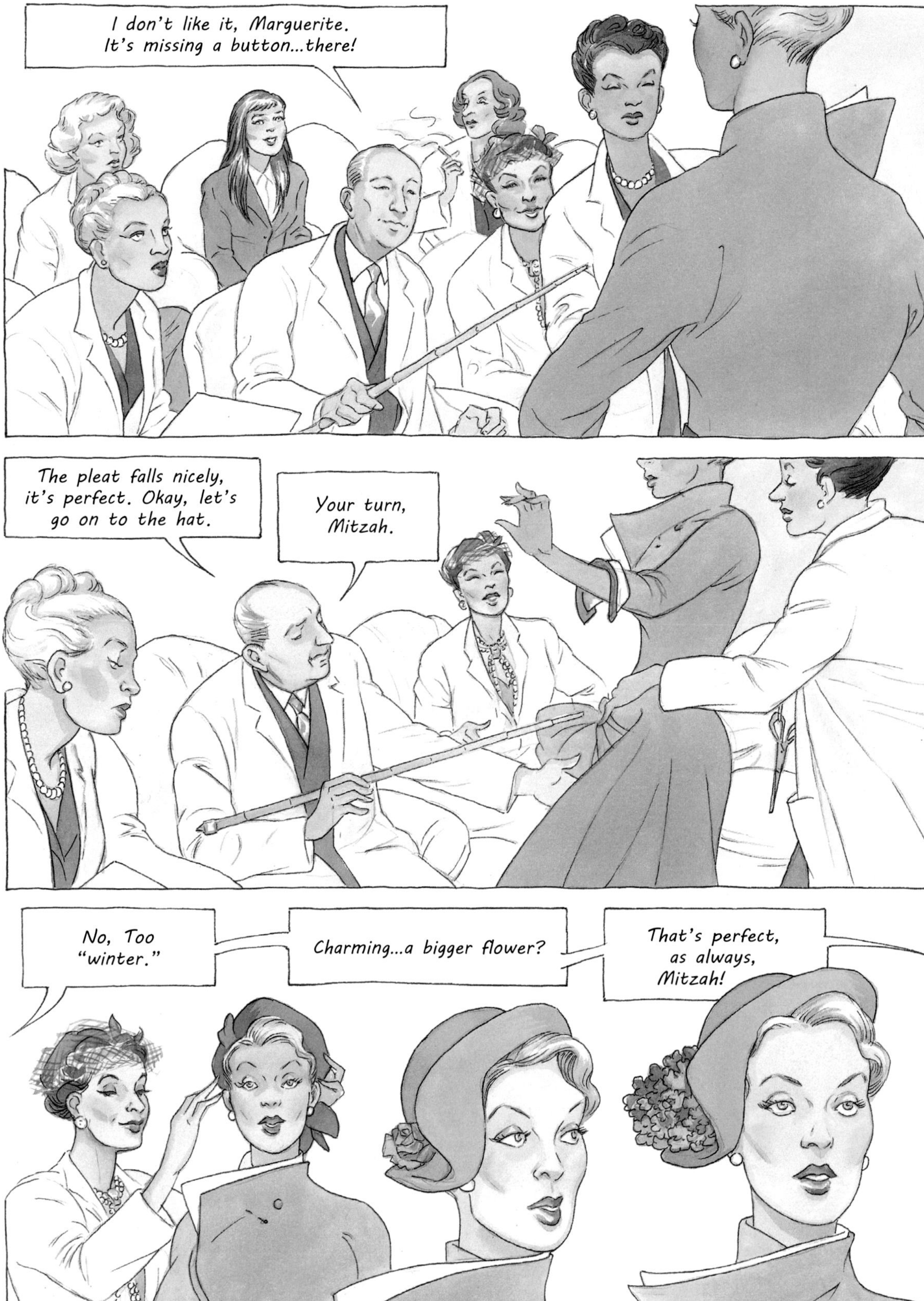
I don't like it, Marguerite. It's missing a button...there!
The pleat falls nicely, it's perfect. Okay, let's go on to the hat.
Your turn, Mitzah.
No, Too "winter."
Charming...a bigger flower?
That's perfect, as always, Mitzah!

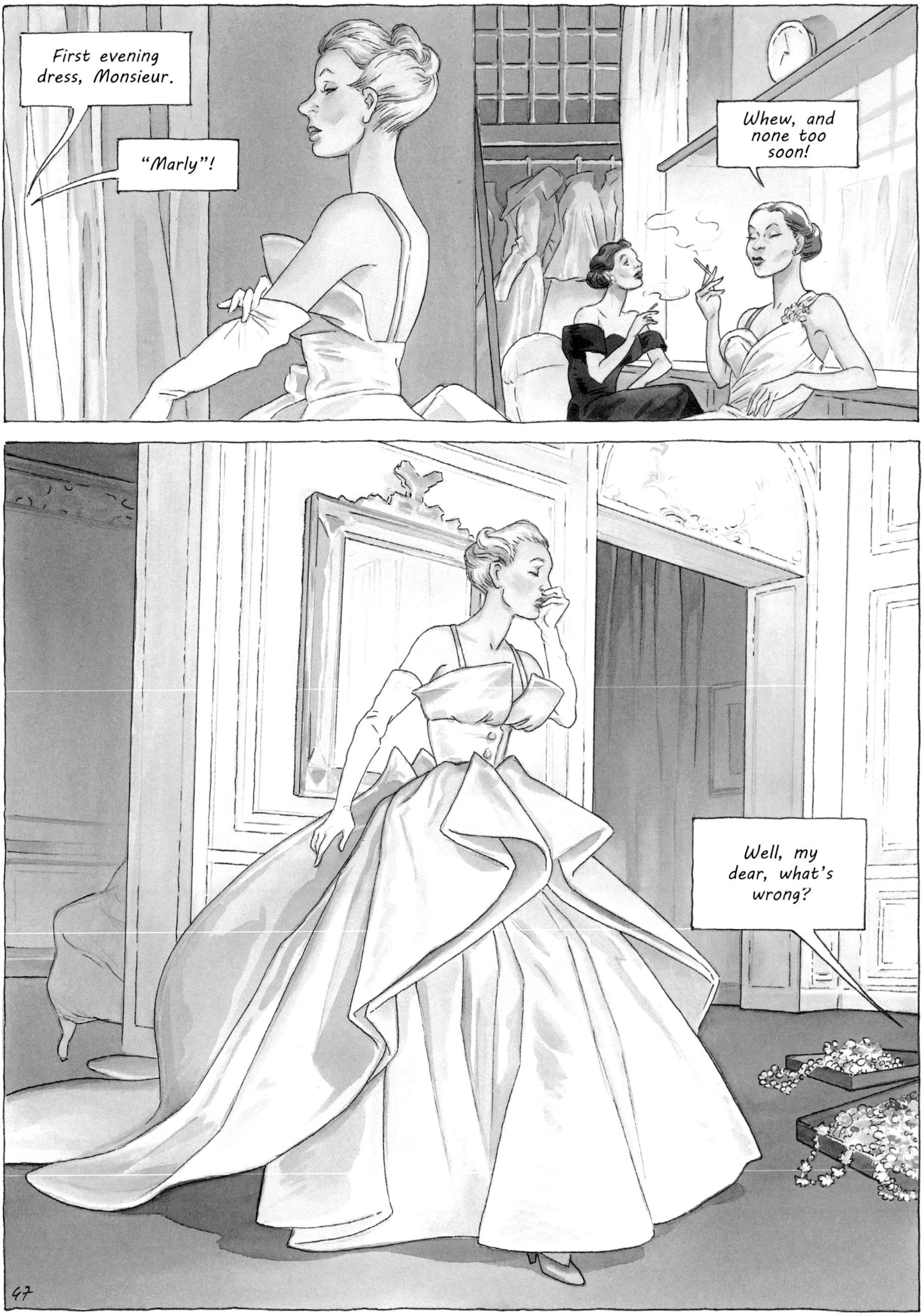
First evening dress, Monsieur.
"Marly"!
Whew, and none too soon!
Well, my dear, what's wrong?
47

For the first time, I found myself inside the enchanted world of high fashion. But I was also going to discover that at Monsieur DIOR's, you know when you'll start the fittings, but never when you'll finish them.

Around midnight, we tackle the gala dresses.

Will "MARLY" wear gloves? Which ones? Or not? Embellished with strings of pearls or rhinestone jewelry? Unless...

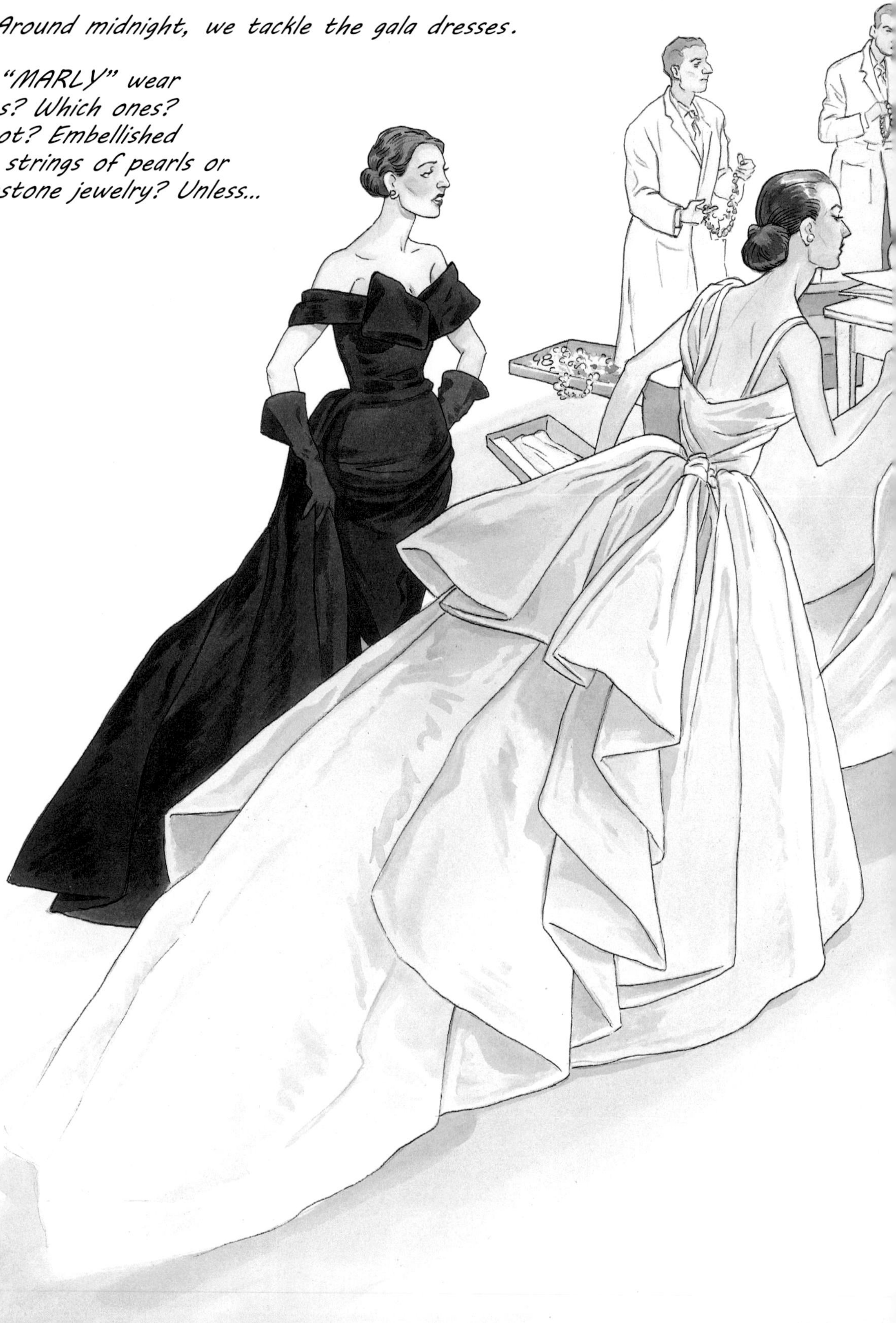

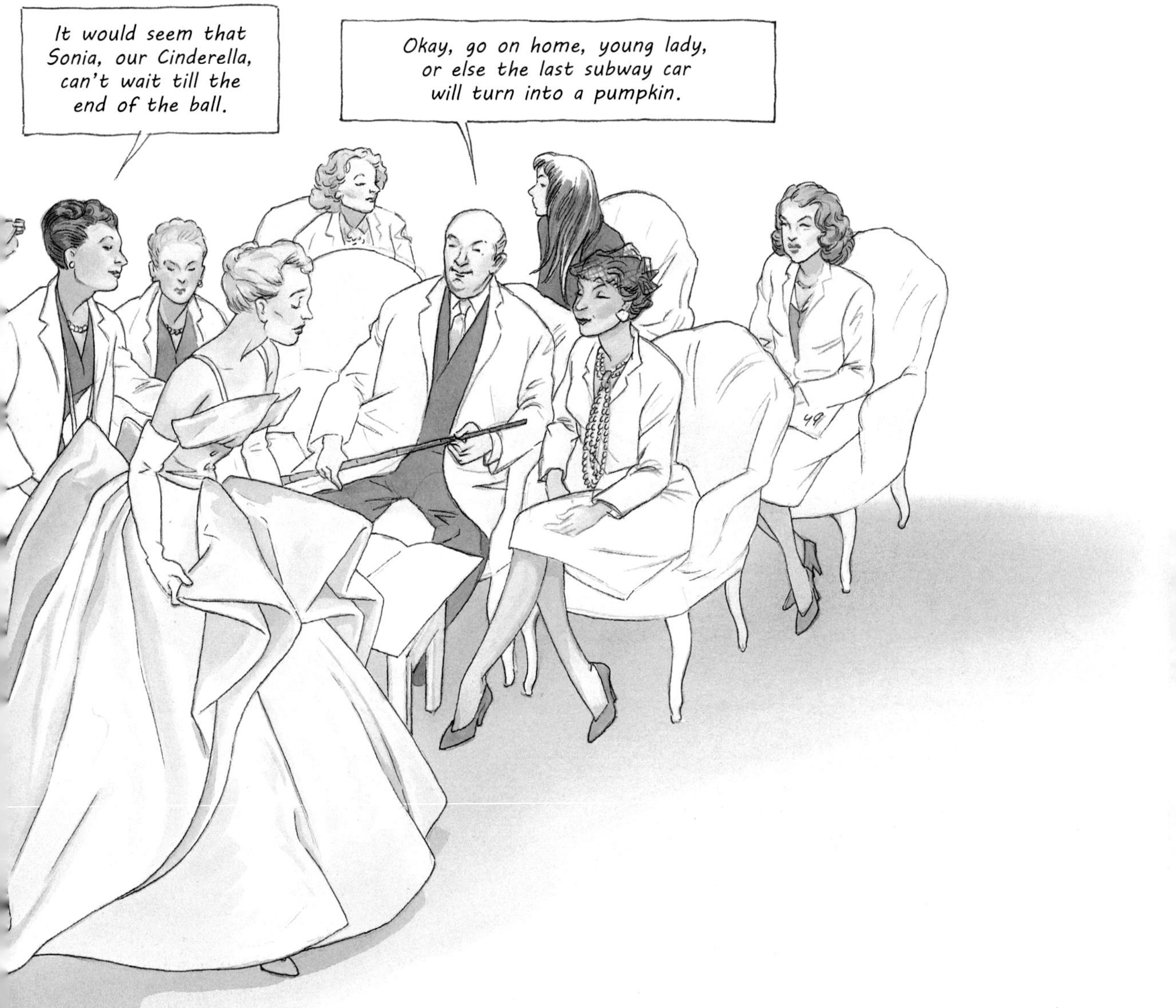
It would seem that Sonia, our Cinderella, can't wait till the end of the ball.
Okay, go on home, young lady, or else the last subway car will turn into a pumpkin.
49

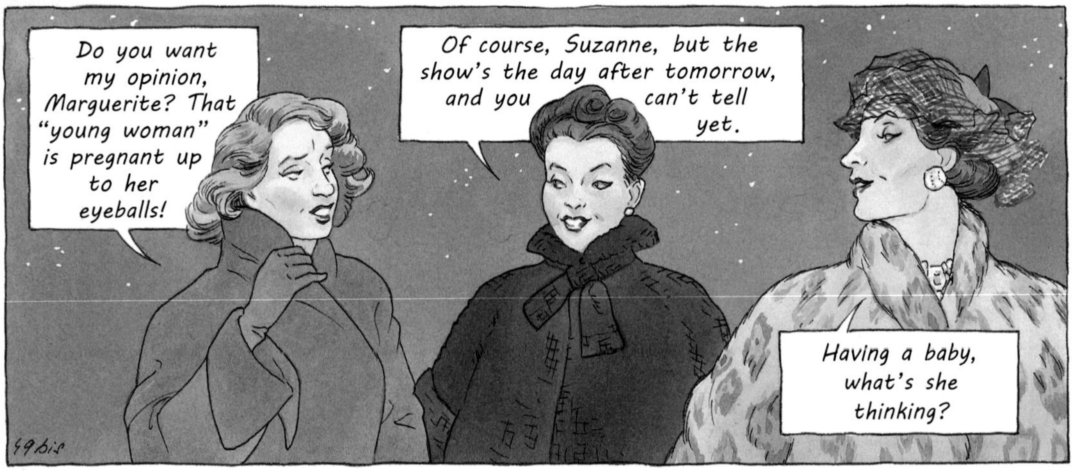
Do you want my opinion, Marguerite? That "young woman" is pregnant up to her eyeballs!
Of course, Suzanne, but the show's the day after tomorrow, and you can't tell yet.
Having a baby, what's she thinking?
49 bis

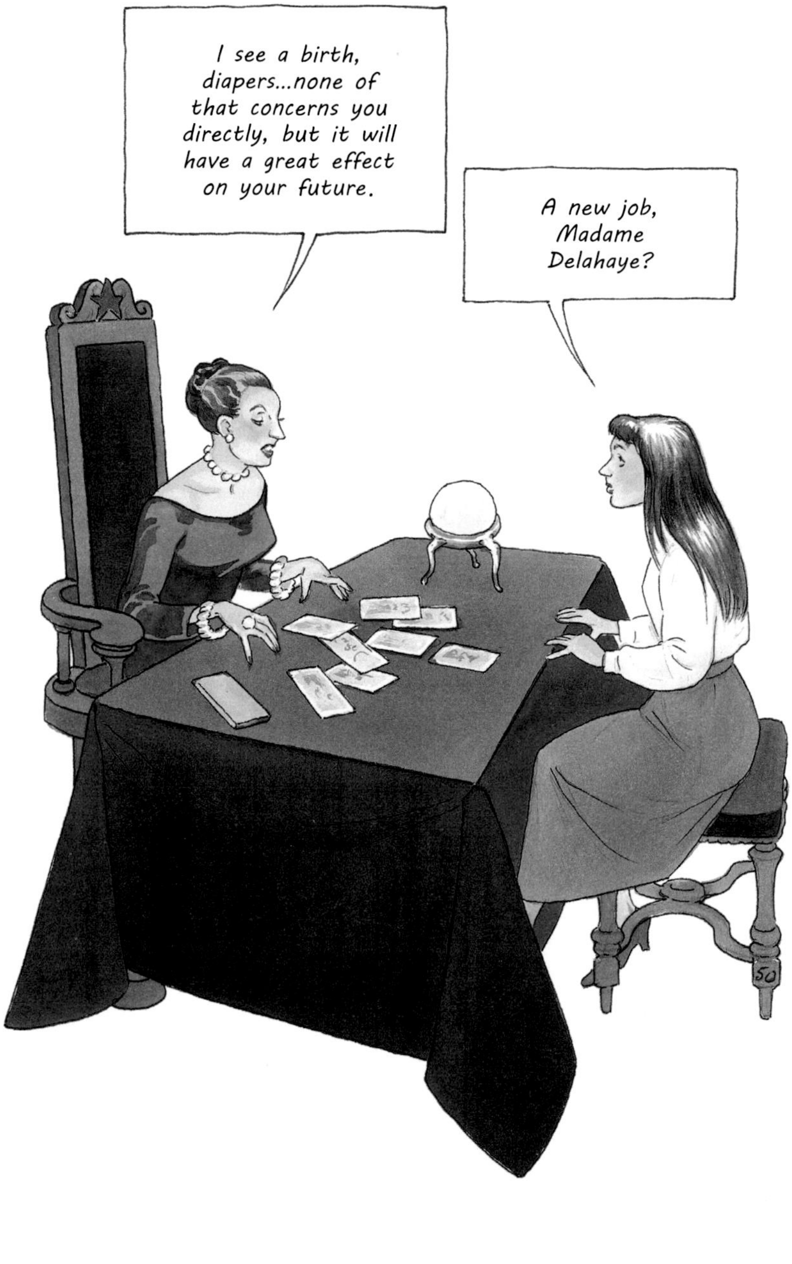
I see a birth, diapers...none of that concerns you directly, but it will have a great effect on your future.
A new job, Madame Delahaye?

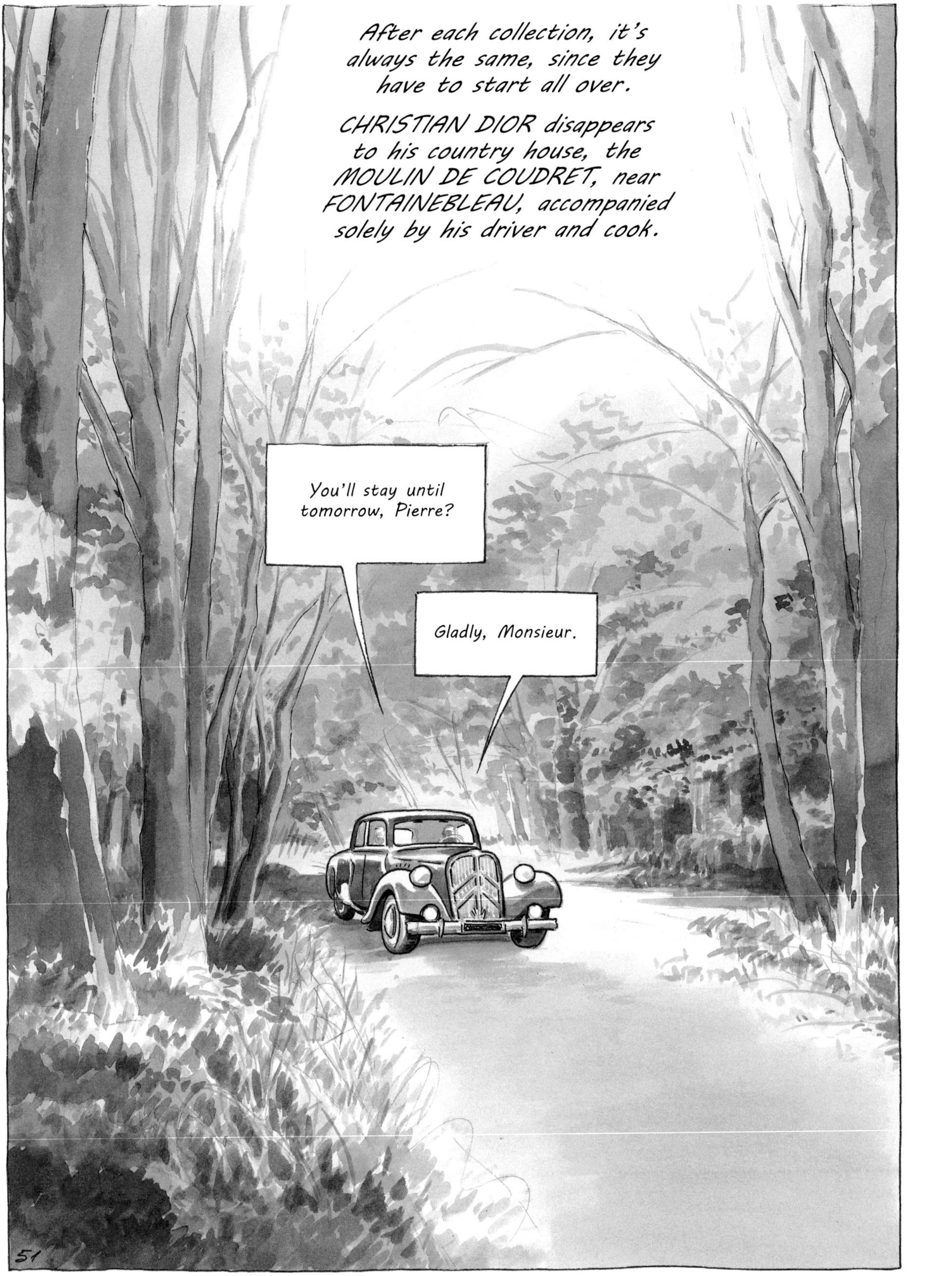
After each collection, it's always the same, since they have to start all over.
CHRISTIAN DIOR disappears to his country house, the MOULIN DE COUDRET, near FONTAINEBLEAU, accompanied solely by his driver and cook.
You'll stay until tomorrow, Pierre?
Gladly, Monsieur.
51

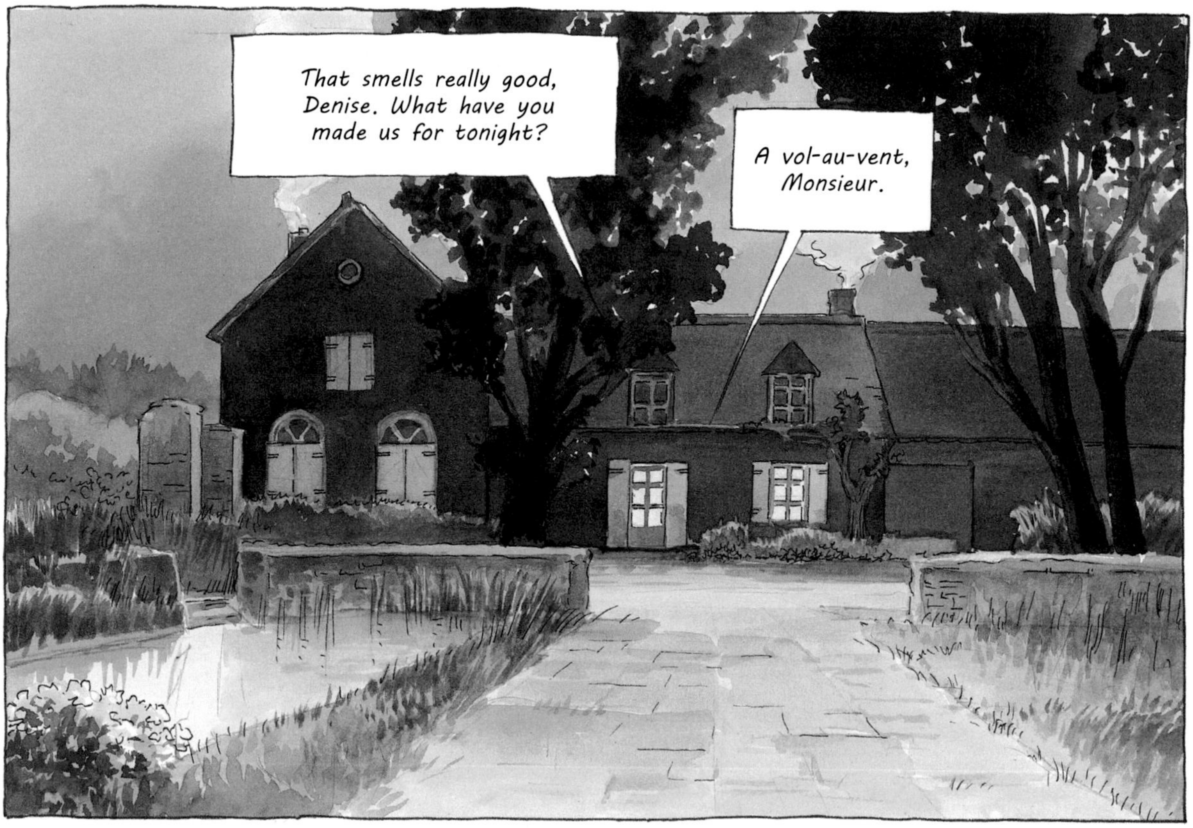
That smells really good, Denise. What have you made us for tonight?
A vol-au-vent, Monsieur.

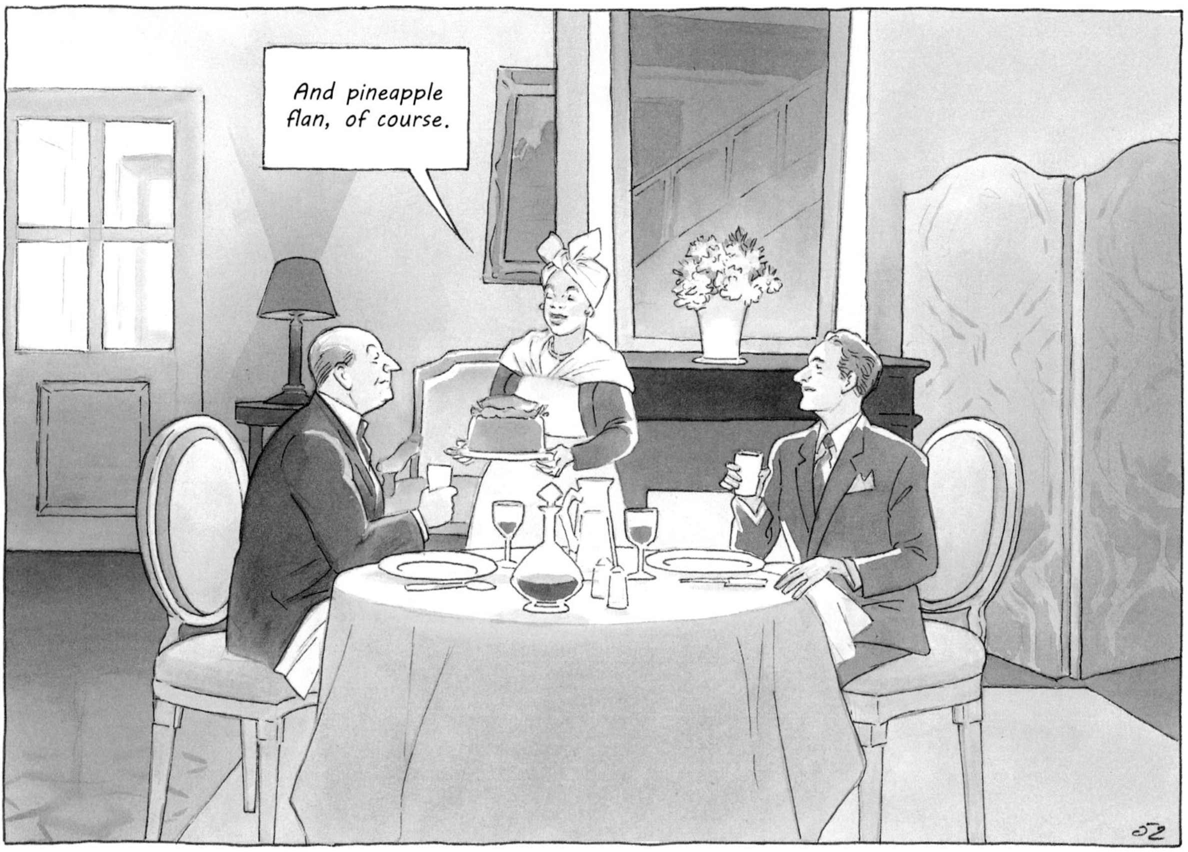
And pineapple flan, of course.

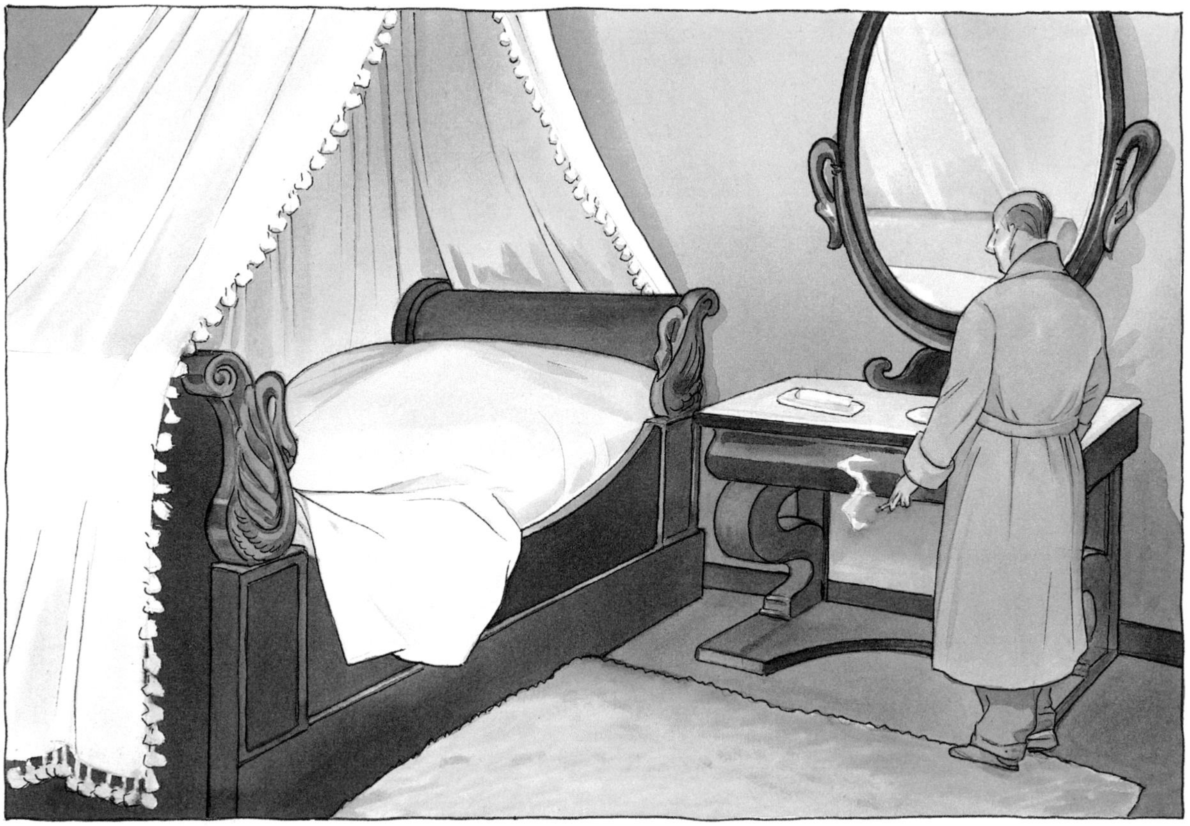

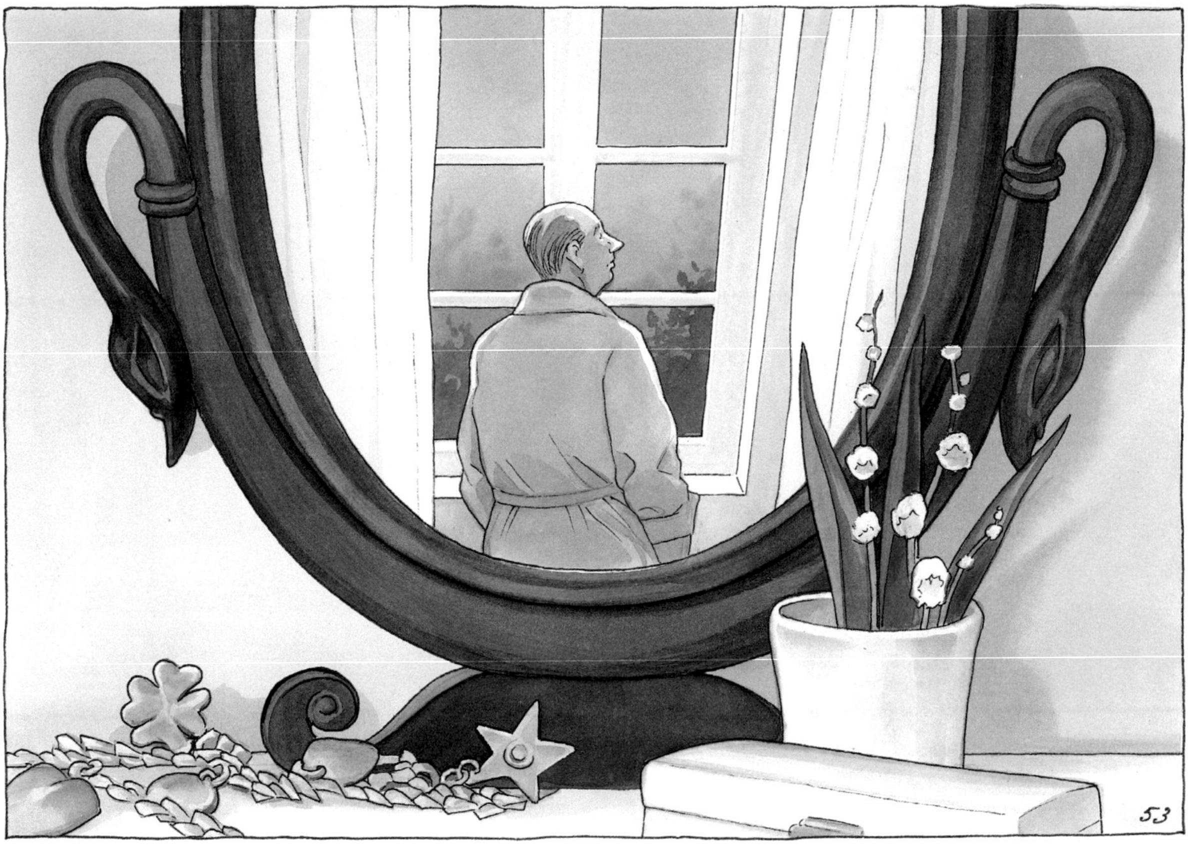
53

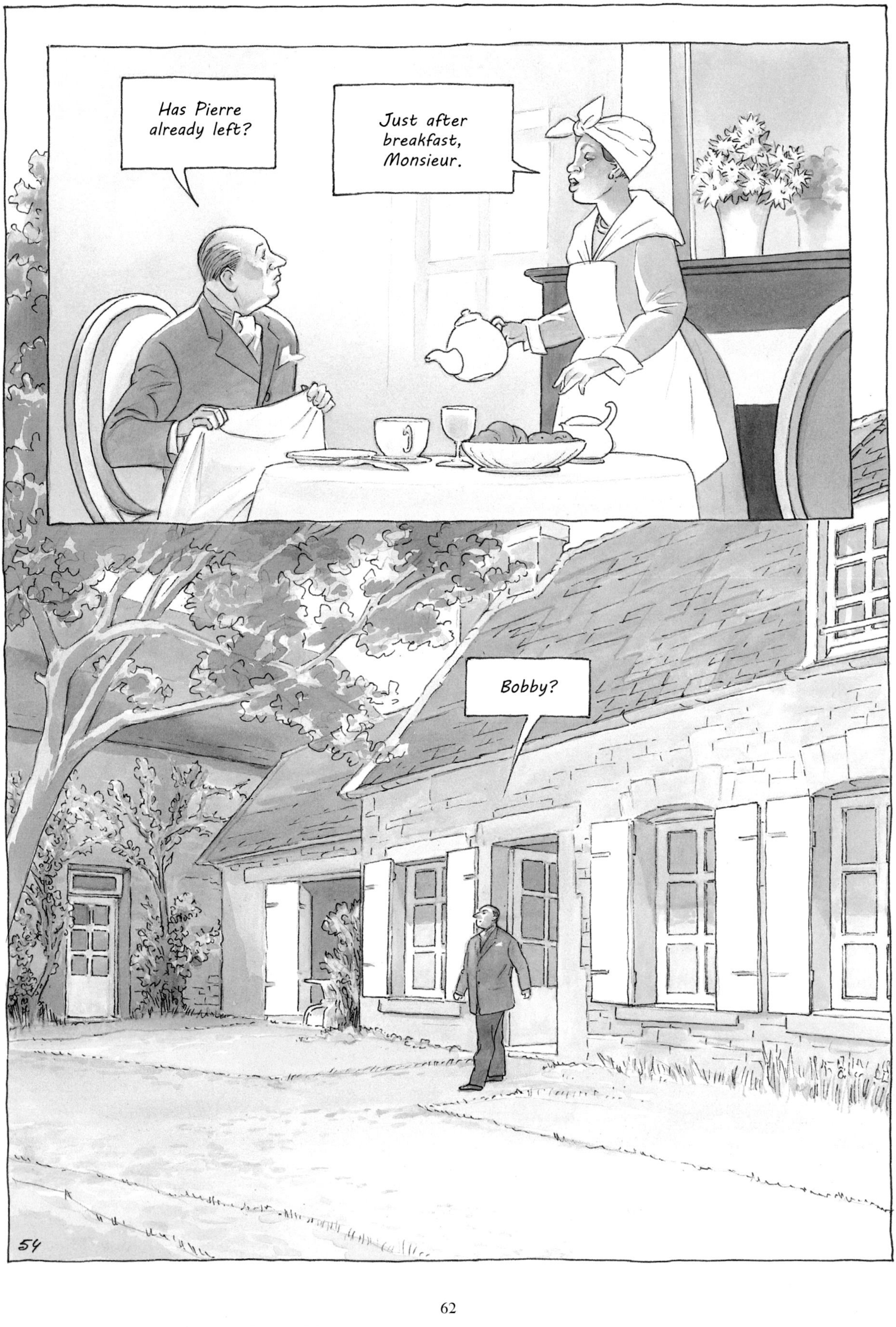
Has Pierre already left?
Just after breakfast, Monsieur.
Bobby?
54

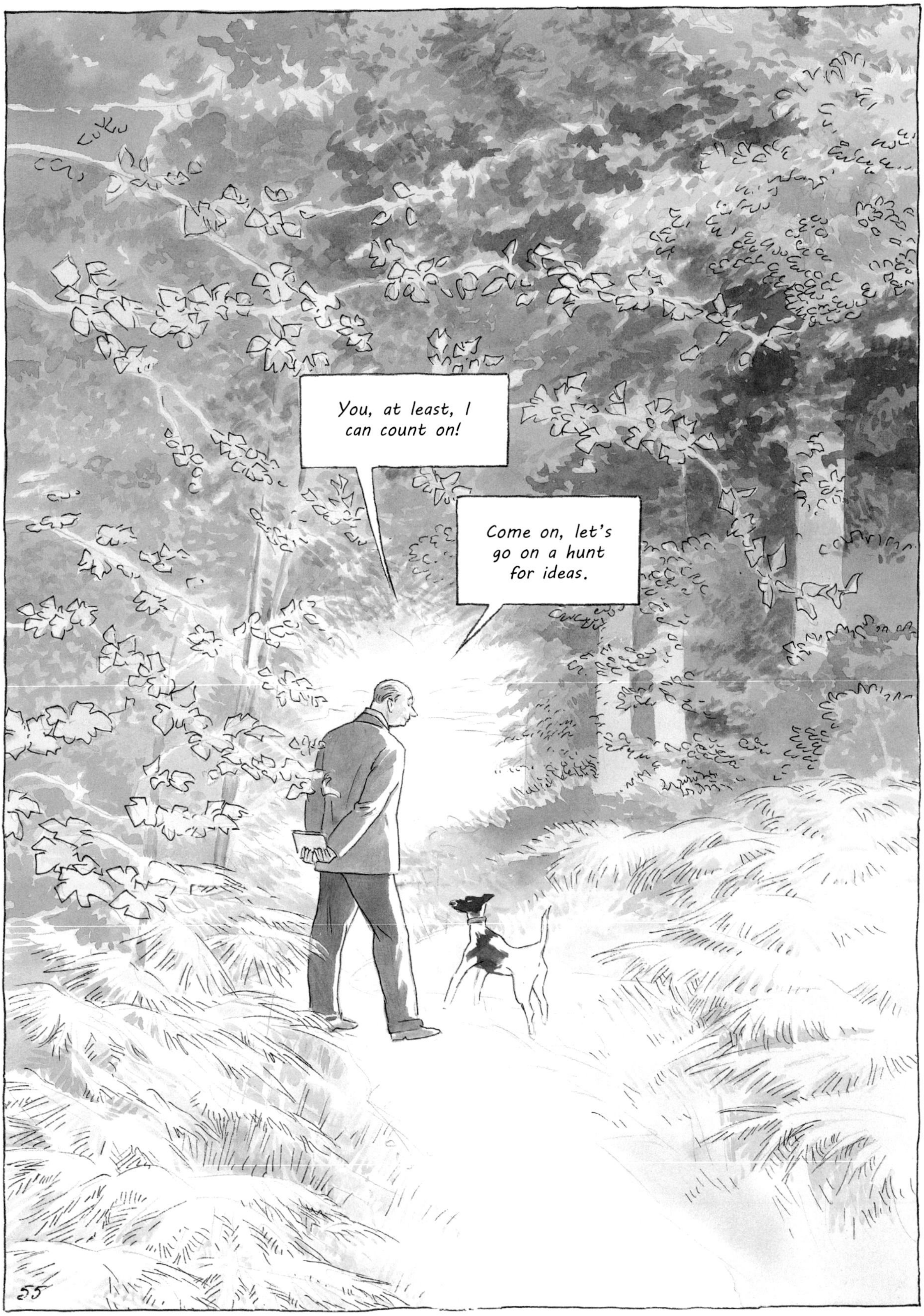
You, at least, I can count on!
Come on, let's go on a hunt for ideas.
55

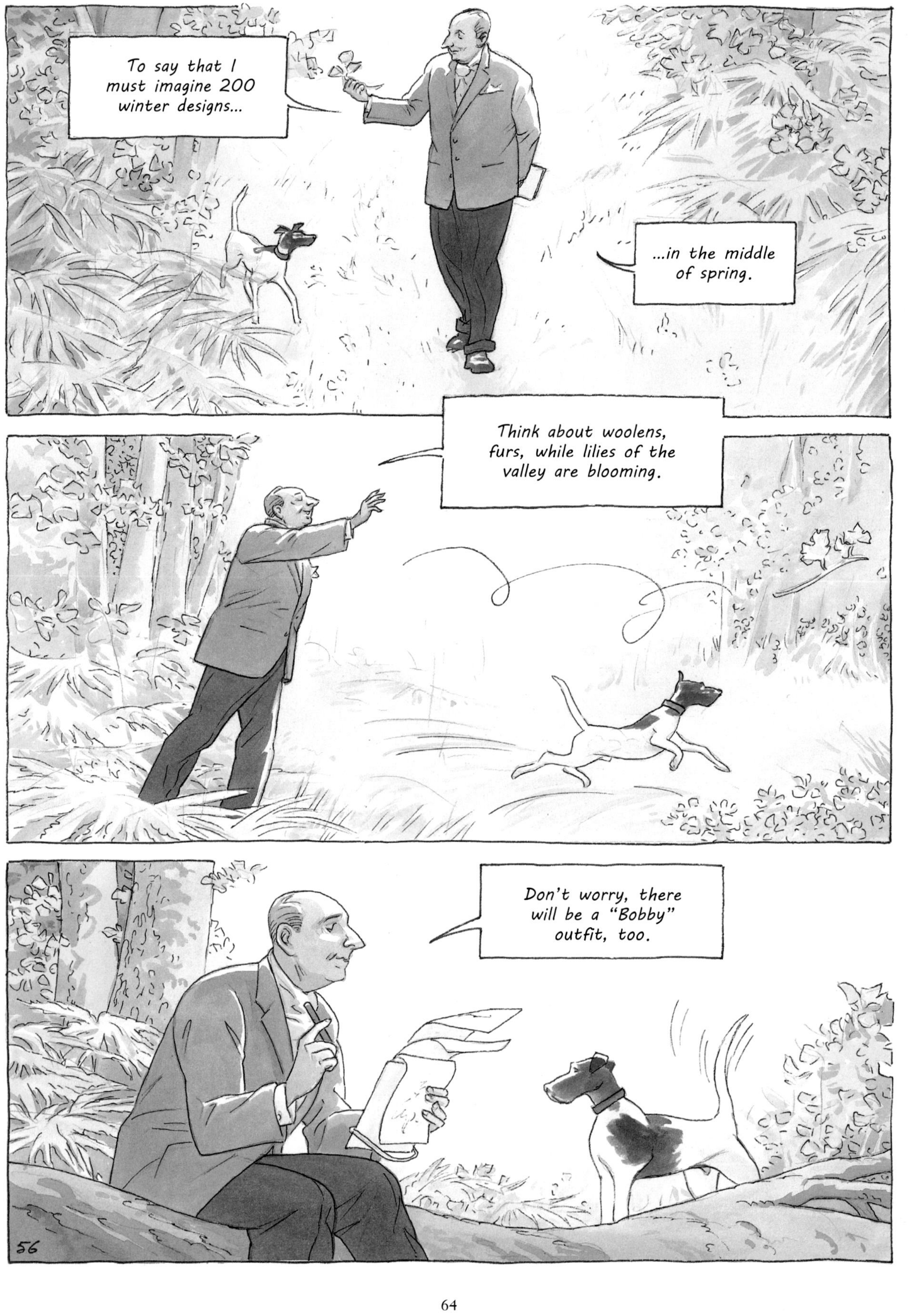
To say that I must imagine 200 winter designs...
...in the middle of spring.
Think about woolens, furs, while lilies of the valley are blooming.
Don't worry, there will be a "Bobby" outfit, too.
56

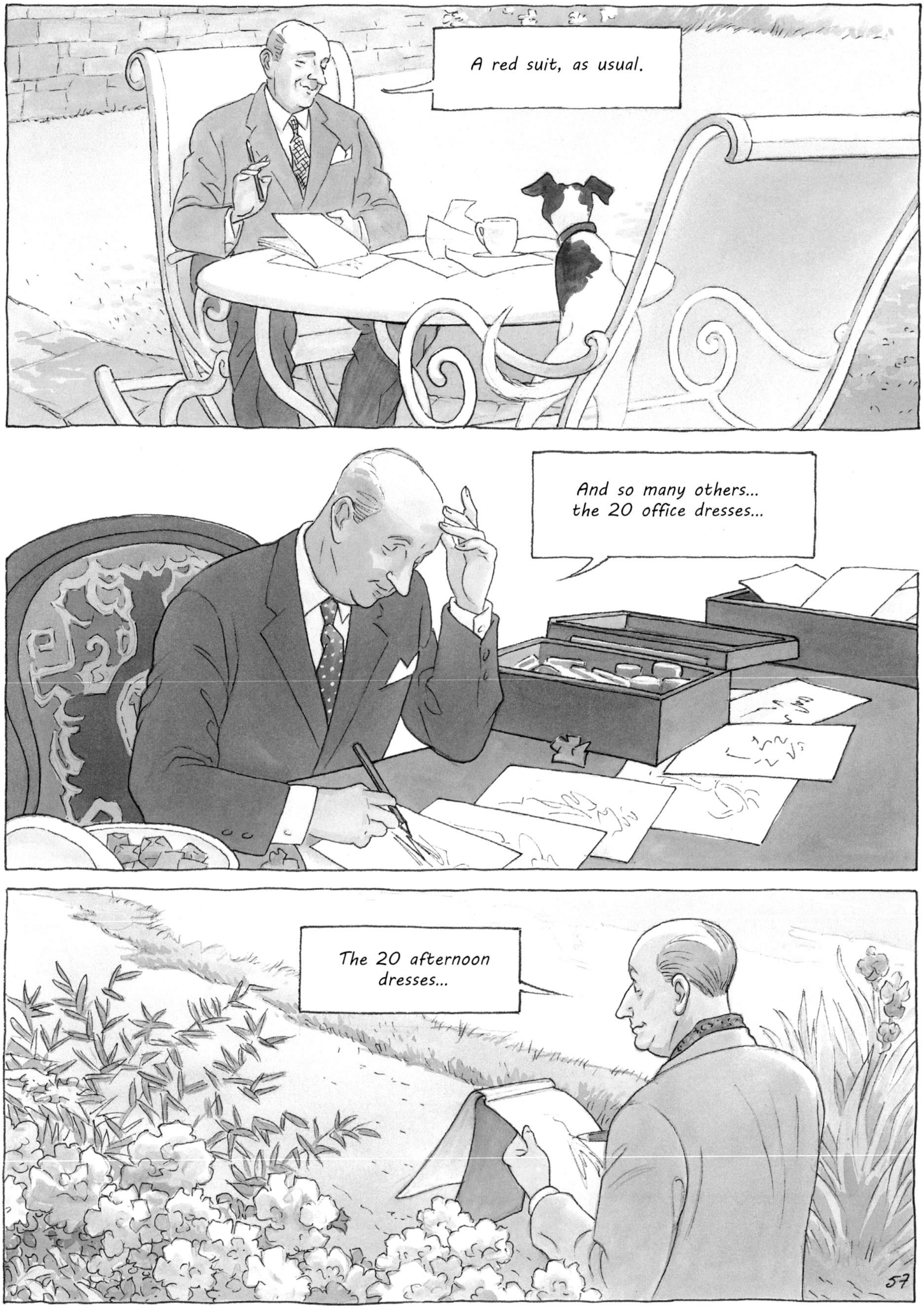
A red suit, as usual.
And so many others... the 20 office dresses...
The 20 afternoon dresses...
57

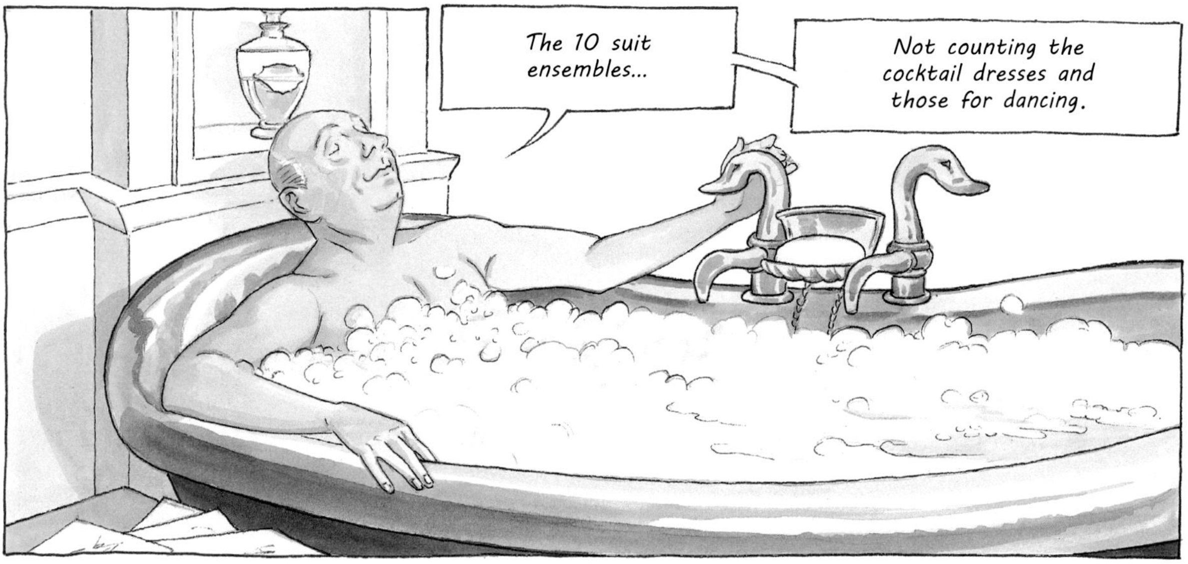
The 10 suit ensembles...
Not counting the cocktail dresses and those for dancing.

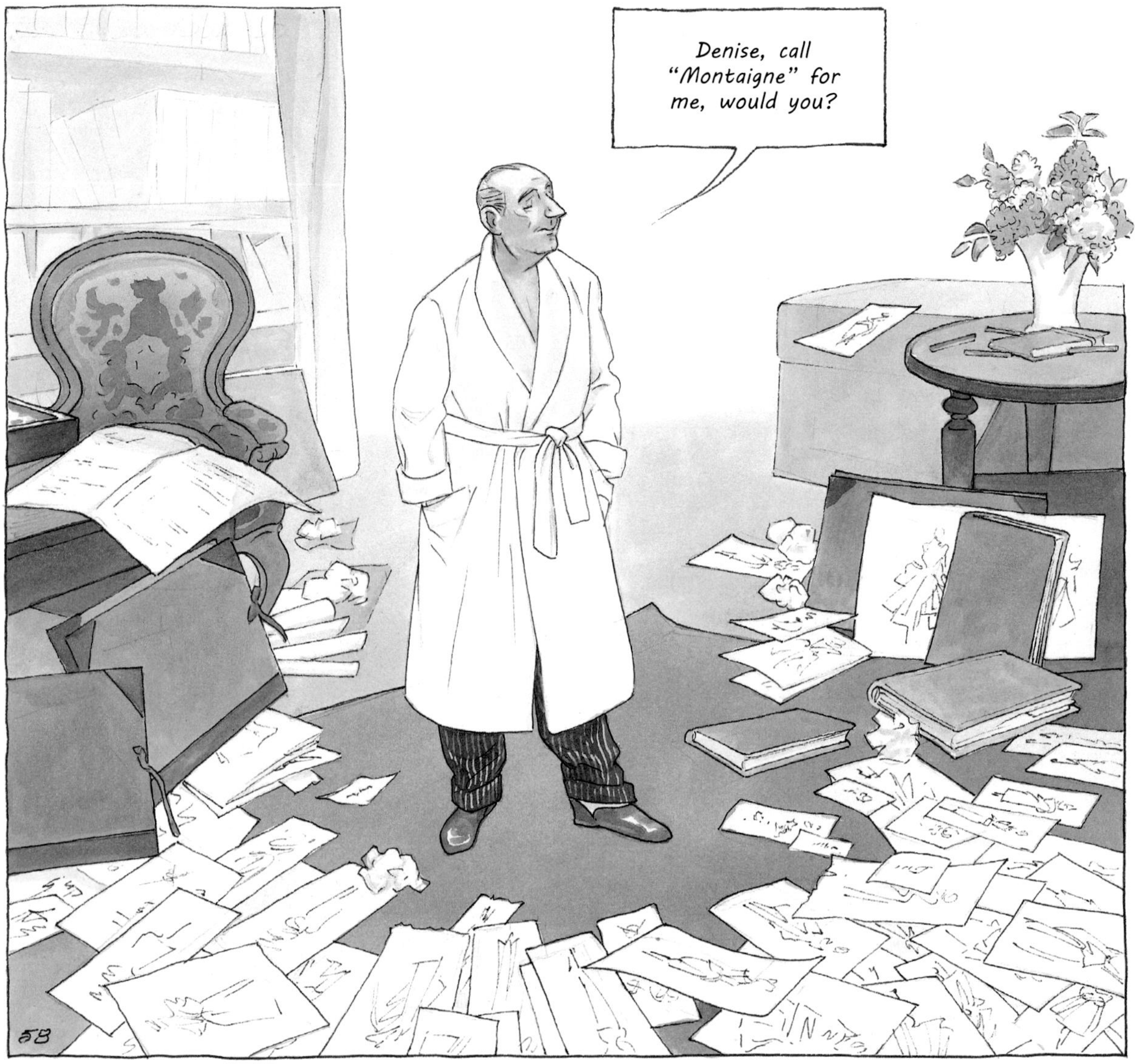
Denise, call "Montaigne" for me, would you?

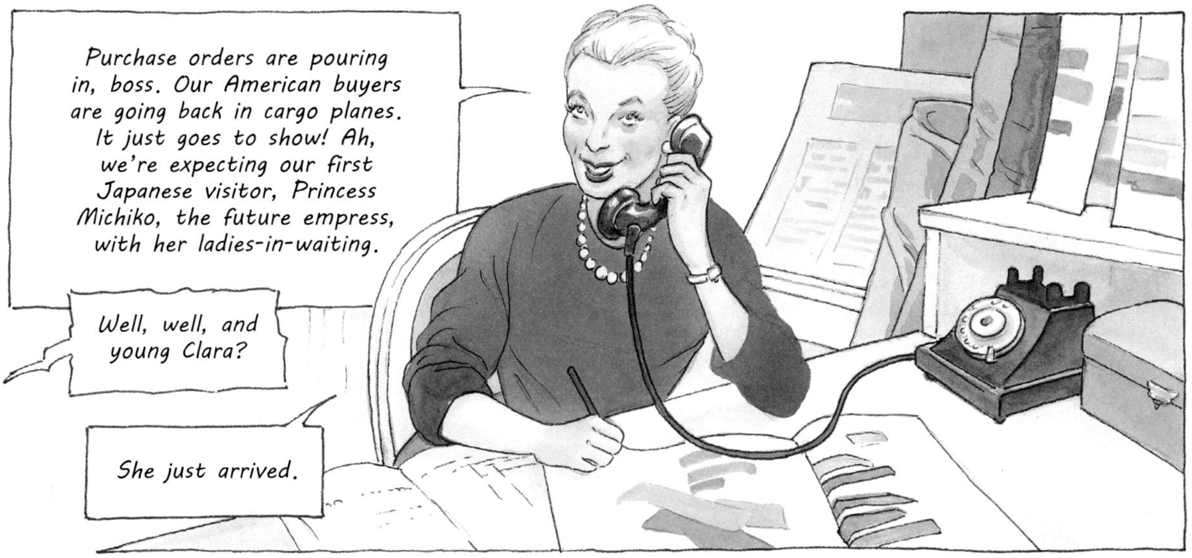
Purchase orders are pouring in, boss. Our American buyers are going back in cargo planes. It just goes to show! Ah, we're expecting our first Japanese visitor, Princess Michiko, the future empress, with her ladies-in-waiting.
Well, well, and young Clara?
She just arrived.

Madame DELAHAYE's Tarot cards spoke true.

SONIA, whose belly filled out, left the salons to give birth in peace and quiet.

Monsieur DIOR had me come to replace her... Me!

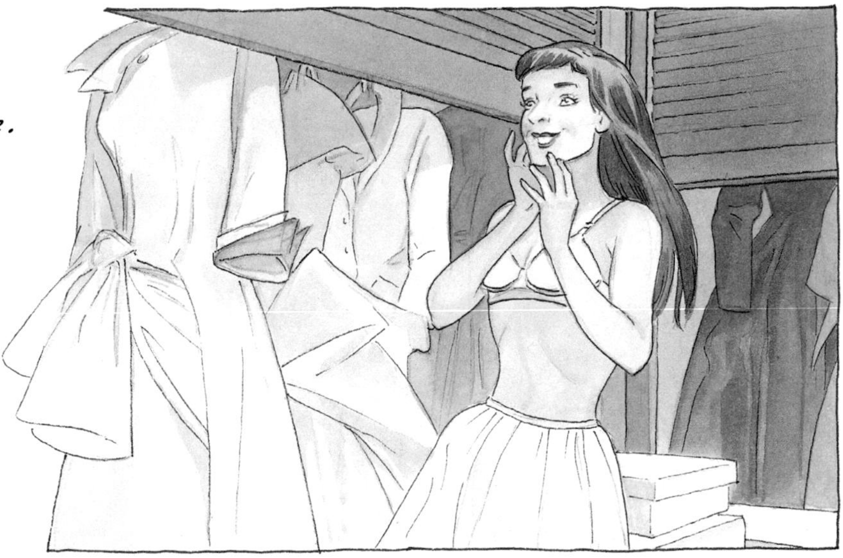

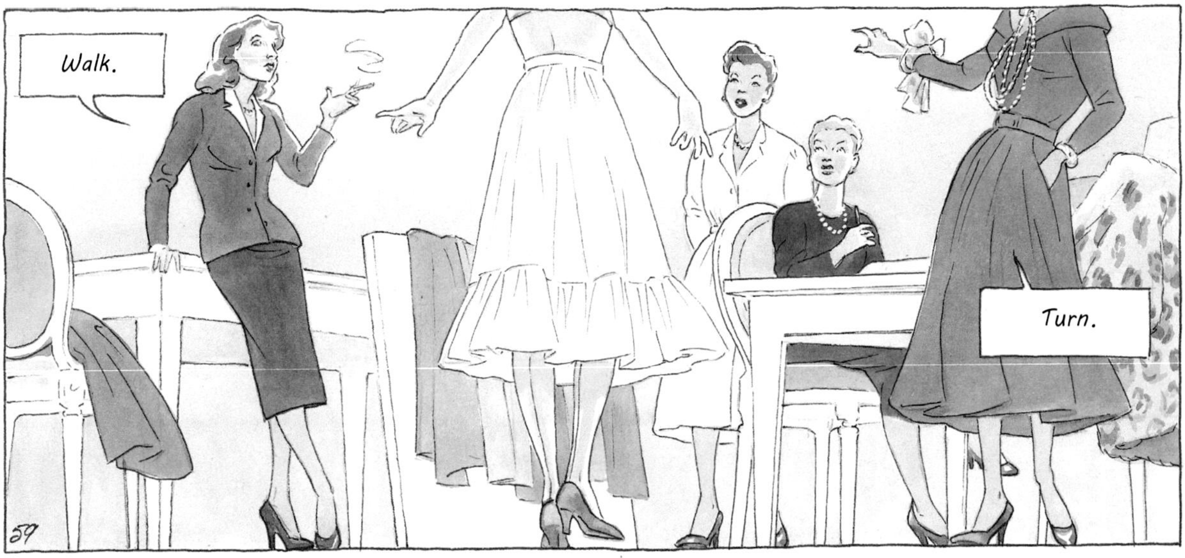
Walk.
Turn.

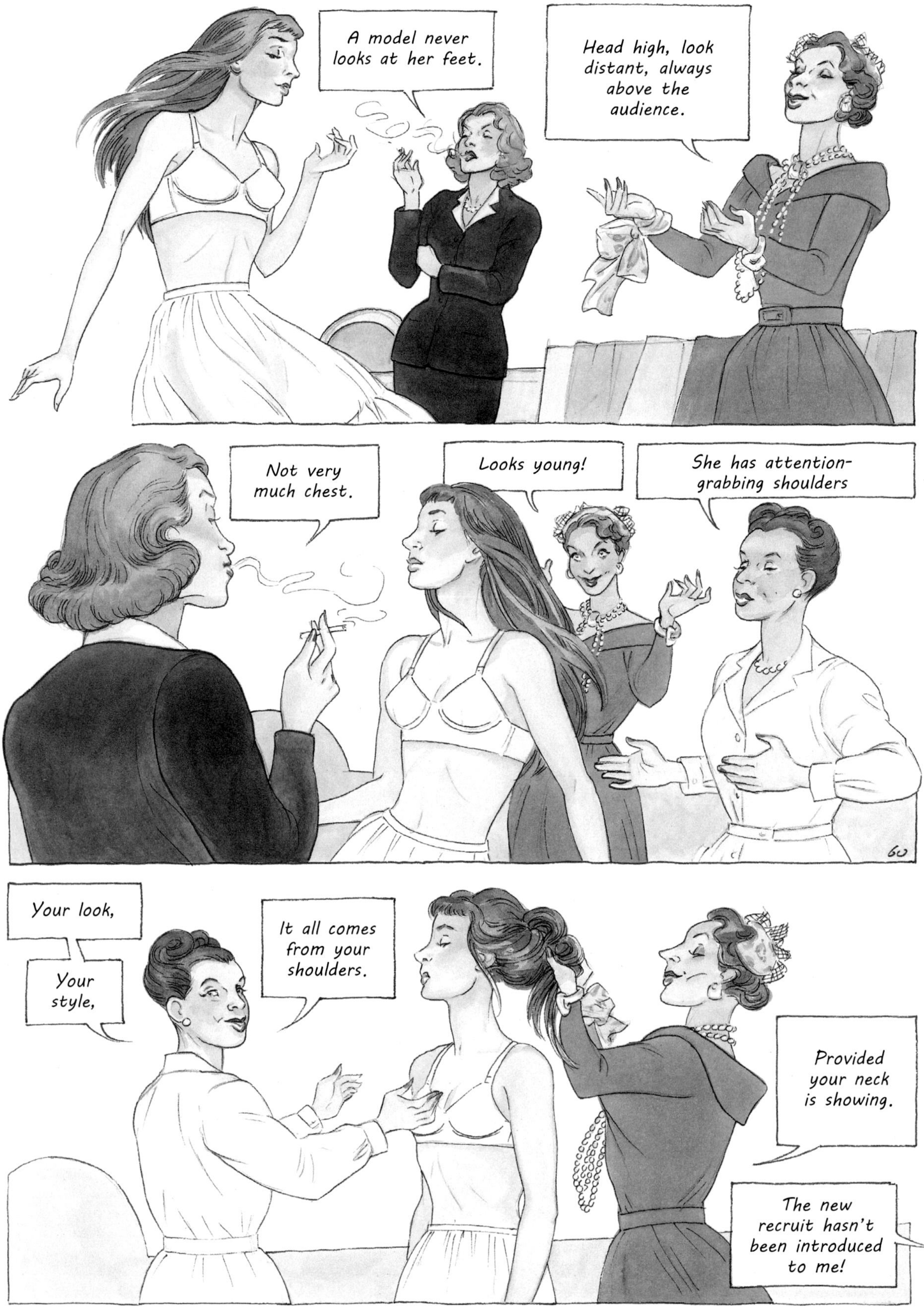
A model never looks at her feet.
Head high, look distant, always above the audience.
Not very much chest.
Looks young!
She has attention-grabbing shoulders
Your look,
Your style,
It all comes from your shoulders.
Provided your neck is showing.
The new recruit hasn't been introduced to me!

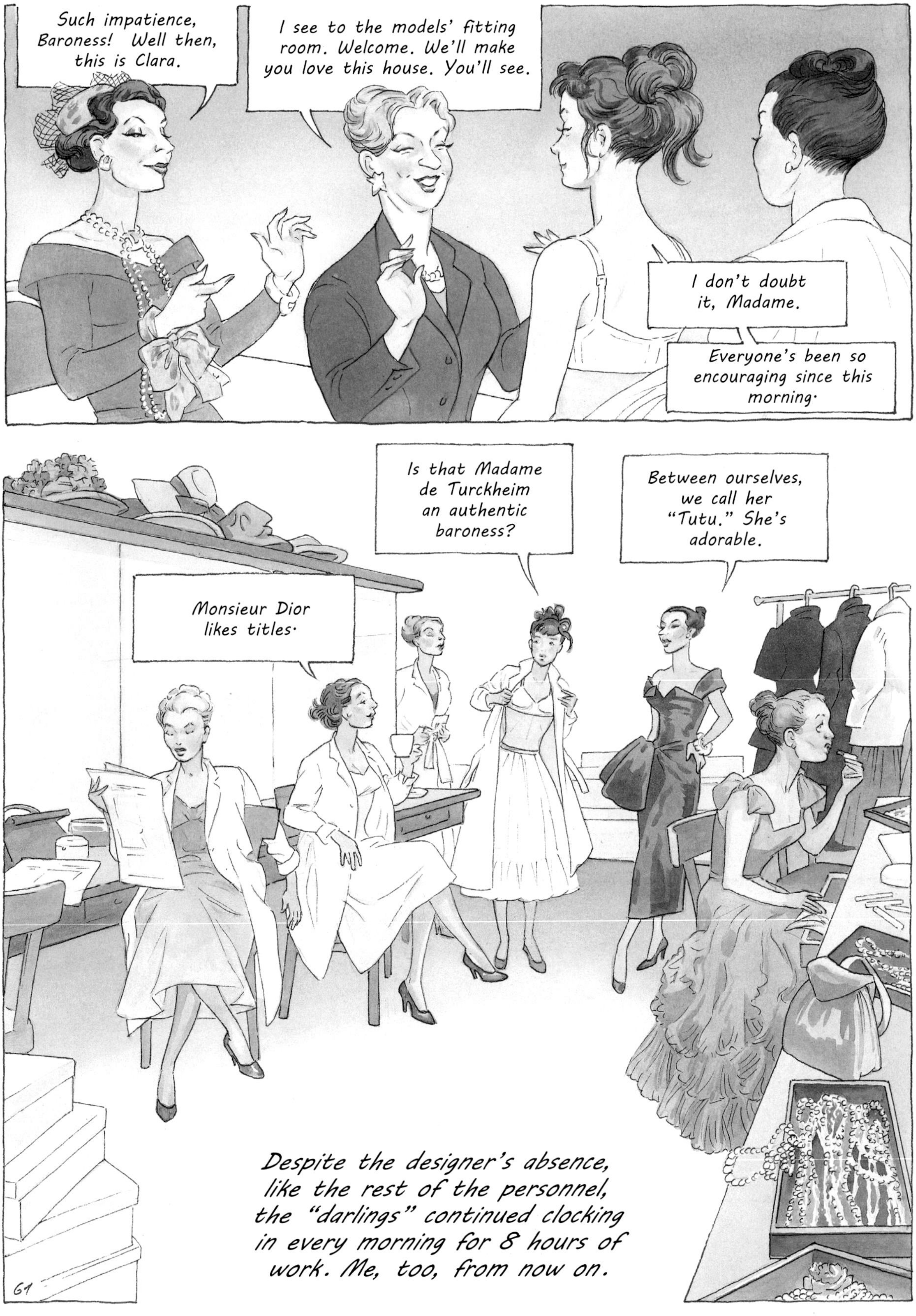
Such impatience, Baroness! Well then, this is Clara.
I see to the models' fitting room. Welcome. We'll make you love this house. You'll see.
I don't doubt it, Madame.
Everyone's been so encouraging since this morning.
Monsieur Dior likes titles.
Is that Madame de Turckheim an authentic baroness?
Between ourselves, we call her "Tutu." She's adorable.
Despite the designer's absence, like the rest of the personnel, the "darlings" continued clocking in every morning for 8 hours of work. Me, too, from now on.

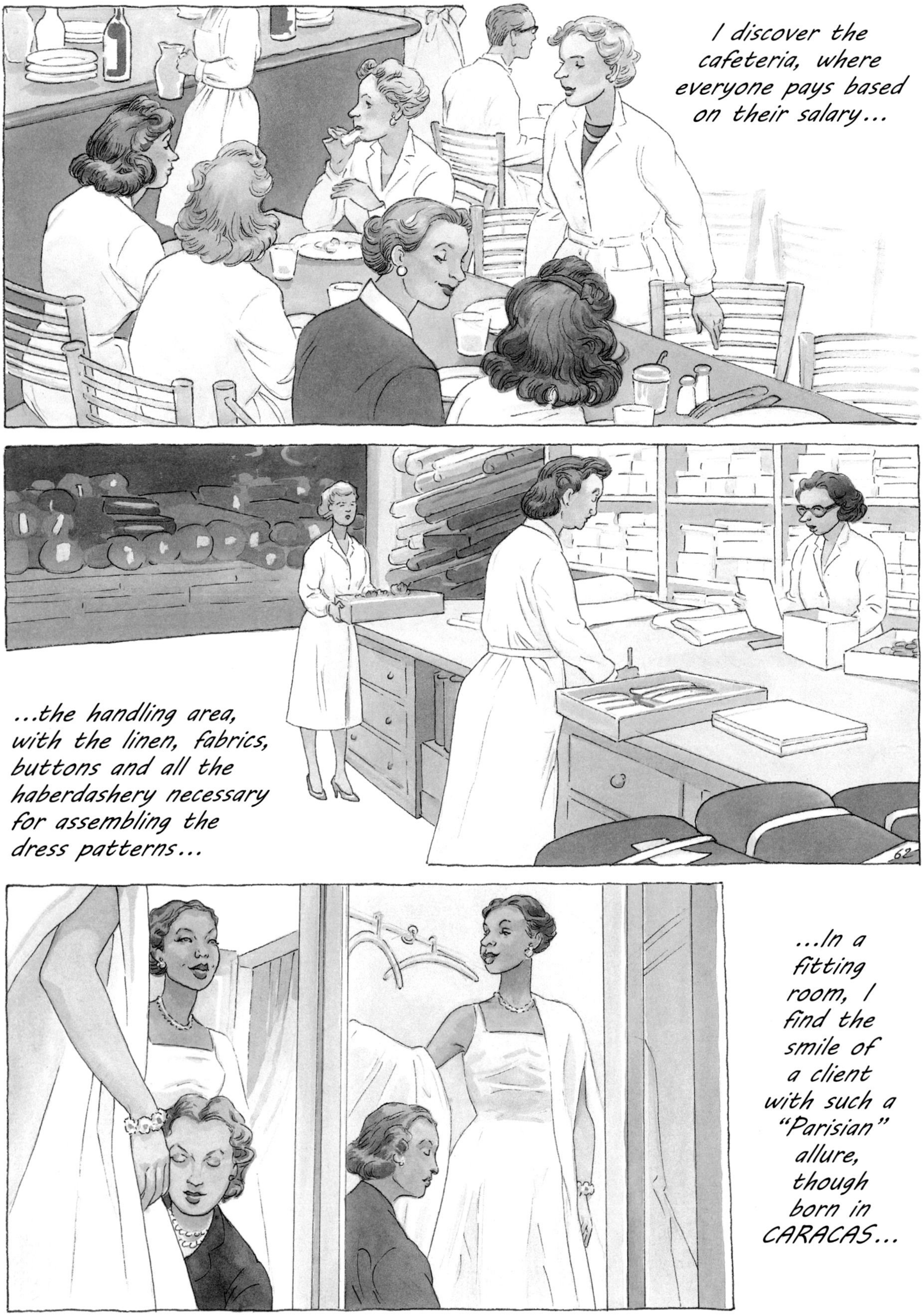
I discover the cafeteria, where everyone pays based on their salary...
...the handling area, with the linen, fabrics, buttons and all the haberdashery necessary for assembling the dress patterns...
...In a fitting room, I find the smile of a client with such a "Parisian" allure, though born in CARACAS...

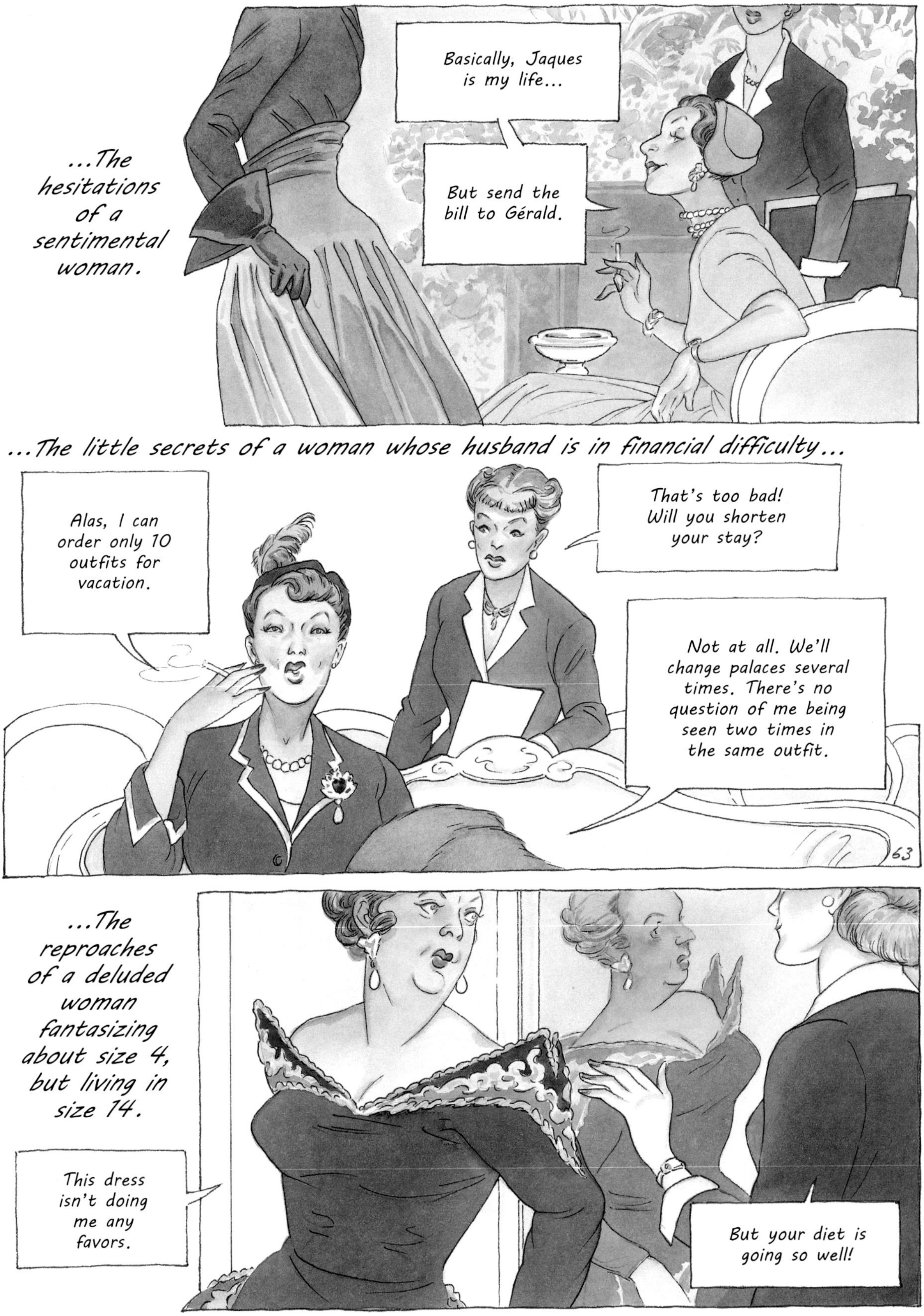

...The hesitations of a sentimental woman.
Basically, Jaques is my life...
But send the bill to Gérald.
...The little secrets of a woman whose husband is in financial difficulty...
Alas, I can order only 10 outfits for vacation.
That's too bad! Will you shorten your stay?
Not at all. We'll change palaces several times. There's no question of me being seen two times in the same outfit.
...The reproaches of a deluded woman fantasizing about size 4, but living in size 14.
This dress isn't doing me any favors.
But your diet is going so well!

And then, one fine morning, Monsieur DIOR is back, laden with a multitude of sketches, which are called "little etchings" in fashion.

Here are my cat scratches.

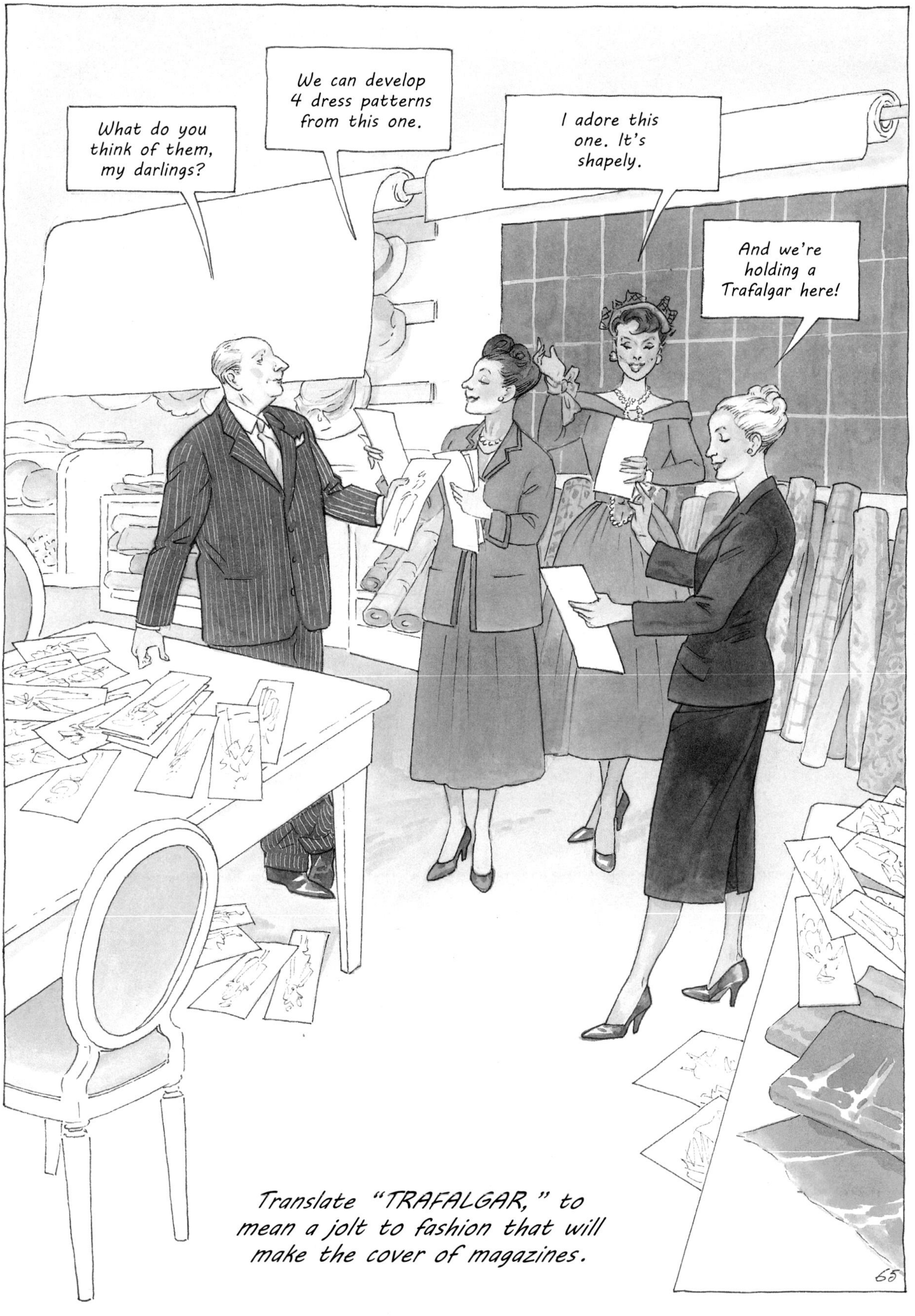
What do you think of them, my darlings?
We can develop 4 dress patterns from this one.
I adore this one. It's shapely.
And we're holding a Trafalgar here!
Translate "TRAFALGAR," to mean a jolt to fashion that will make the cover of magazines.
65

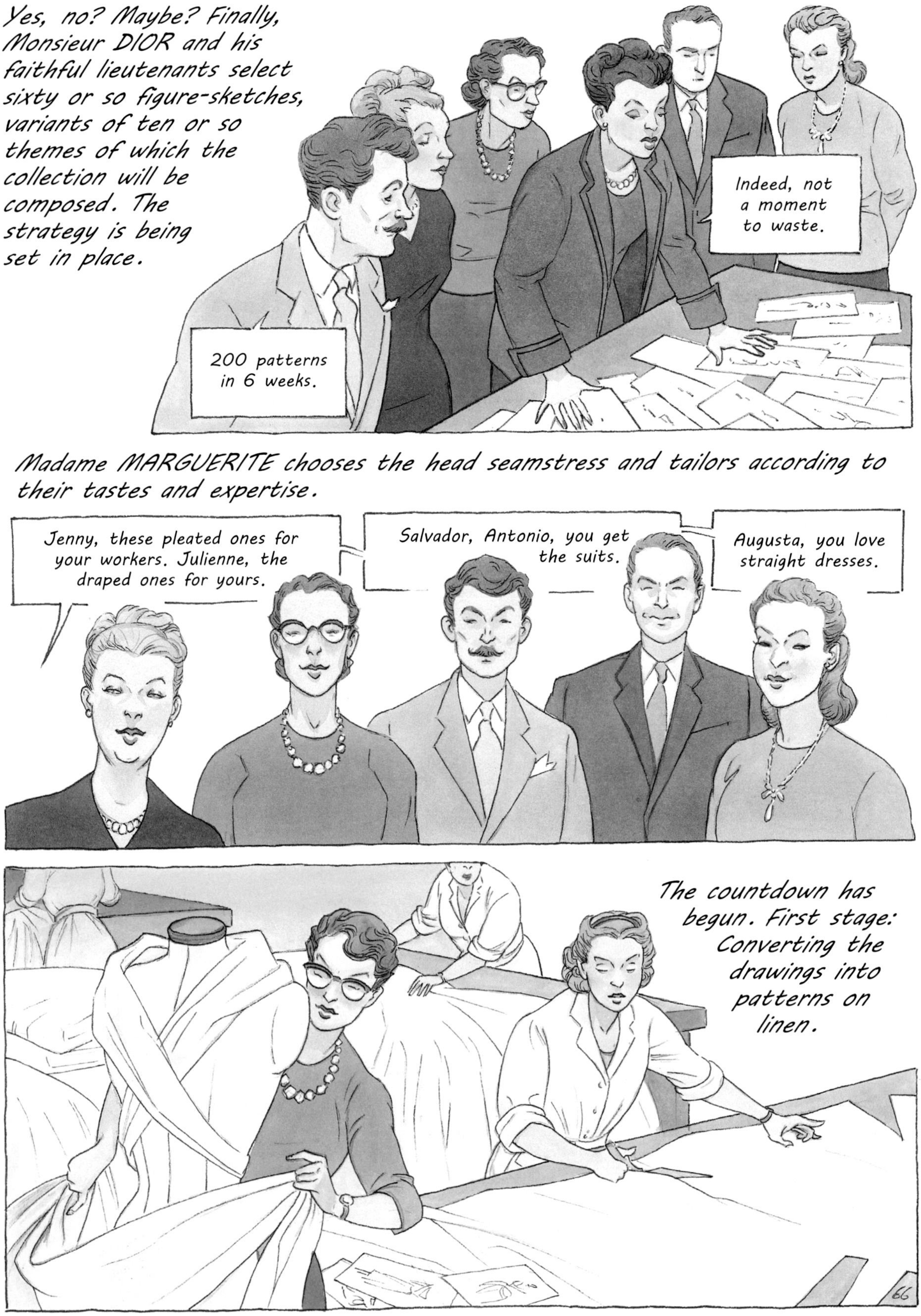
Yes, no? Maybe? Finally, Monsieur DIOR and his faithful lieutenants select sixty or so figure-sketches, variants of ten or so themes of which the collection will be composed. The strategy is being set in place.
200 patterns in 6 weeks.
Indeed, not a moment to waste.
Madame MARGUERITE chooses the head seamstress and tailors according to their tastes and expertise.
Jenny, these pleated ones for your workers. Julienne, the draped ones for yours.
Salvador, Antonio, you get the suits.
Augusta, you love straight dresses.
The countdown has begun. First stage: Converting the drawings into patterns on linen.

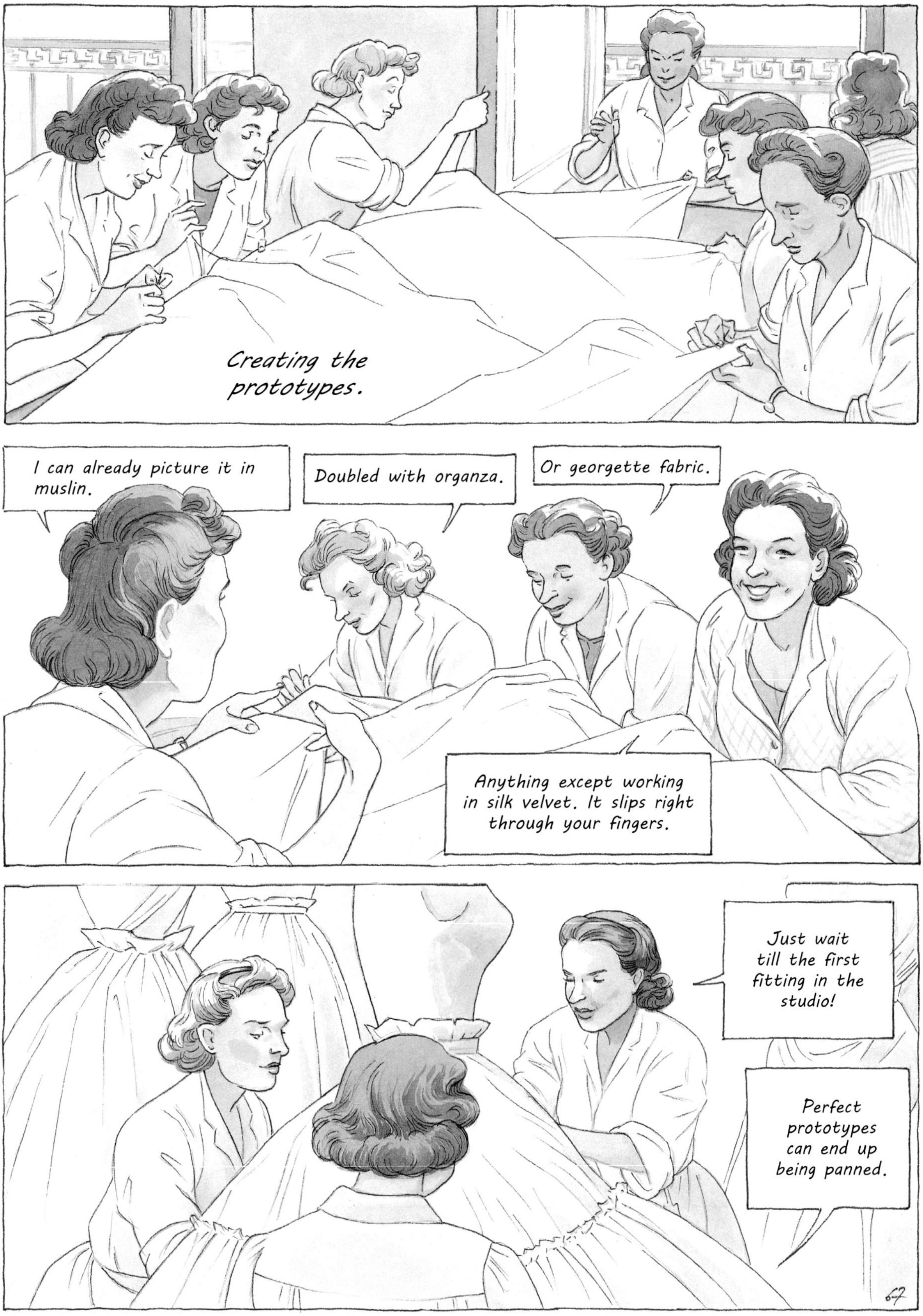
Creating the prototypes.
I can already picture it in muslin.
Doubled with organza.
Or georgette fabric.
Anything except working in silk velvet. It slips right through your fingers.
Just wait till the first fitting in the studio!
Perfect prototypes can end up being panned.
67

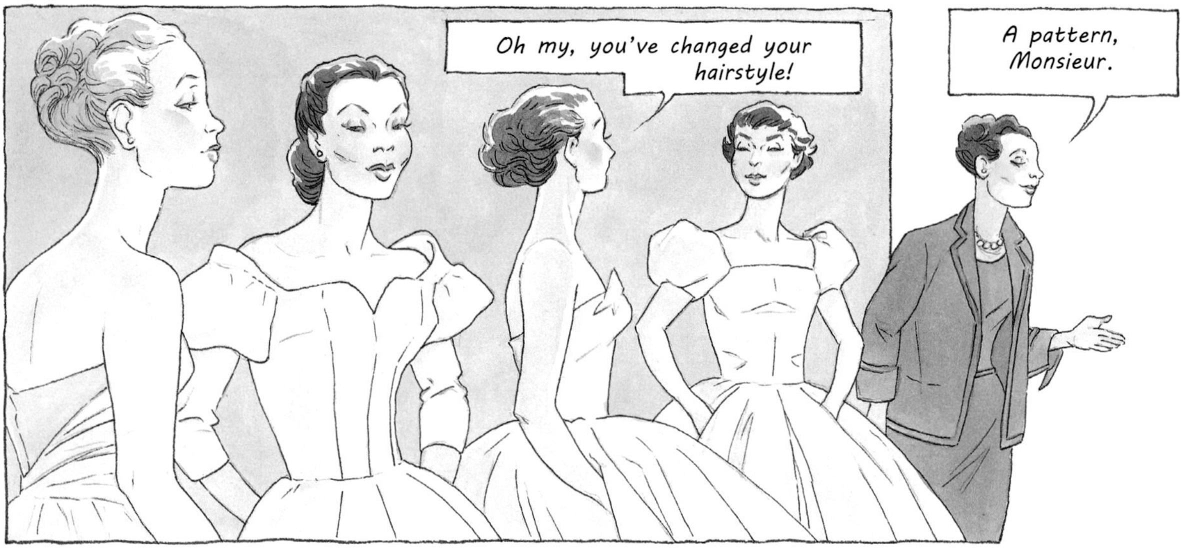
Oh my, you've changed your hairstyle!
A pattern, Monsieur.

Second stage: The studio fitting.

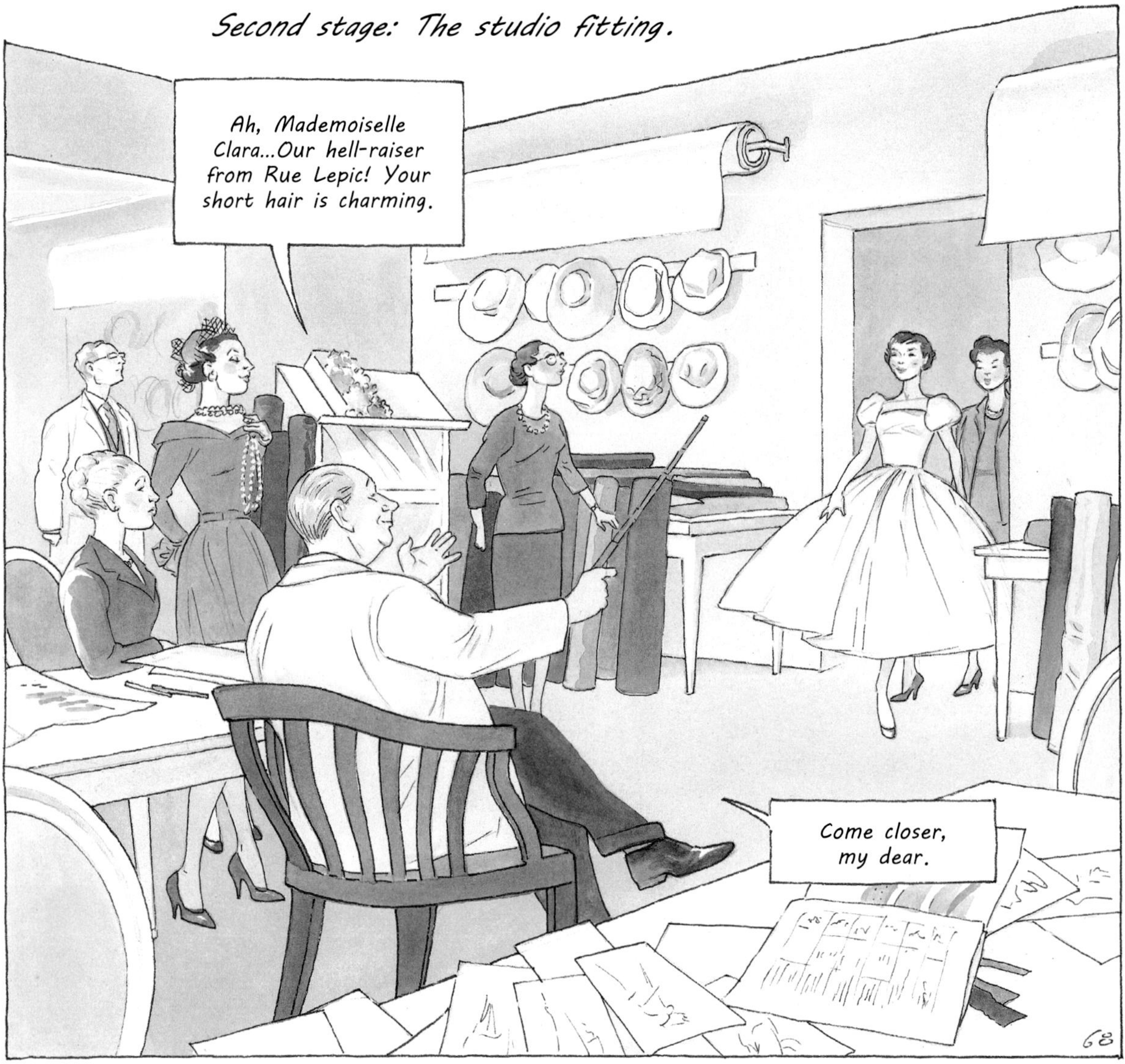
Ah, Mademoiselle Clara...Our hell-raiser from Rue Lepic! Your short hair is charming.
Come closer, my dear.

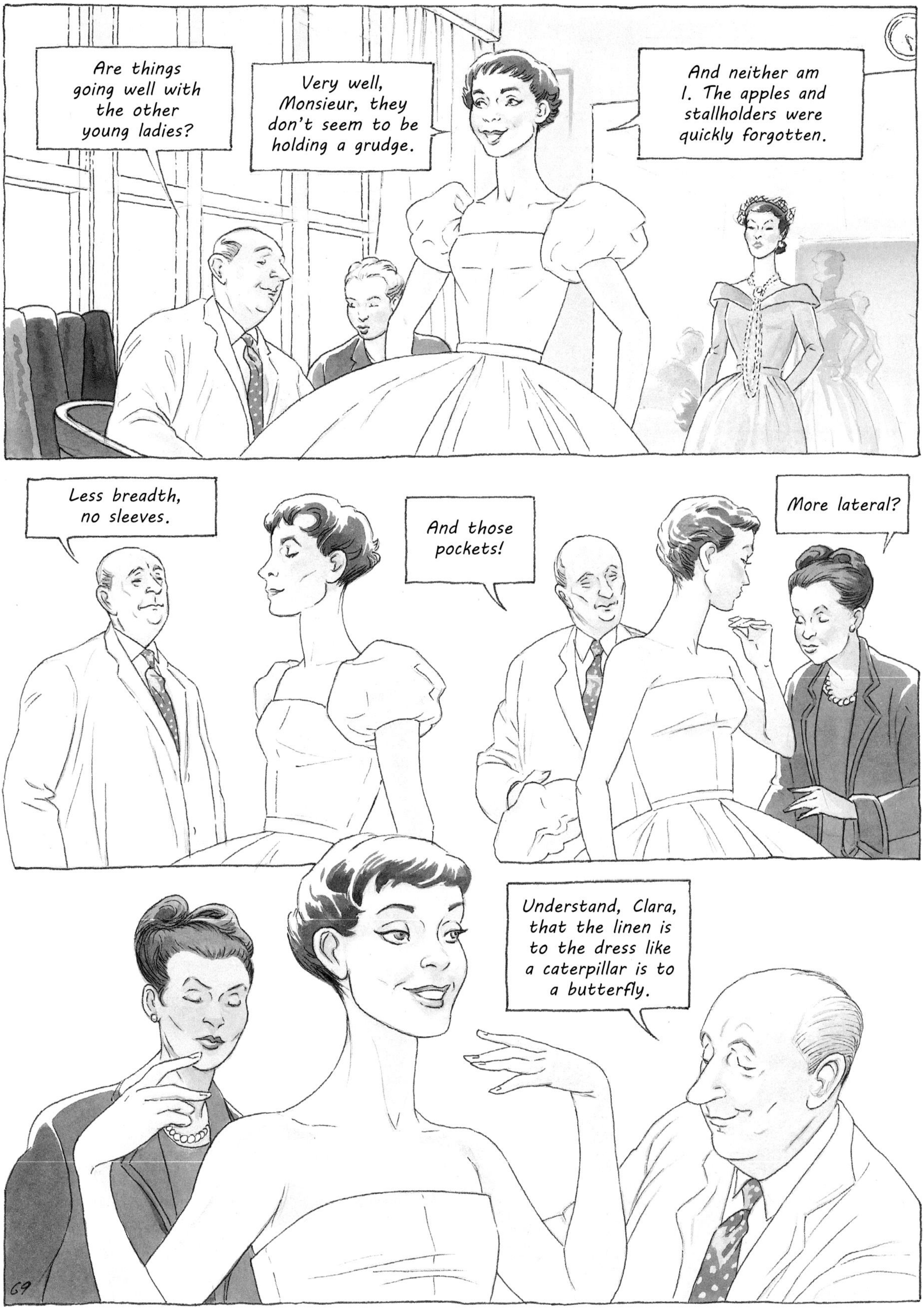
Are things going well with the other young ladies?
Very well, Monsieur, they don't seem to be holding a grudge.
And neither am I. The apples and stallholders were quickly forgotten.
Less breadth, no sleeves.
And those pockets!
More lateral?
Understand, Clara, that the linen is to the dress like a caterpillar is to a butterfly.

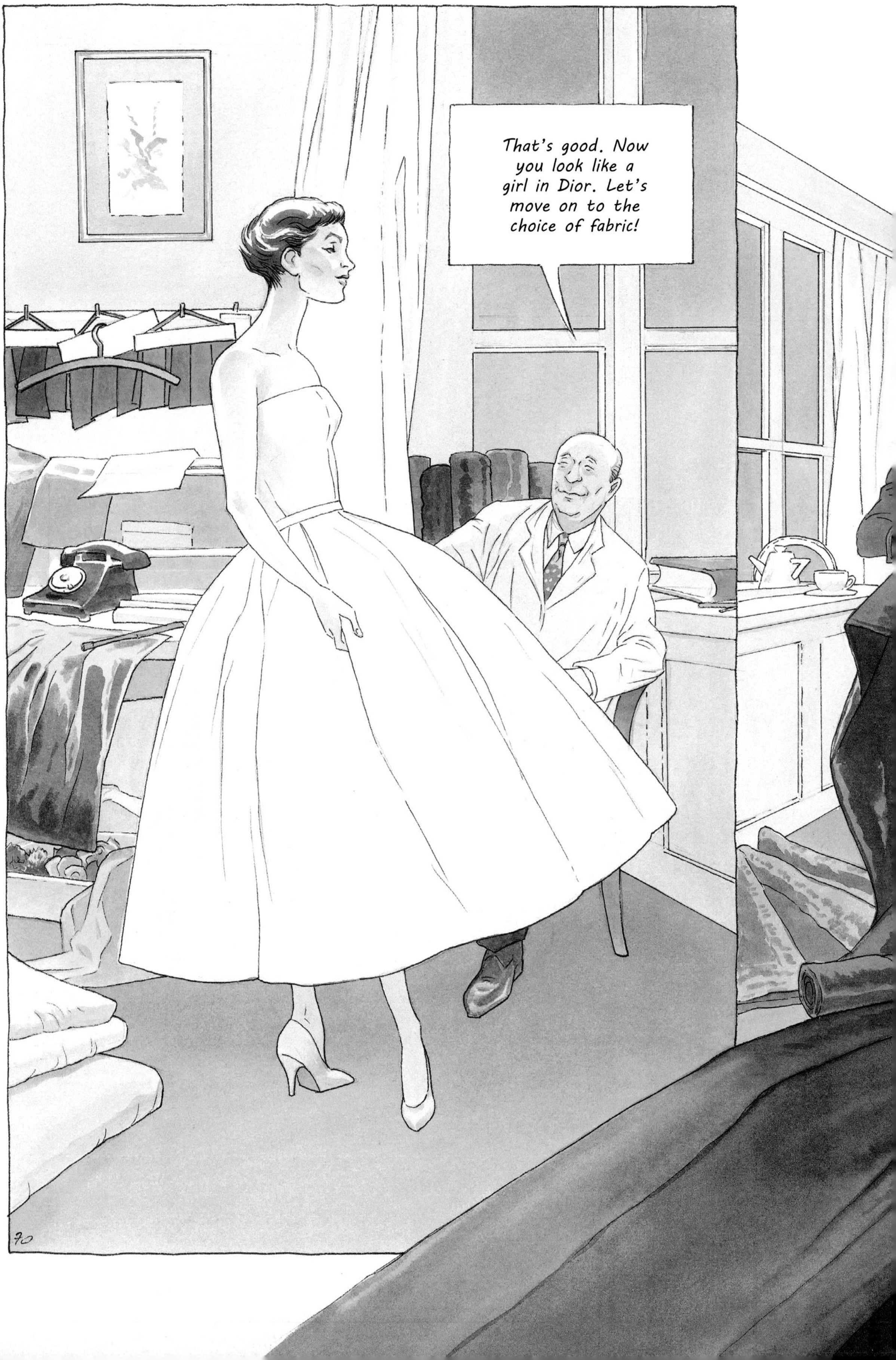
That's good. Now you look like a girl in Dior. Let's move on to the choice of fabric!

Silk, of course! It's obvious. Brocade, crepe de chine, rep or surah?
No. A red taffeta leaning towards garnet, crimson, ruby?
I dream of getting out of my heels.
I dream of a toasted ham and cheese.
But I'm in Dior, so grin and bear it!

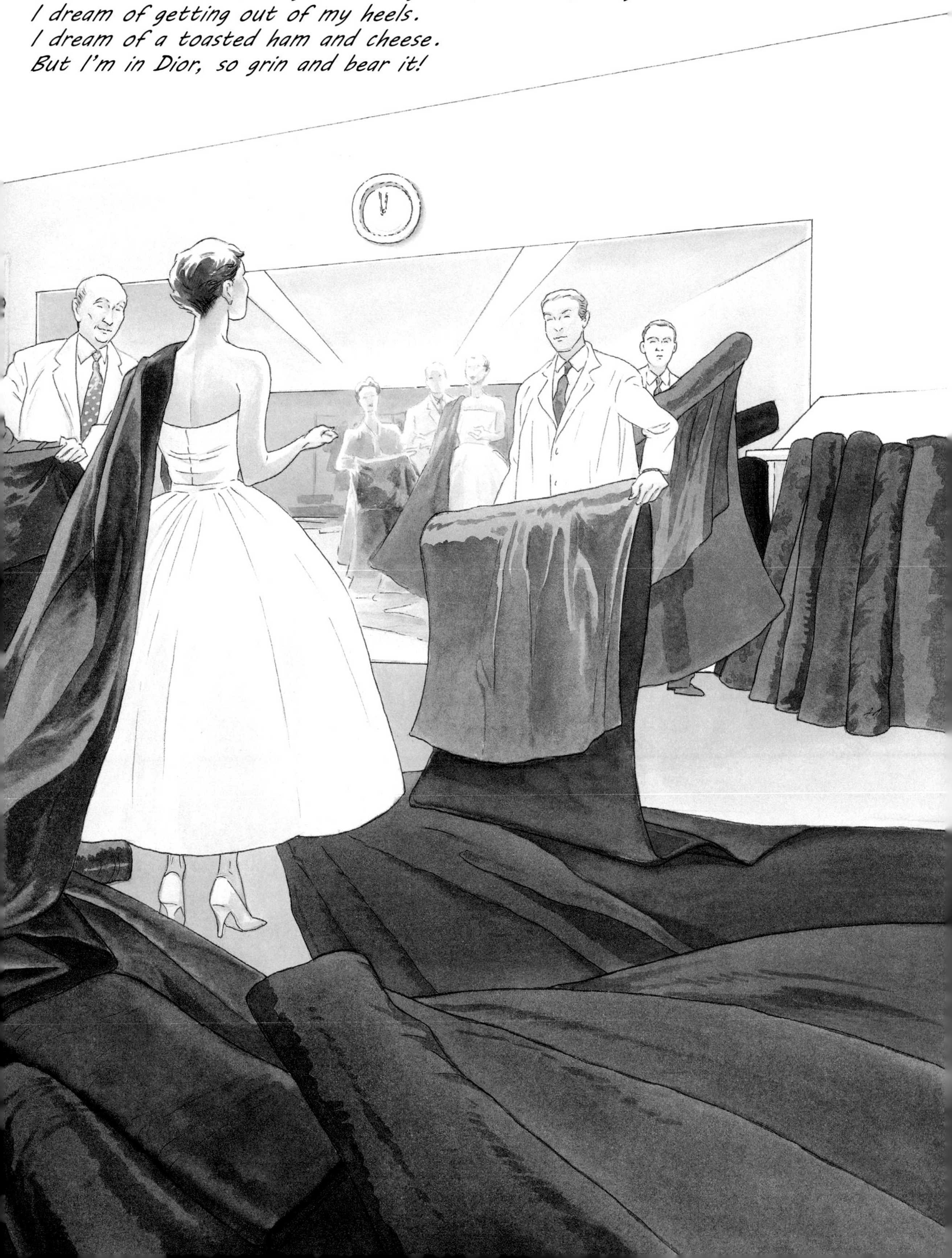

I'm in Dior and miss the last train.

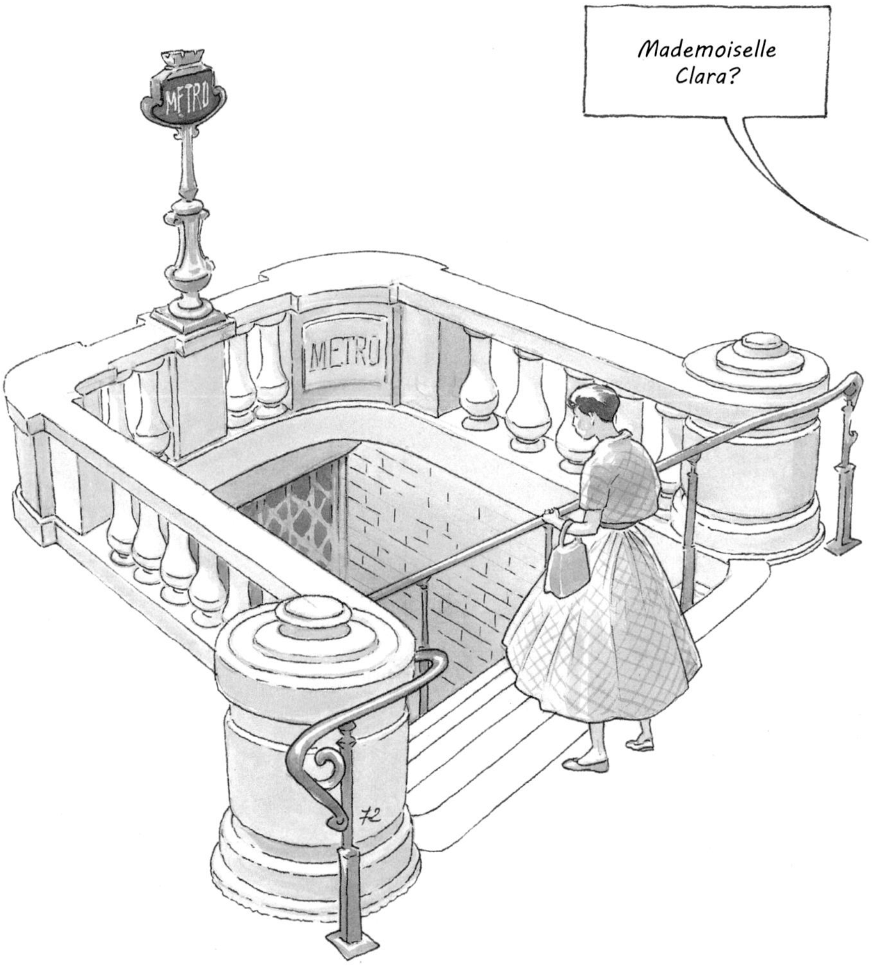
Mademoiselle Clara?
METRO
METRO

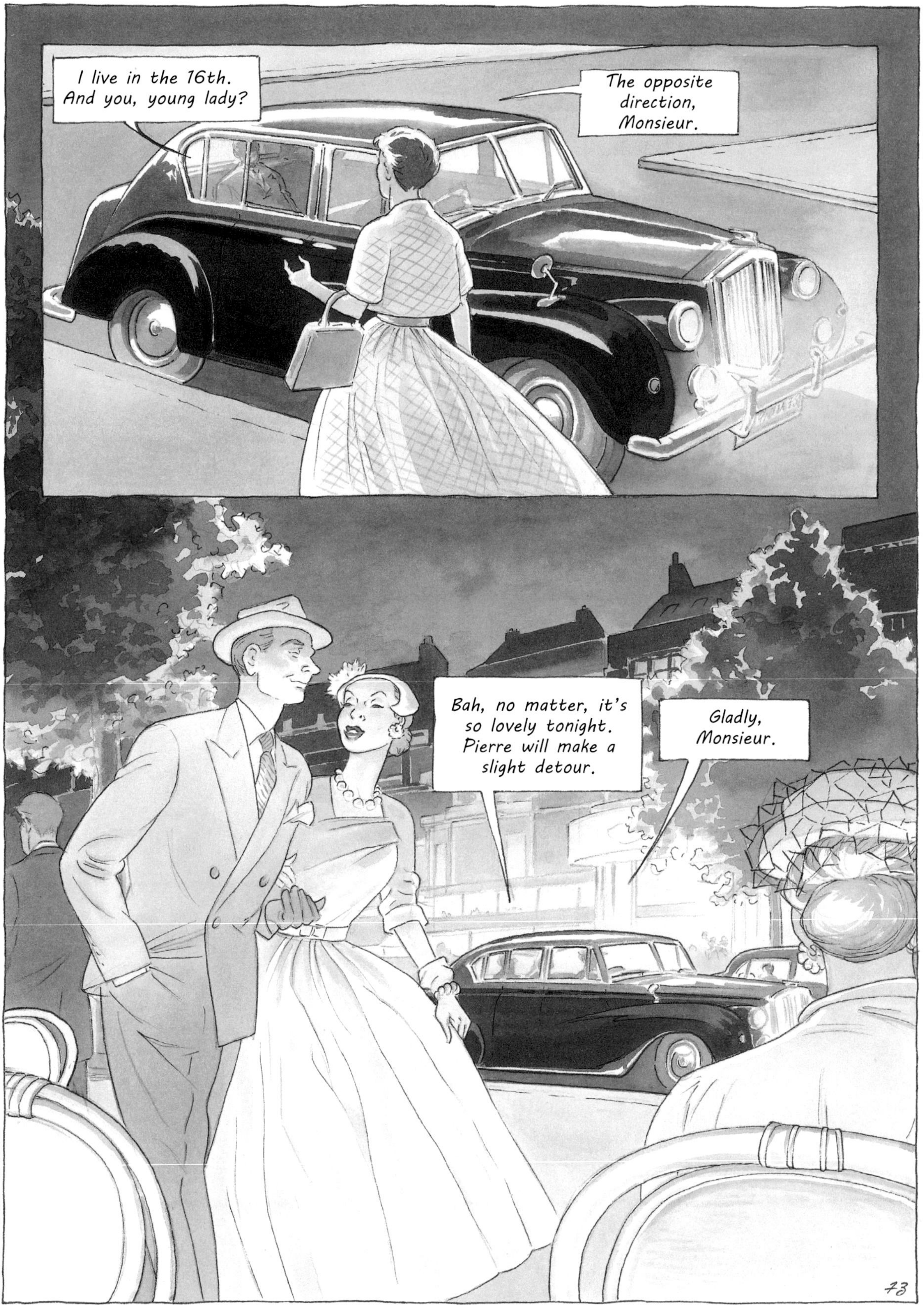
I live in the 16th. And you, young lady?
The opposite direction, Monsieur.
Bah, no matter, it's so lovely tonight. Pierre will make a slight detour.
Gladly, Monsieur.
73

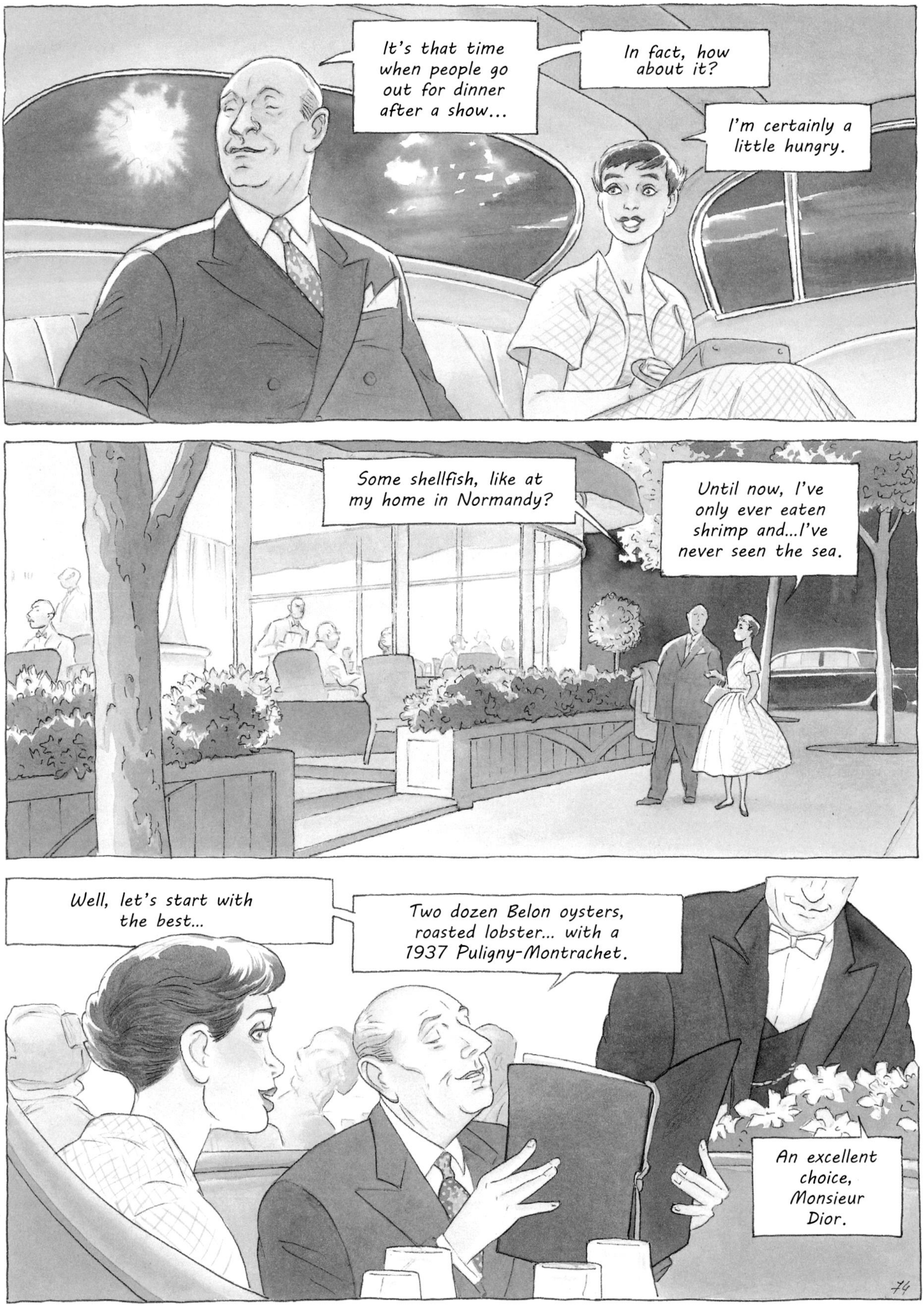
It's that time when people go out for dinner after a show...
In fact, how about it?
I'm certainly a little hungry.
Some shellfish, like at my home in Normandy?
Until now, I've only ever eaten shrimp and...I've never seen the sea.
Well, let's start with the best...
Two dozen Belon oysters, roasted lobster... with a 1937 Puligny-Montrachet.
An excellent choice, Monsieur Dior.

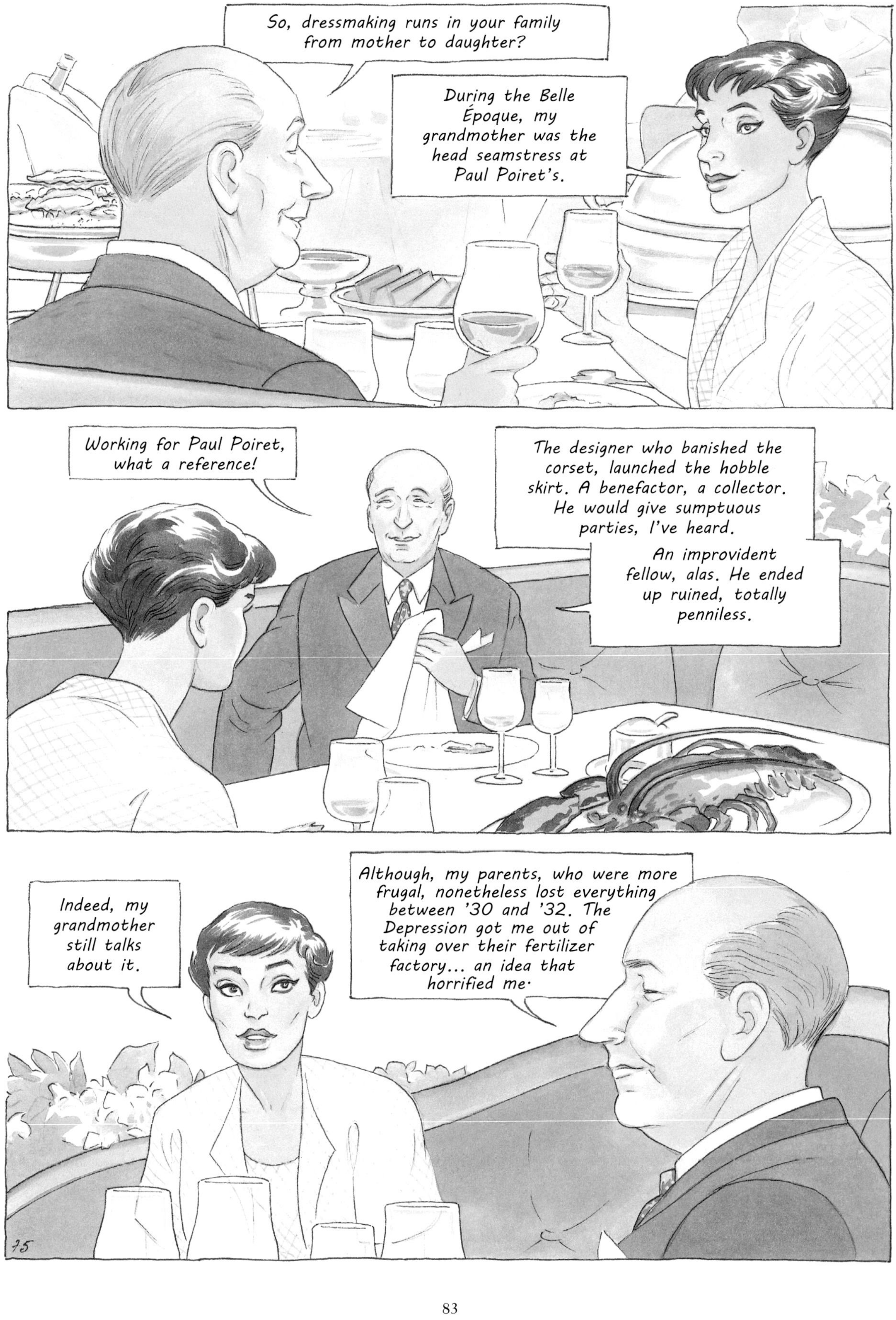

So, dressmaking runs in your family from mother to daughter?
During the Belle Époque, my grandmother was the head seamstress at Paul Poiret's.
Working for Paul Poiret, what a reference!
The designer who banished the corset, launched the hobble skirt. A benefactor, a collector. He would give sumptuous parties, I've heard.
An improvident fellow, alas. He ended up ruined, totally penniless.
Indeed, my grandmother still talks about it.
Although, my parents, who were more frugal, nonetheless lost everything between '30 and '32. The Depression got me out of taking over their fertilizer factory... an idea that horrified me.

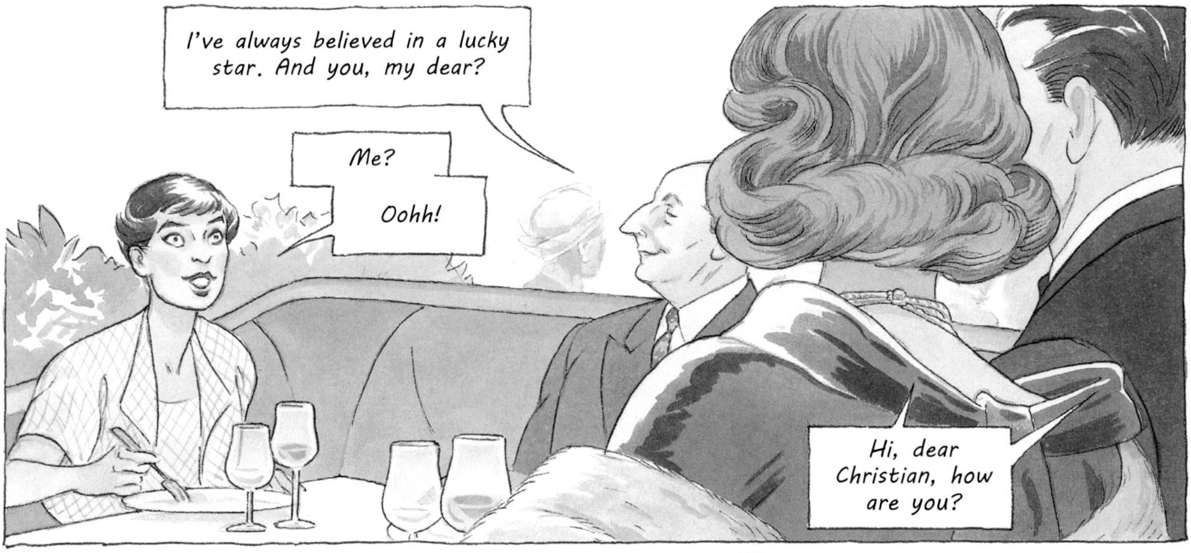
I've always believed in a lucky star. And you, my dear?
Me?
Oohh!
Hi, dear Christian, how are you?

To hell with my self-revelations! HUMPHREY BOGART and LAUREN BACALL, whom I saw in the black and white films "THE BIG SLEEP" and "KEY LARGO," are here, suddenly, before my eyes, in color!

This night is shining especially brightly, and I, in turn, transform from gray to technicolor with Monsieur Dior's words:

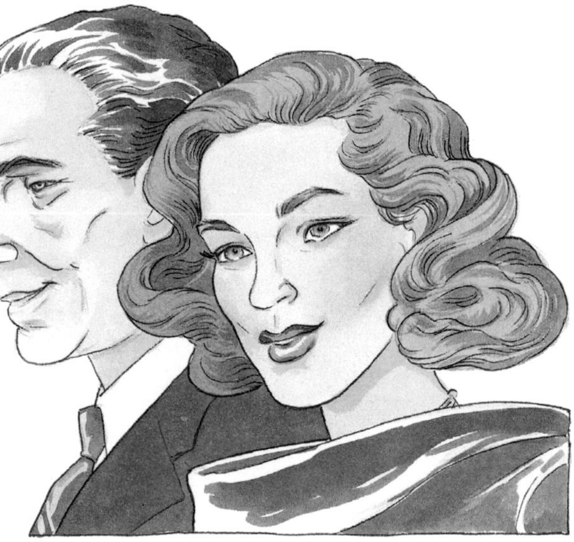

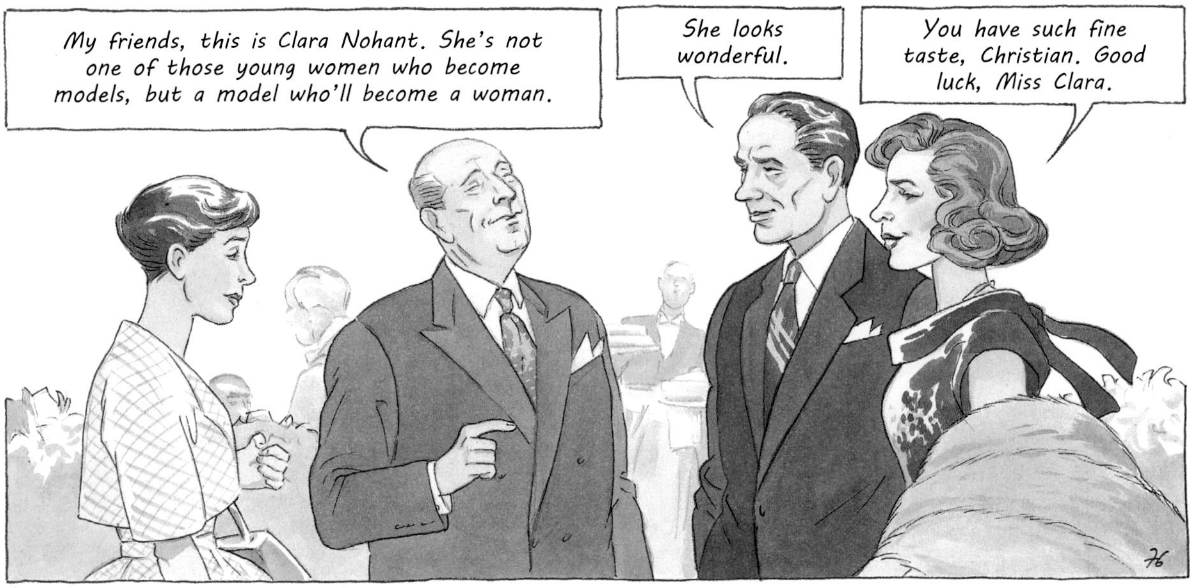
My friends, this is Clara Nohant. She's not one of those young women who become models, but a model who'll become a woman.
She looks wonderful.
You have such fine taste, Christian. Good luck, Miss Clara.

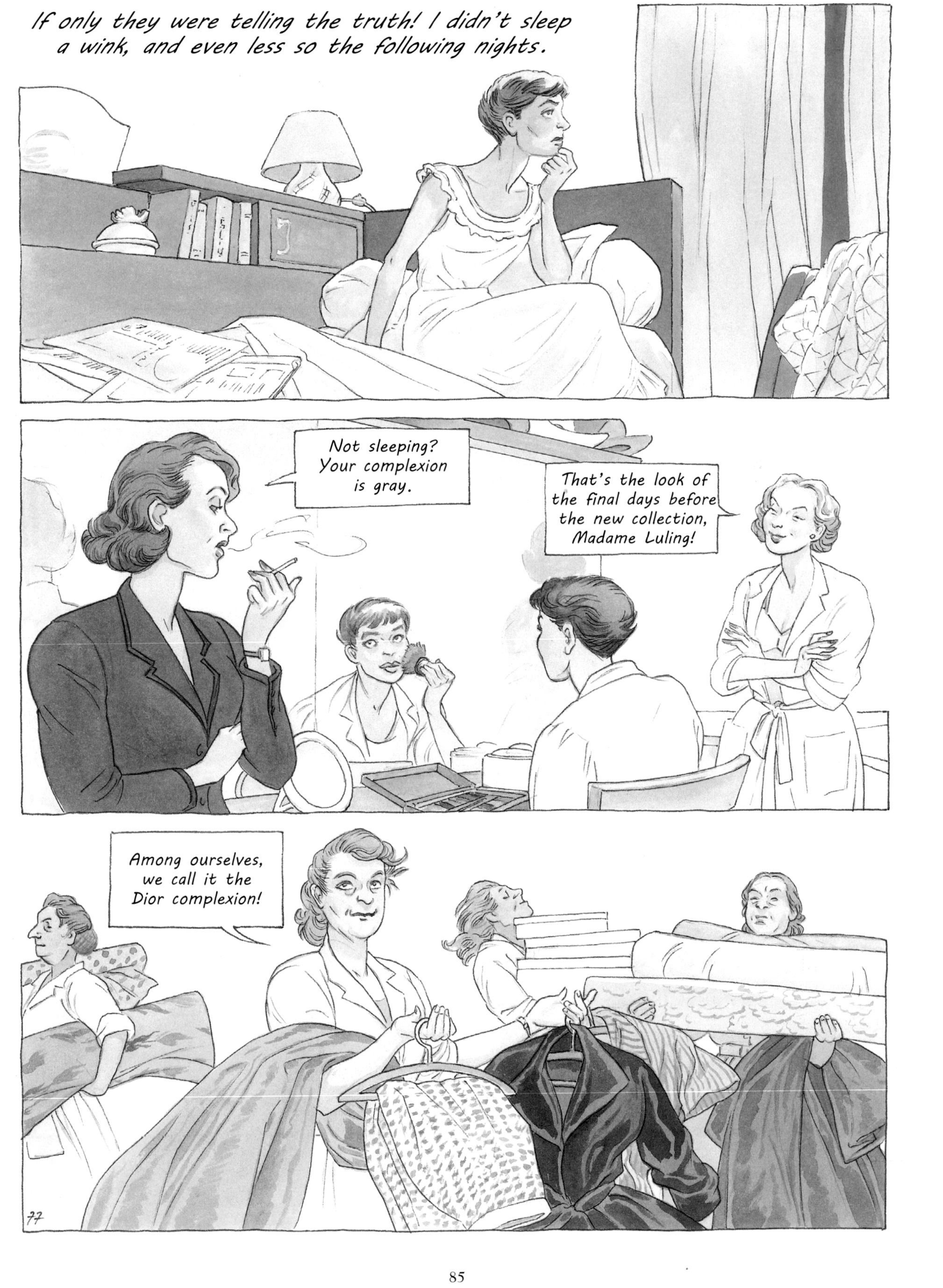
If only they were telling the truth! I didn't sleep a wink, and even less so the following nights.
Not sleeping? Your complexion is gray.
That's the look of the final days before the new collection, Madame Luling!
Among ourselves, we call it the Dior complexion!
77

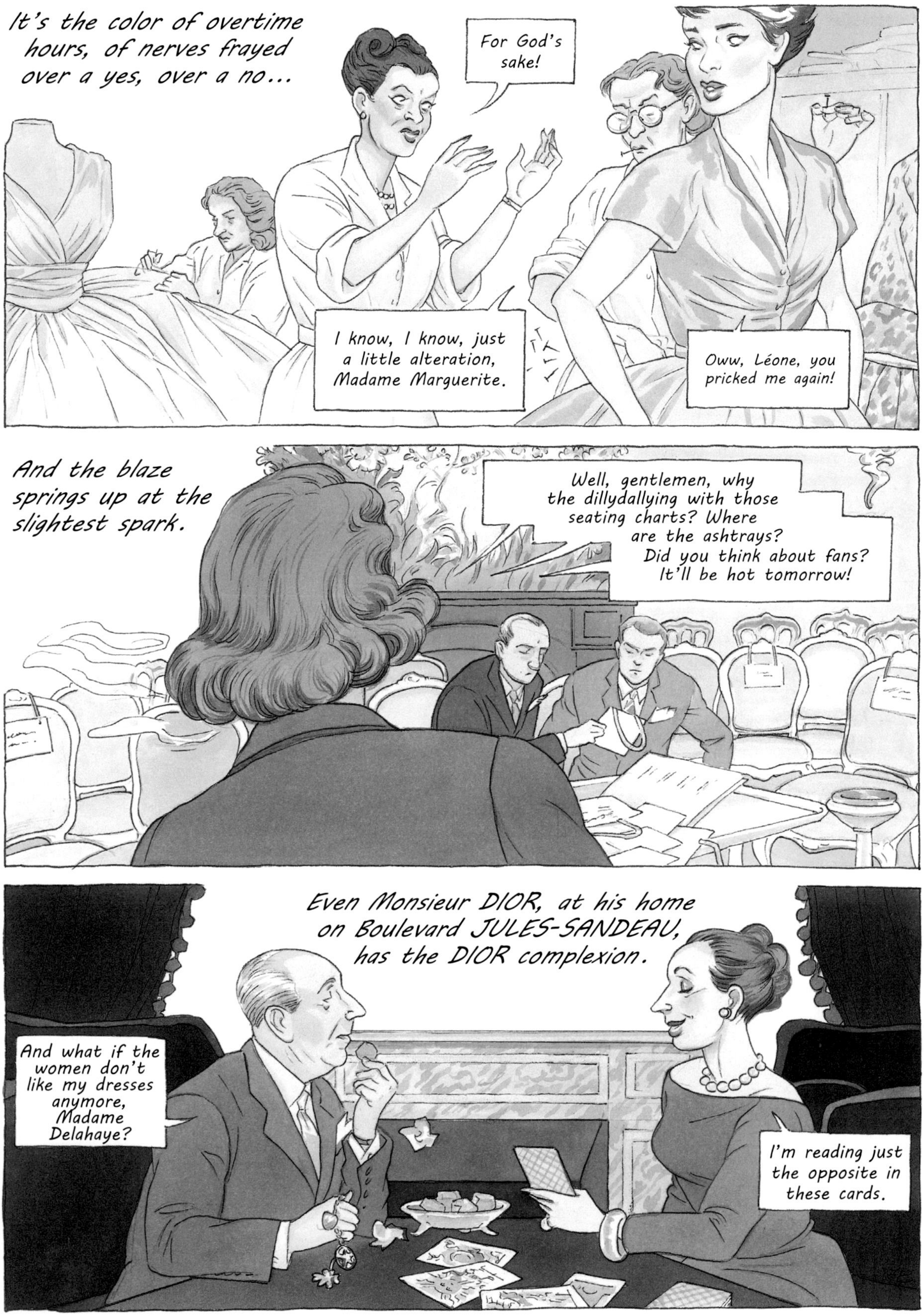
It's the color of overtime hours, of nerves frayed over a yes, over a no...
For God's sake!
I know, I know, just a little alteration, Madame Marguerite.
Oww, Léone, you pricked me again!
And the blaze springs up at the slightest spark.
Well, gentlemen, why the dillydallying with those seating charts? Where are the ashtrays? Did you think about fans? It'll be hot tomorrow!
Even Monsieur DIOR, at his home on Boulevard JULES-SANDEAU, has the DIOR complexion.
And what if the women don't like my dresses anymore, Madame Delahaye?
I'm reading just the opposite in these cards.

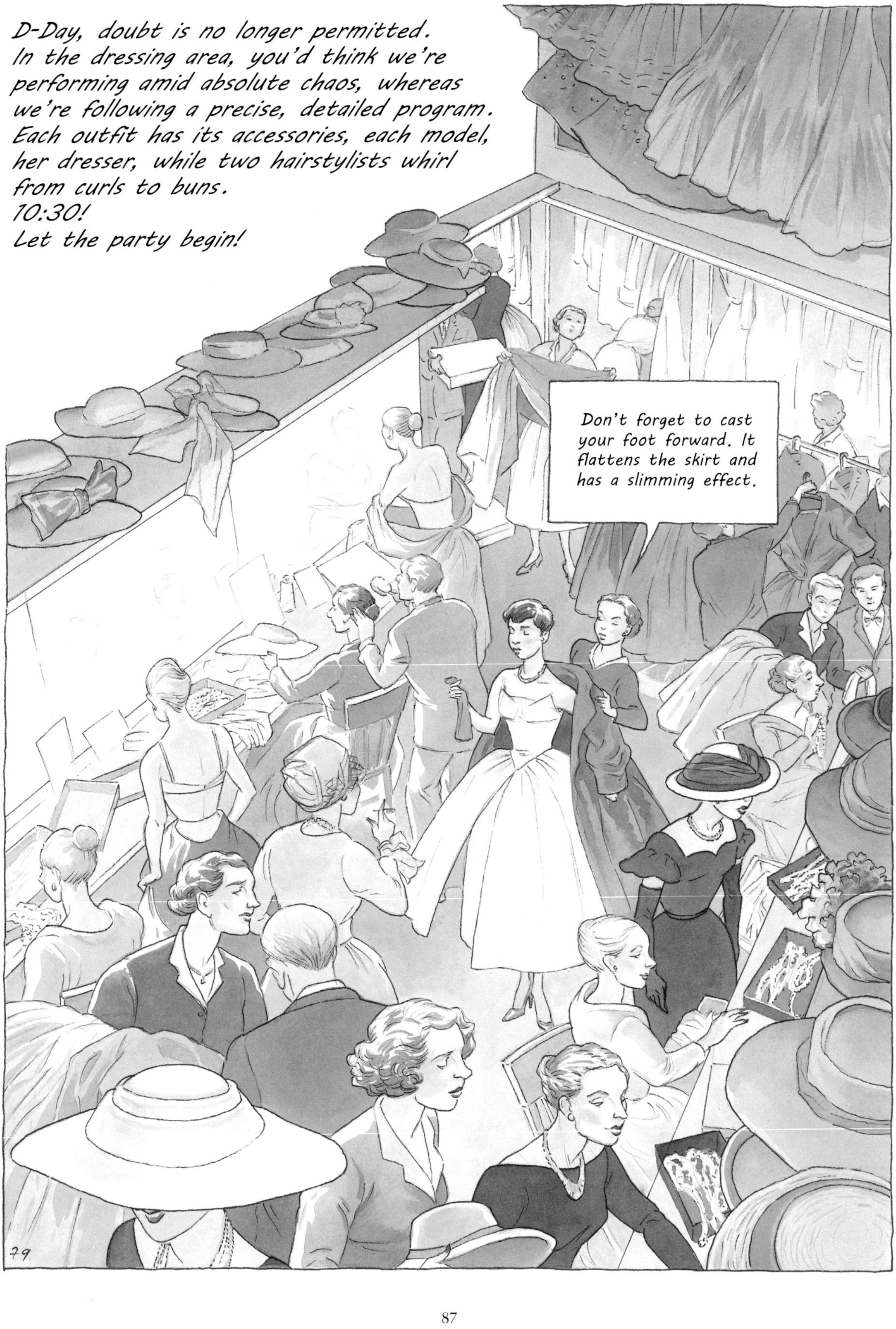
D-Day, doubt is no longer permitted.
In the dressing area, you'd think we're performing amid absolute chaos, whereas we're following a precise, detailed program.
Each outfit has its accessories, each model, her dresser, while two hairstylists whirl from curls to buns.
10:30!
Let the party begin!
Don't forget to cast your foot forward. It flattens the skirt and has a slimming effect.
79

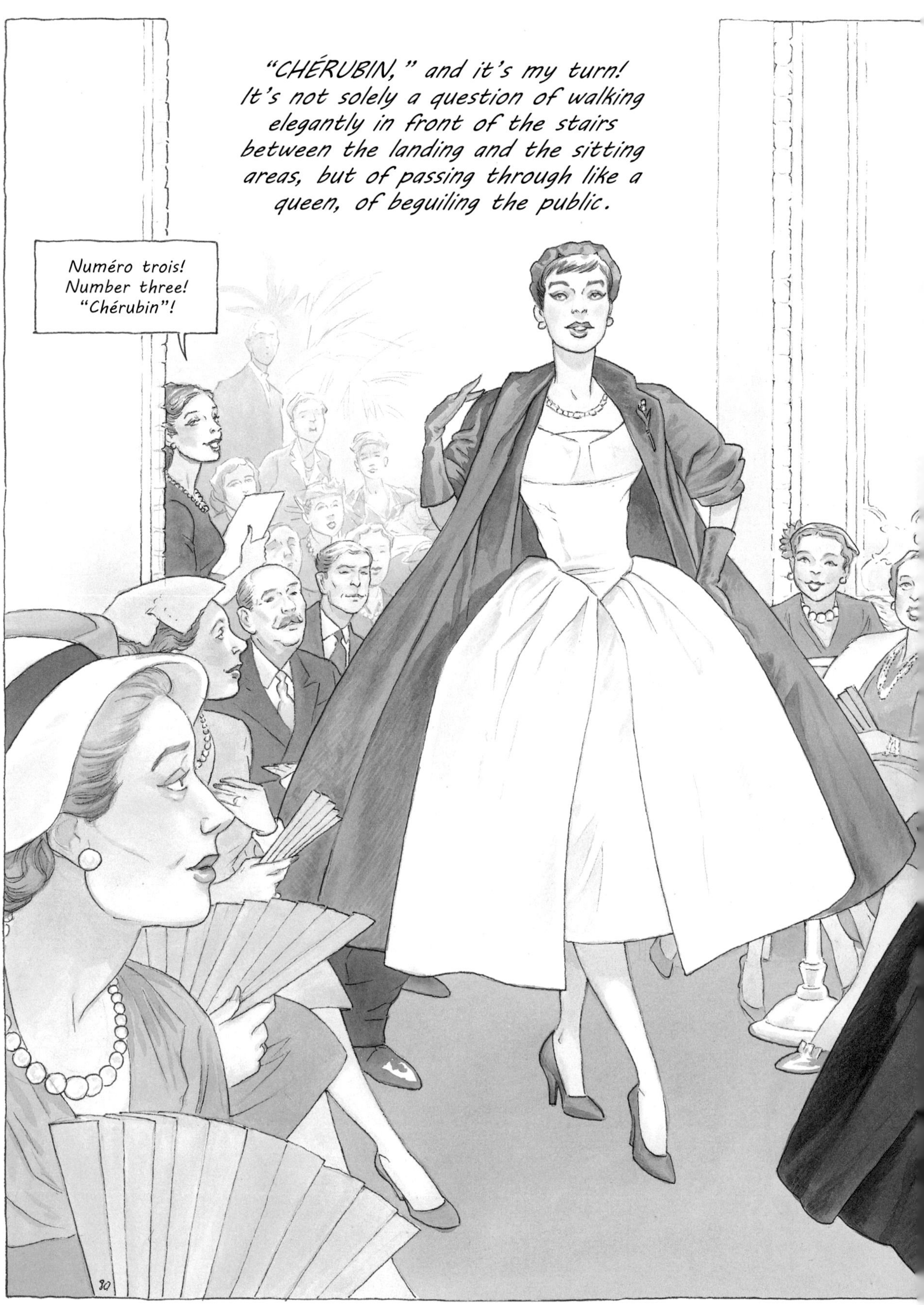
"CHÉRUBIN," and it's my turn! It's not solely a question of walking elegantly in front of the stairs between the landing and the sitting areas, but of passing through like a queen, of beguiling the public.
Numéro trois! Number three! "Chérubin"!

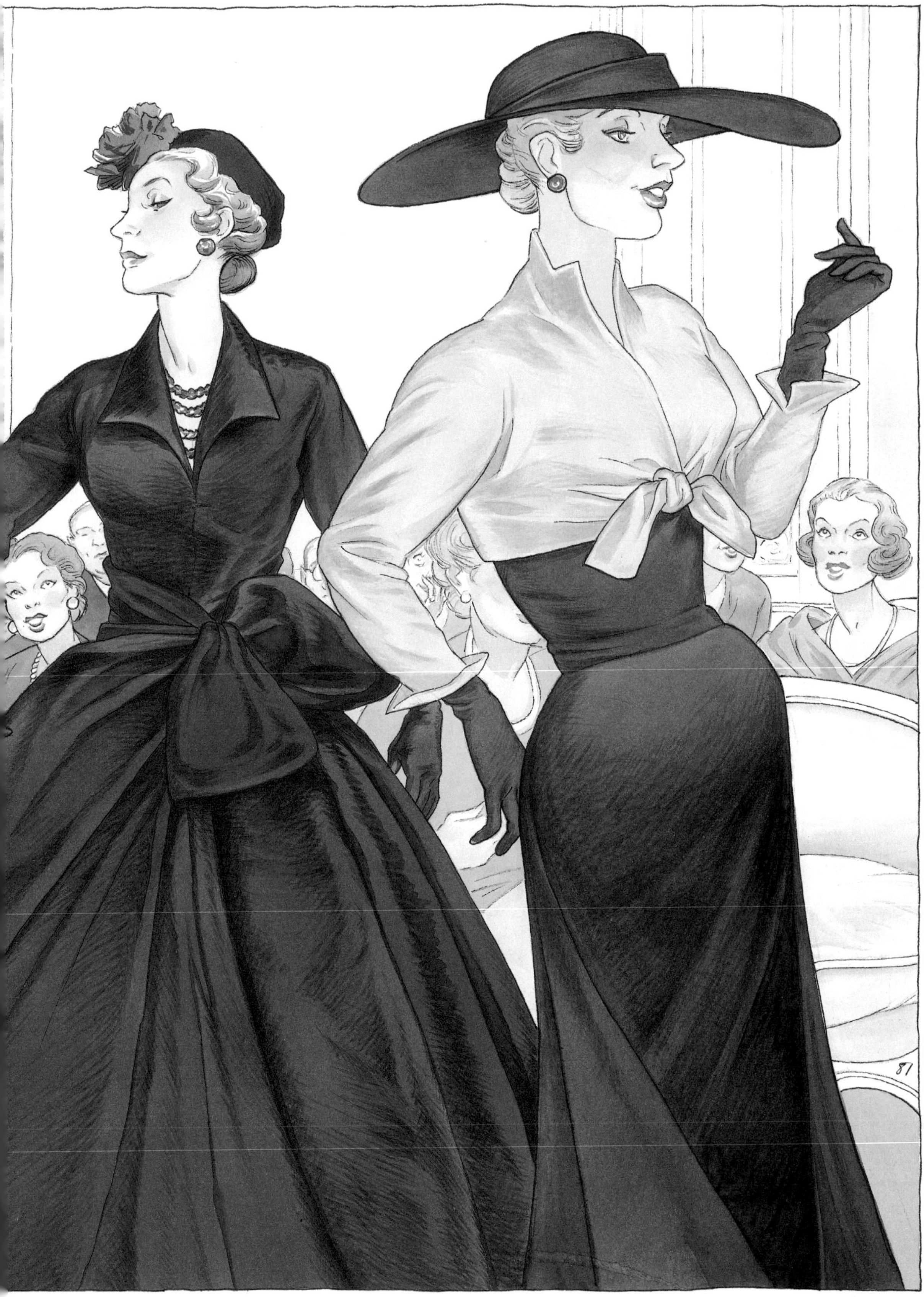

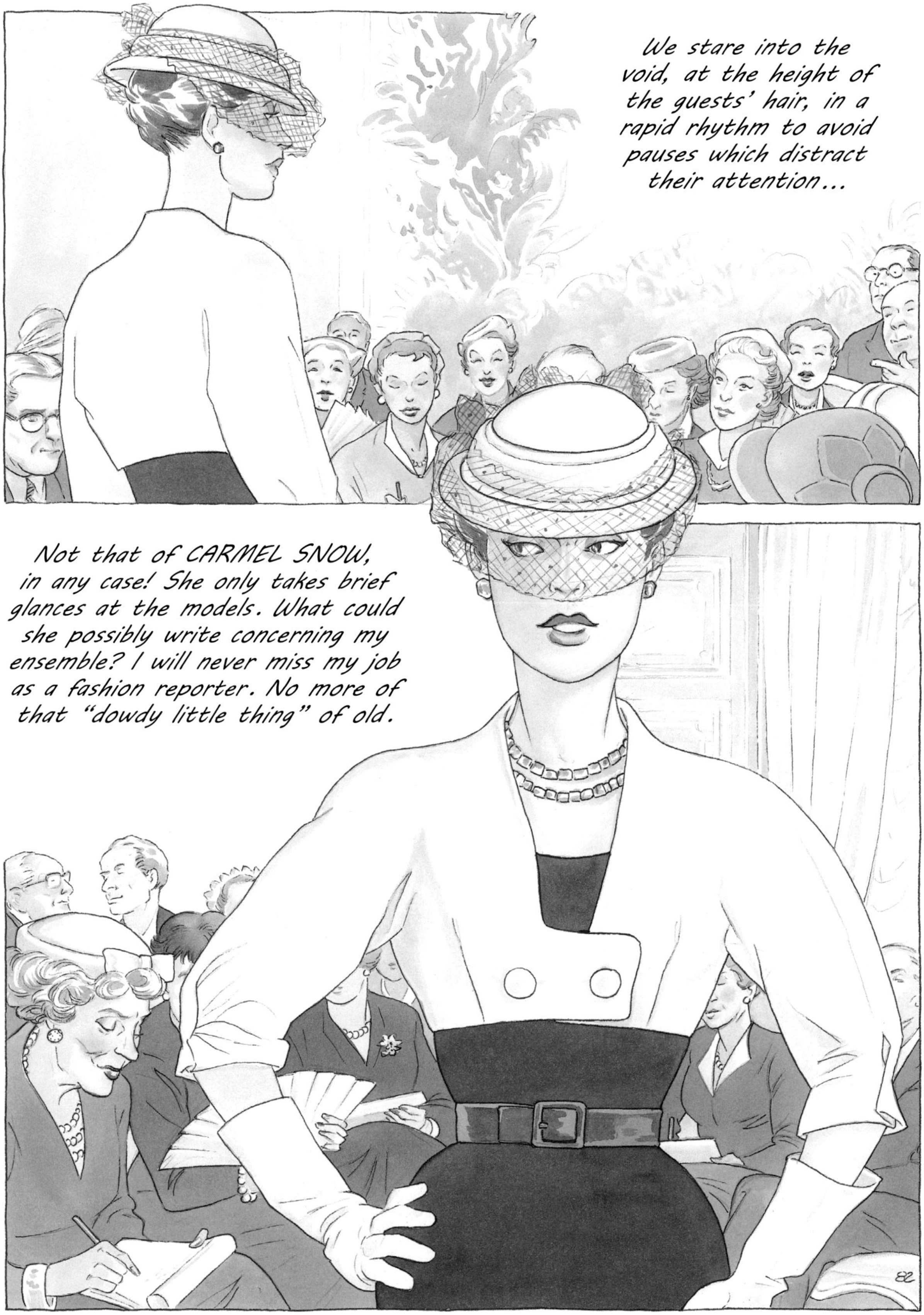
We stare into the void, at the height of the guests' hair, in a rapid rhythm to avoid pauses which distract their attention...
Not that of CARMEL SNOW, in any case! She only takes brief glances at the models. What could she possibly write concerning my ensemble? I will never miss my job as a fashion reporter. No more of that "dowdy little thing" of old.

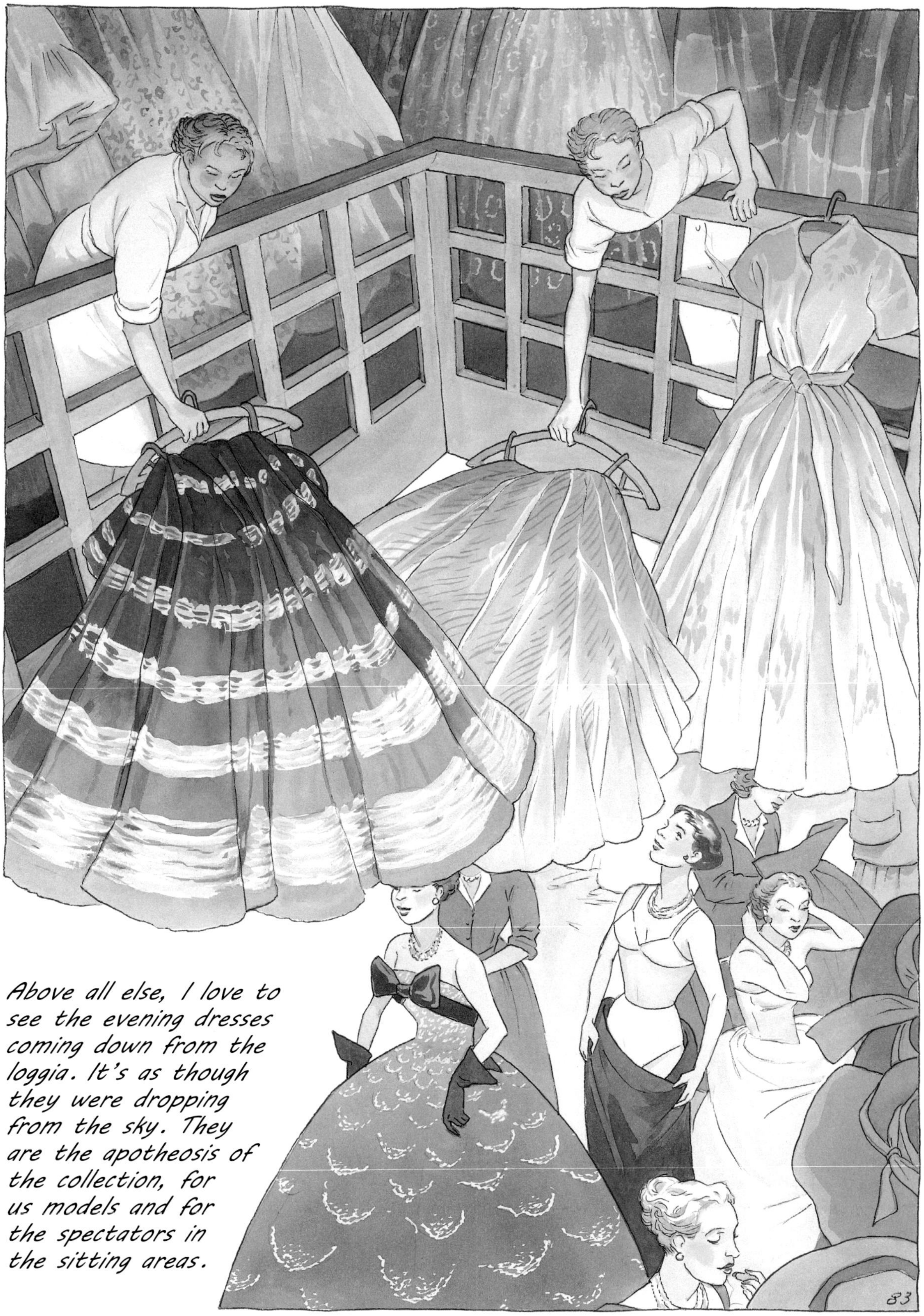
Above all else, I love to see the evening dresses coming down from the loggia. It's as though they were dropping from the sky. They are the apotheosis of the collection, for us models and for the spectators in the sitting areas.
83

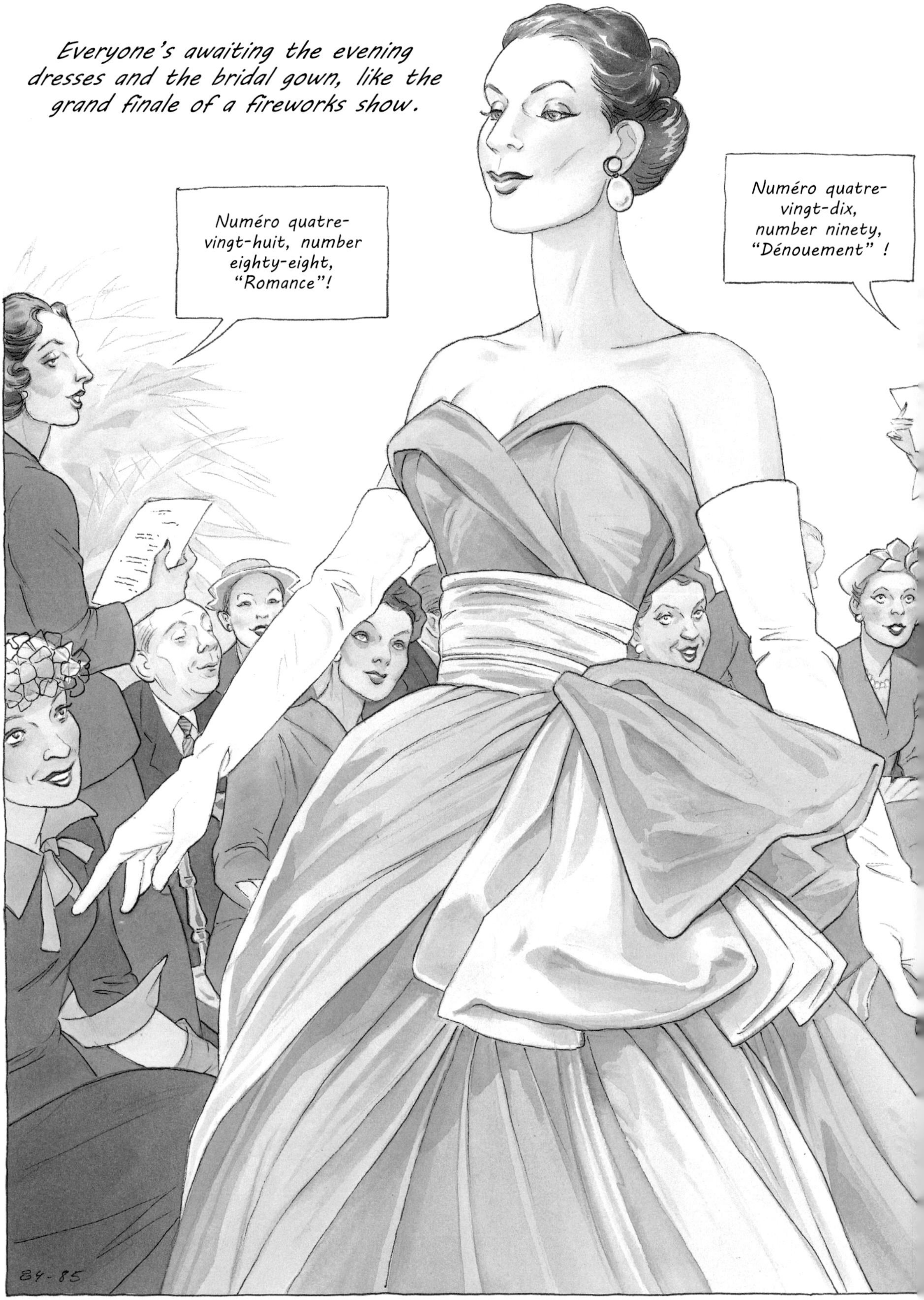
Everyone's awaiting the evening dresses and the bridal gown, like the grand finale of a fireworks show.
Numéro quatre-vingt-huit, number eighty-eight, "Romance"!
Numéro quatre-vingt-dix, number ninety, "Dénouement" !
84-85

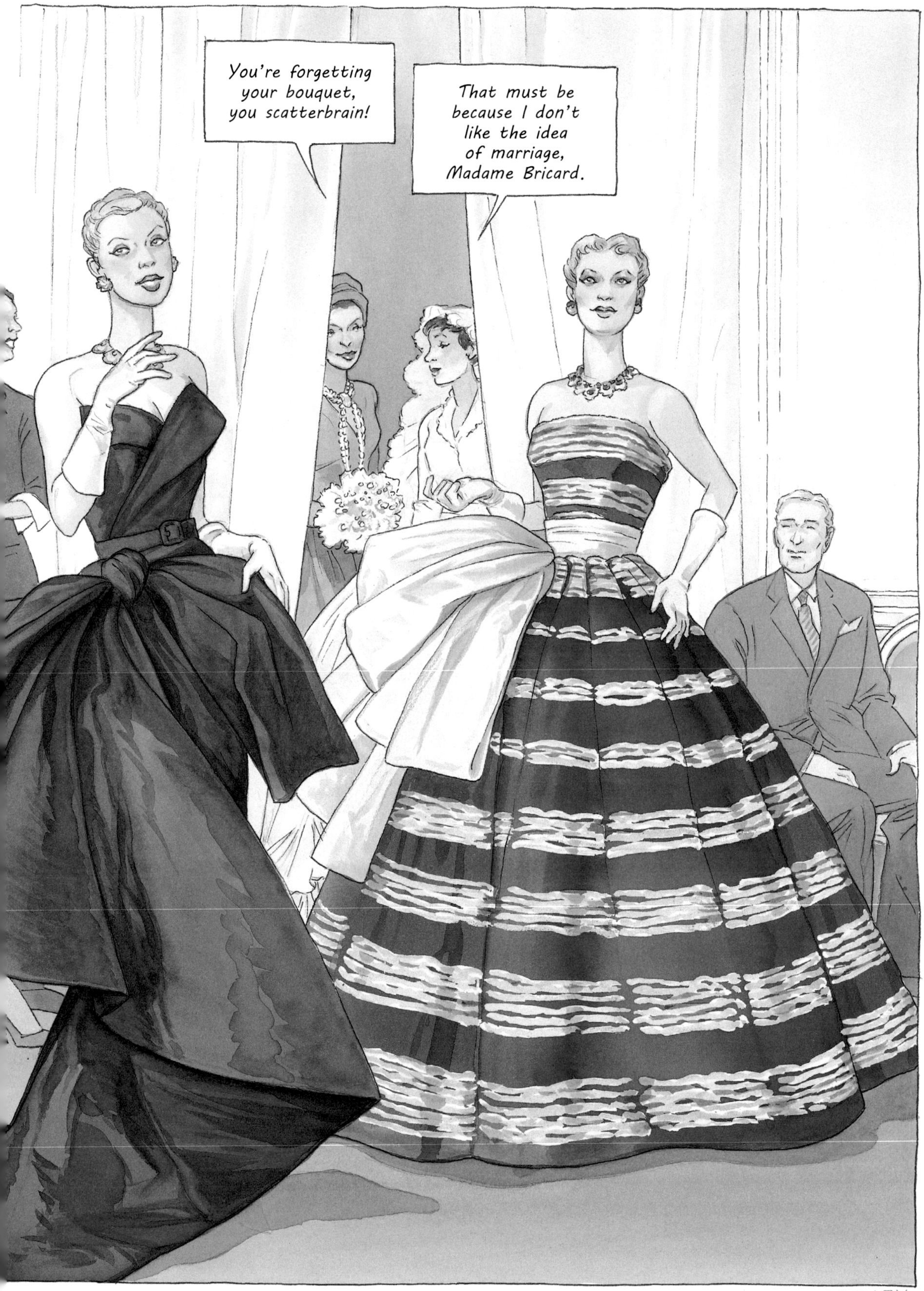
You're forgetting your bouquet, you scatterbrain!
That must be because I don't like the idea of marriage, Madame Bricard.

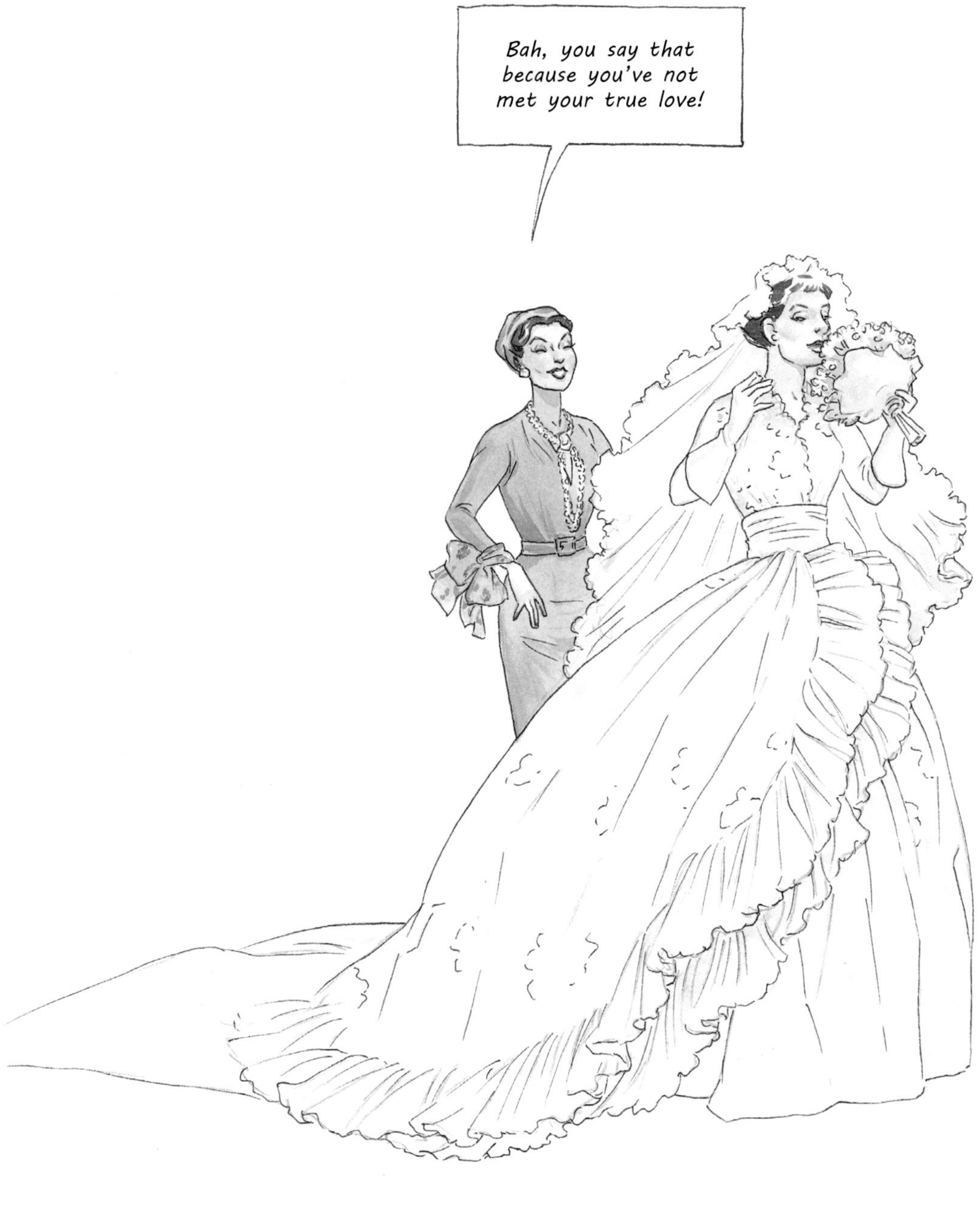
Bah, you say that because you've not met your true love!

I wasn't afraid of men either in life or during the fashion shows, but I dreaded certain professional buyers. They paid dearly for access rights to the collections in advance of their acquisitions.

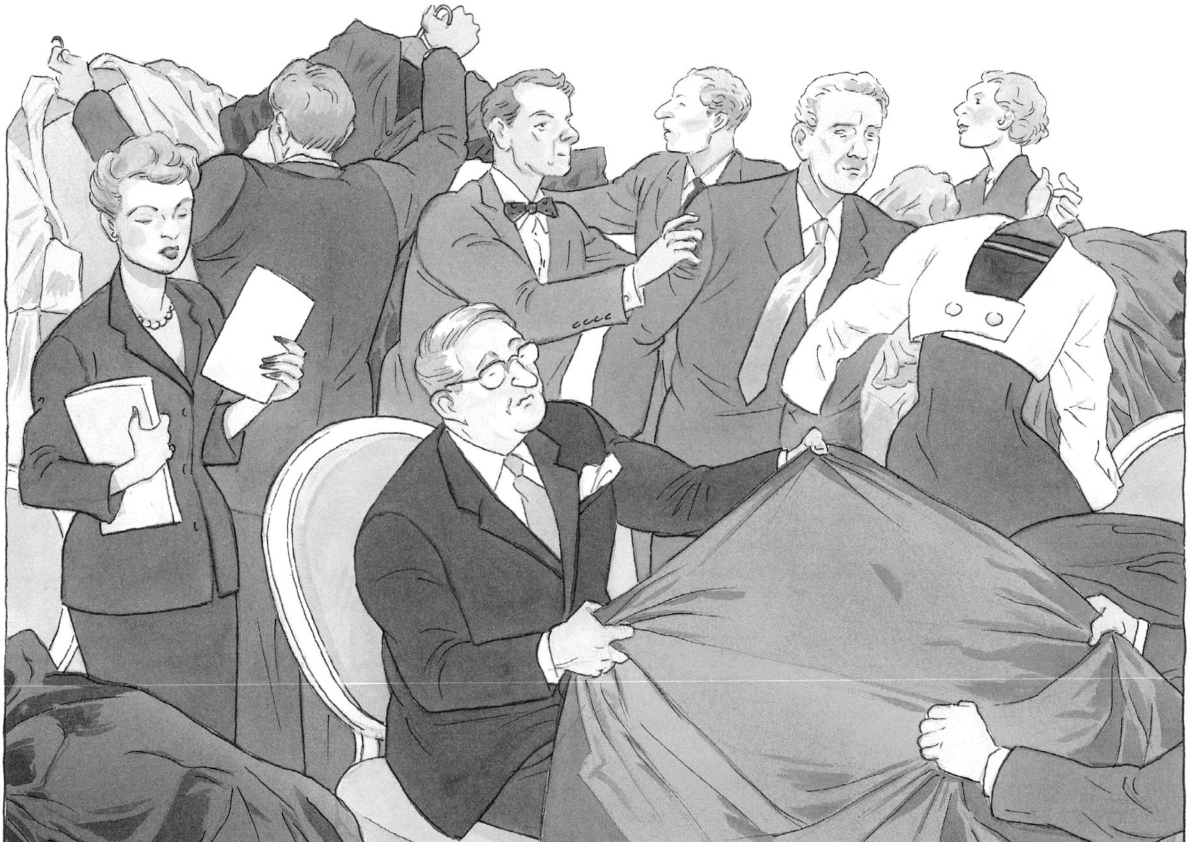

As if that gave them the right to finger, paw at, and dissect the clothing we'd worn a few days earlier.

They were insatiable, tireless.

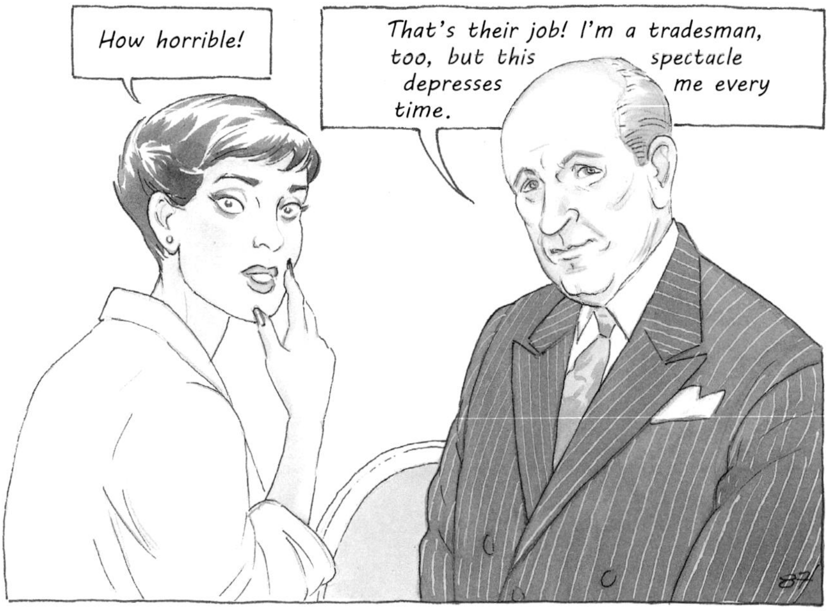
How horrible!
That's their job! I'm a tradesman, too, but this spectacle depresses me every time.

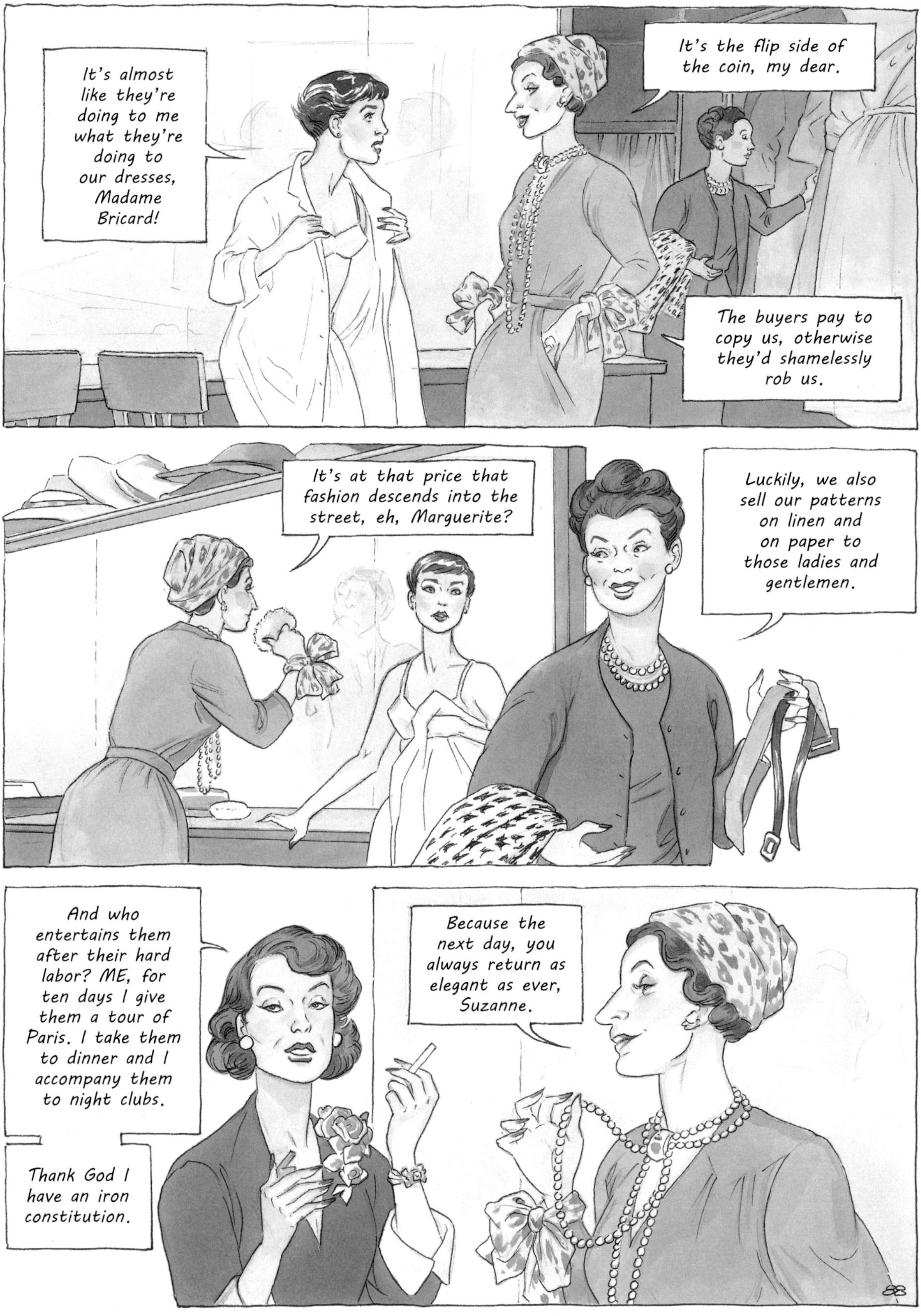
It's almost like they're doing to me what they're doing to our dresses, Madame Bricard!
It's the flip side of the coin, my dear.
The buyers pay to copy us, otherwise they'd shamelessly rob us.
It's at that price that fashion descends into the street, eh, Marguerite?
Luckily, we also sell our patterns on linen and on paper to those ladies and gentlemen.
And who entertains them after their hard labor? ME, for ten days I give them a tour of Paris. I take them to dinner and I accompany them to night clubs.
Thank God I have an iron constitution.
Because the next day, you always return as elegant as ever, Suzanne.

It's time to tell of my very first trip abroad, in July 1954. The Duchess of MARLBOROUGH, the head of the English Red Cross, had asked the DIOR house to present a fashion show during a gala benefitting its charitable work, at her home, BLENHEIM PALACE, in OXFORDSHIRE.

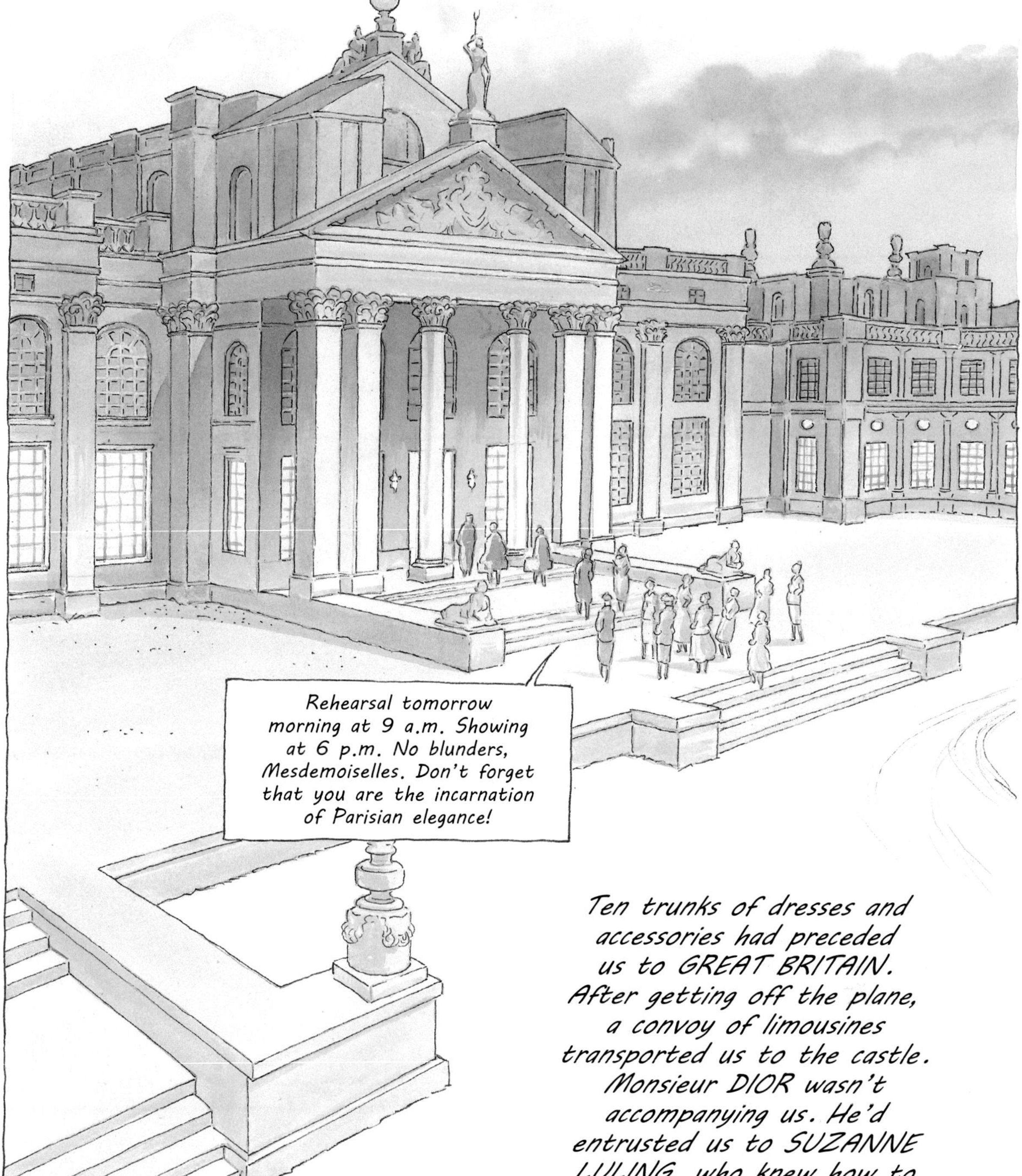
Rehearsal tomorrow morning at 9 a.m. Showing at 6 p.m. No blunders, Mesdemoiselles. Don't forget that you are the incarnation of Parisian elegance!
Ten trunks of dresses and accessories had preceded us to GREAT BRITAIN. After getting off the plane, a convoy of limousines transported us to the castle. Monsieur DIOR wasn't accompanying us. He'd entrusted us to SUZANNE LULING, who knew how to motivate her troops, as usual.

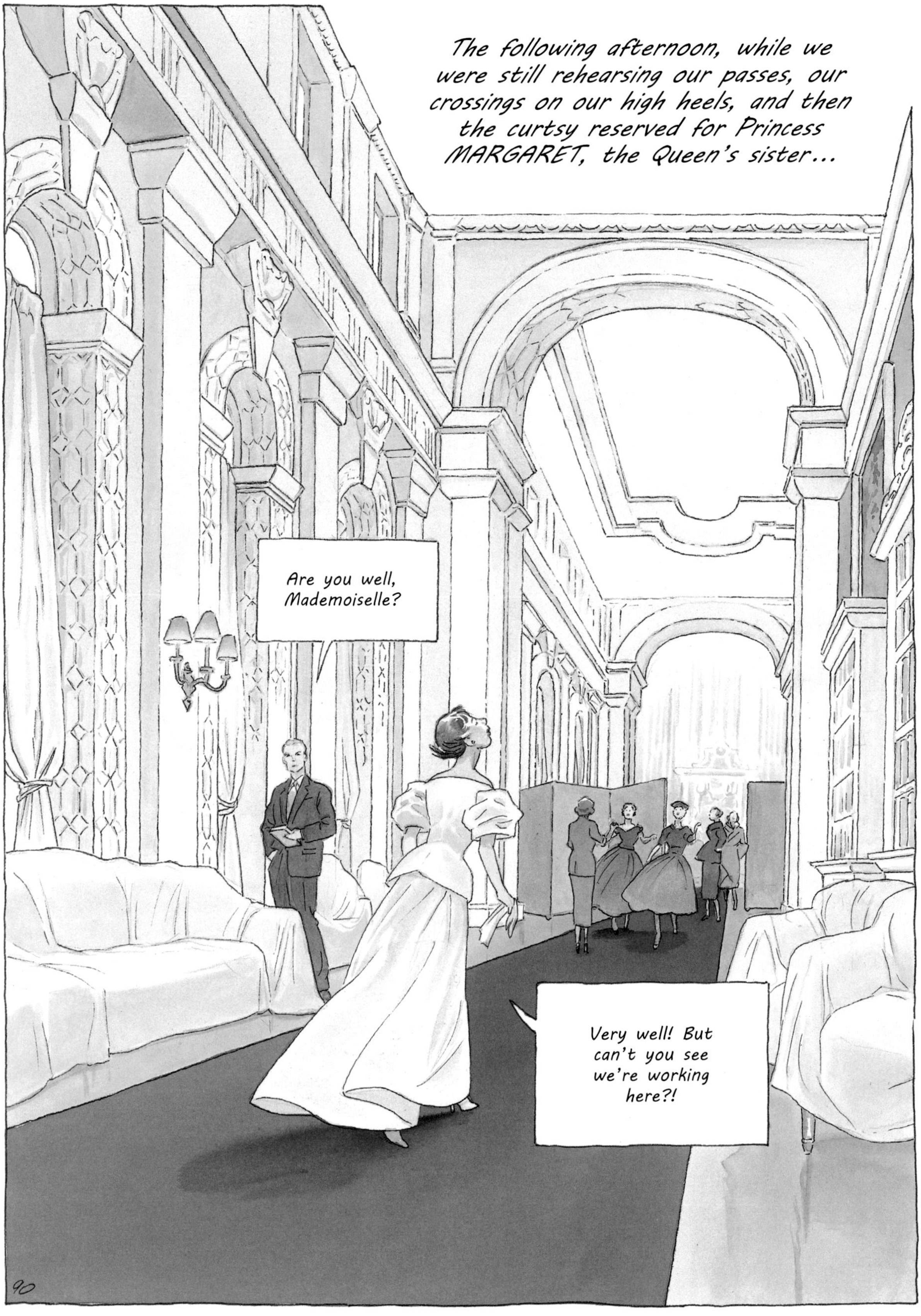
The following afternoon, while we were still rehearsing our passes, our crossings on our high heels, and then the curtsy reserved for Princess MARGARET, the Queen's sister...
Are you well, Mademoiselle?
Very well! But can't you see we're working here?!
90

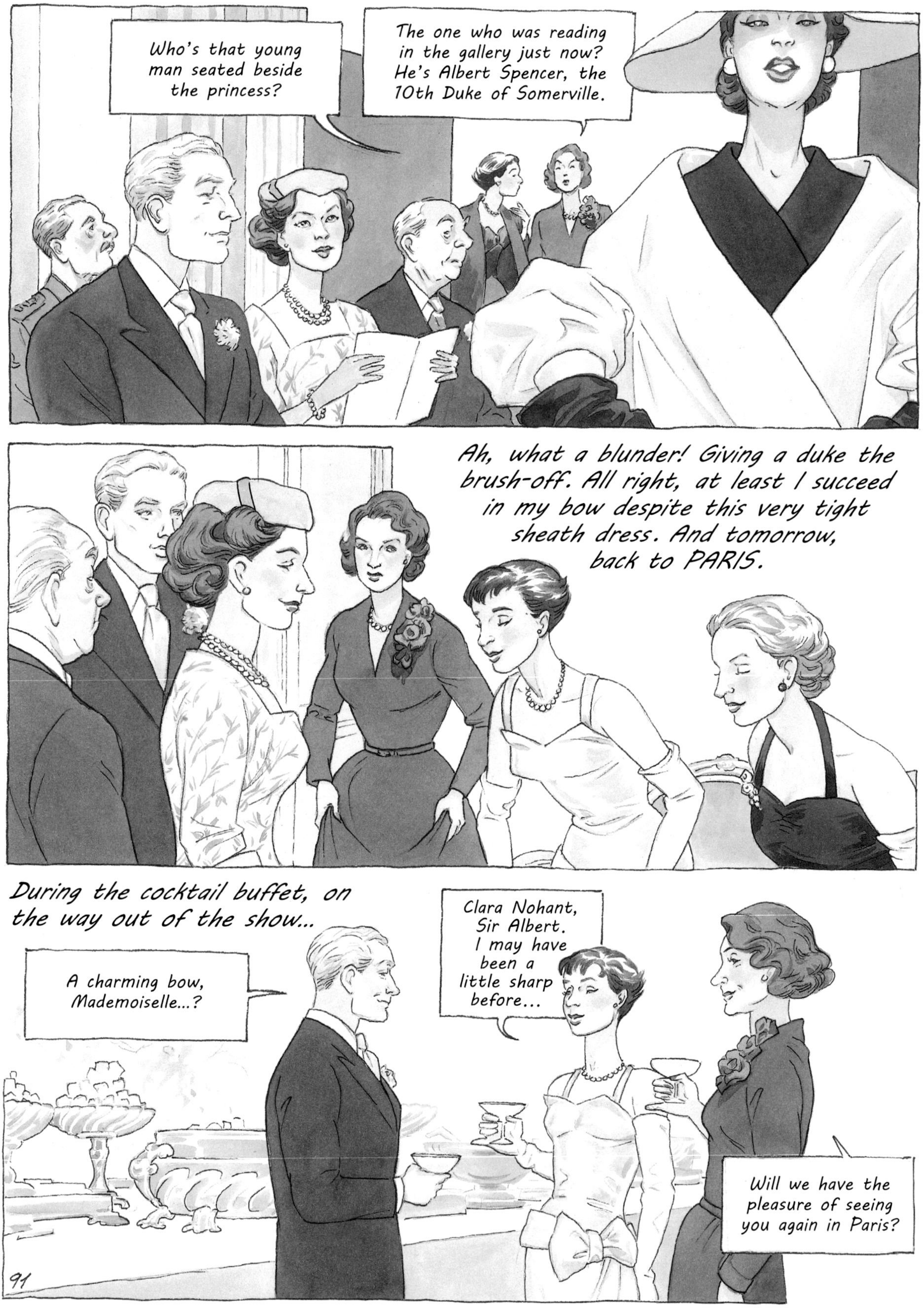
Who's that young man seated beside the princess?
The one who was reading in the gallery just now? He's Albert Spencer, the 10th Duke of Somerville.
Ah, what a blunder! Giving a duke the brush-off. All right, at least I succeed in my bow despite this very tight sheath dress. And tomorrow, back to PARIS.
During the cocktail buffet, on the way out of the show...
A charming bow, Mademoiselle...?
Clara Nohant, Sir Albert. I may have been a little sharp before...
Will we have the pleasure of seeing you again in Paris?
91

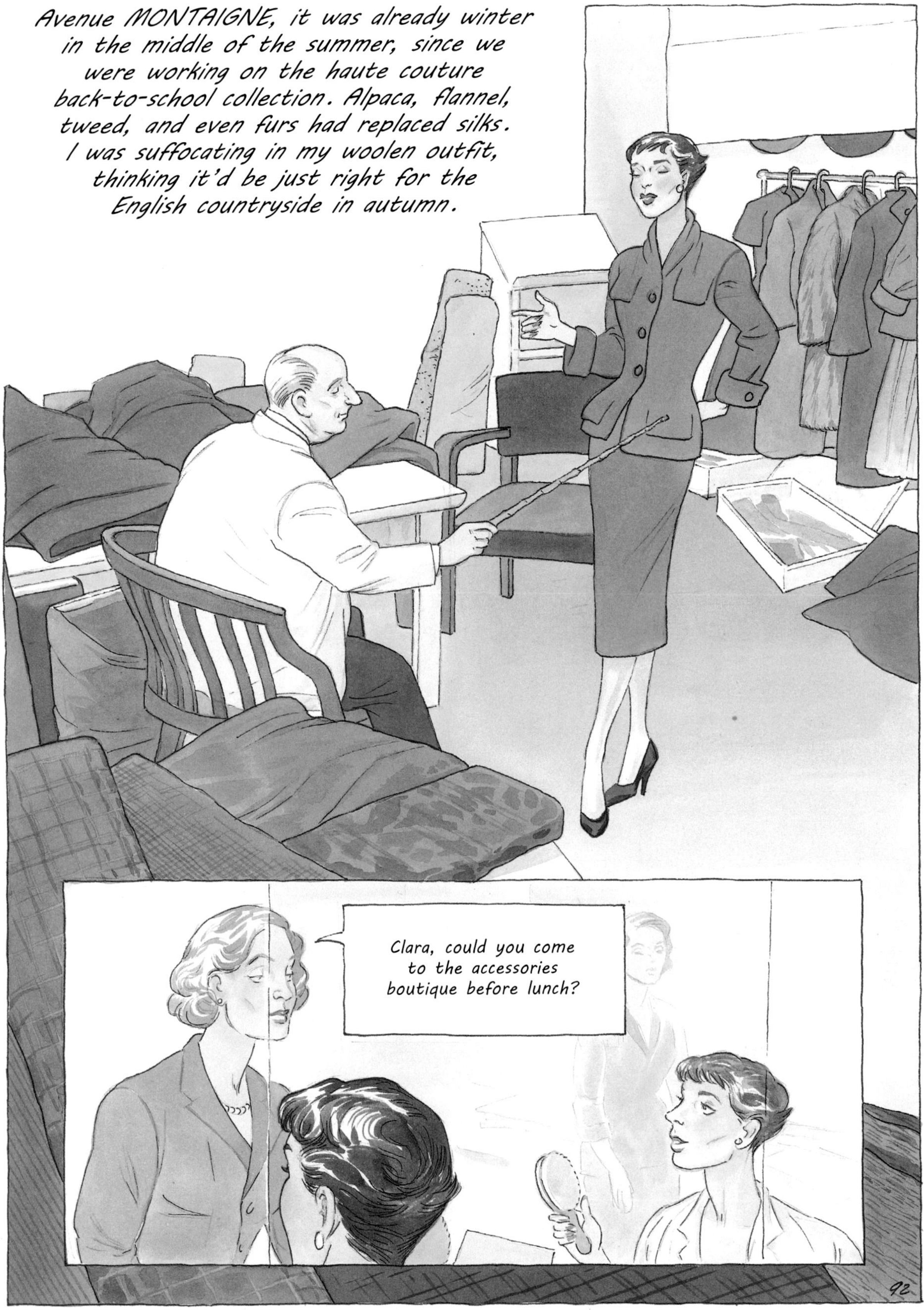
Avenue MONTAIGNE, it was already winter in the middle of the summer, since we were working on the haute couture back-to-school collection. Alpaca, flannel, tweed, and even furs had replaced silks. I was suffocating in my woolen outfit, thinking it'd be just right for the English countryside in autumn.
Clara, could you come to the accessories boutique before lunch?

Dear Mademoiselle Nohant, you can save my life!

I wish to give a handbag and gloves to a very elegant lady...

Lady Caroline Somerville, my mother.

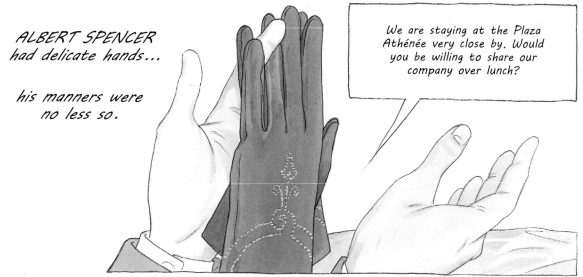

ALBERT SPENCER had delicate hands...

his manners were no less so.

We are staying at the Plaza Athénée very close by. Would you be willing to share our company over lunch?

From that day on, there were many lunches, dinners, balls, until...

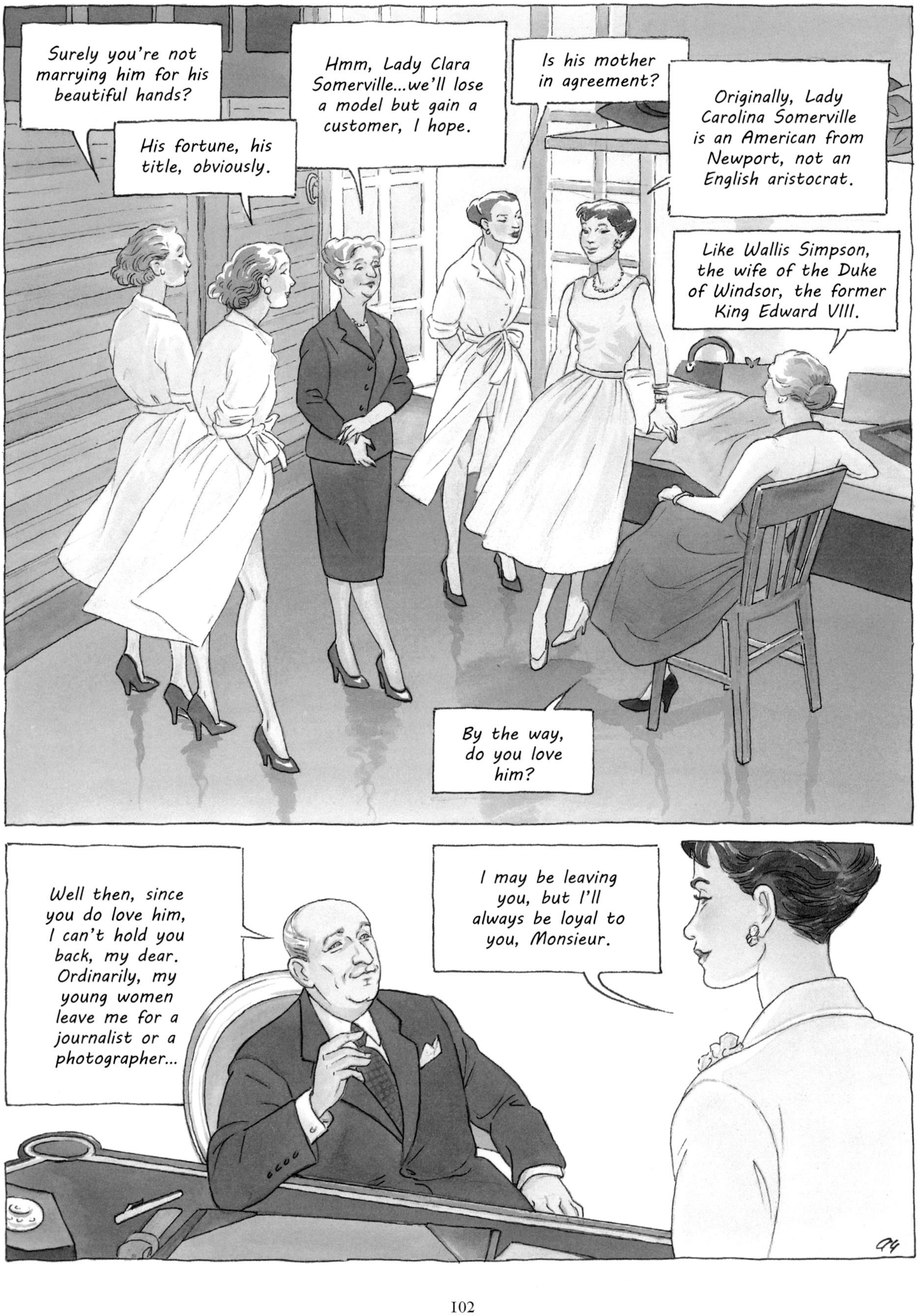

Surely you're not marrying him for his beautiful hands?
His fortune, his title, obviously.
Hmm, Lady Clara Somerville...we'll lose a model but gain a customer, I hope.
Is his mother in agreement?
Originally, Lady Carolina Somerville is an American from Newport, not an English aristocrat.
Like Wallis Simpson, the wife of the Duke of Windsor, the former King Edward VIII.
By the way, do you love him?
Well then, since you do love him, I can't hold you back, my dear. Ordinarily, my young women leave me for a journalist or a photographer...
I may be leaving you, but I'll always be loyal to you, Monsieur.

I have to tell you about my wedding dress, signed DIOR...

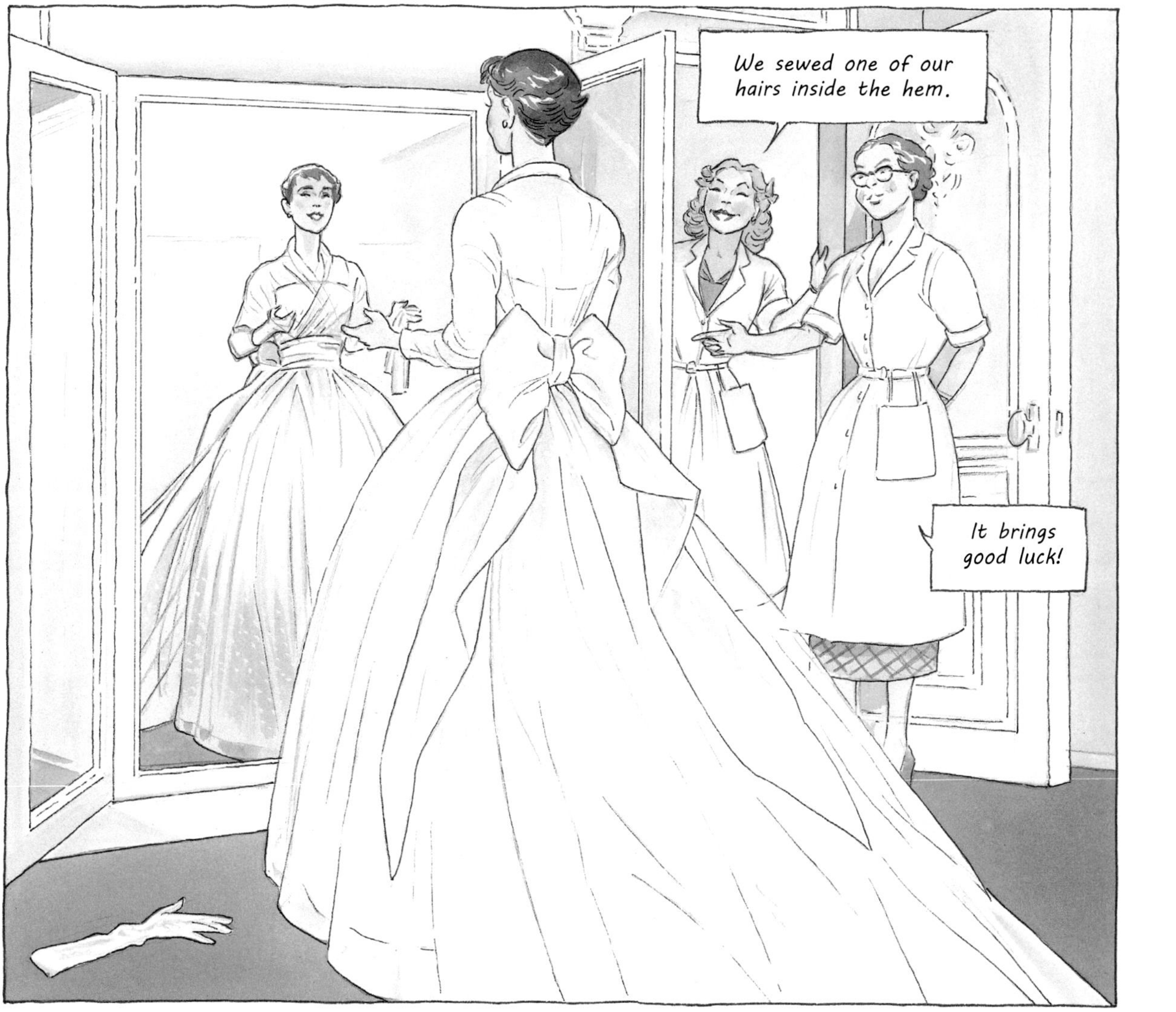

We sewed one of our hairs inside the hem.
It brings good luck!

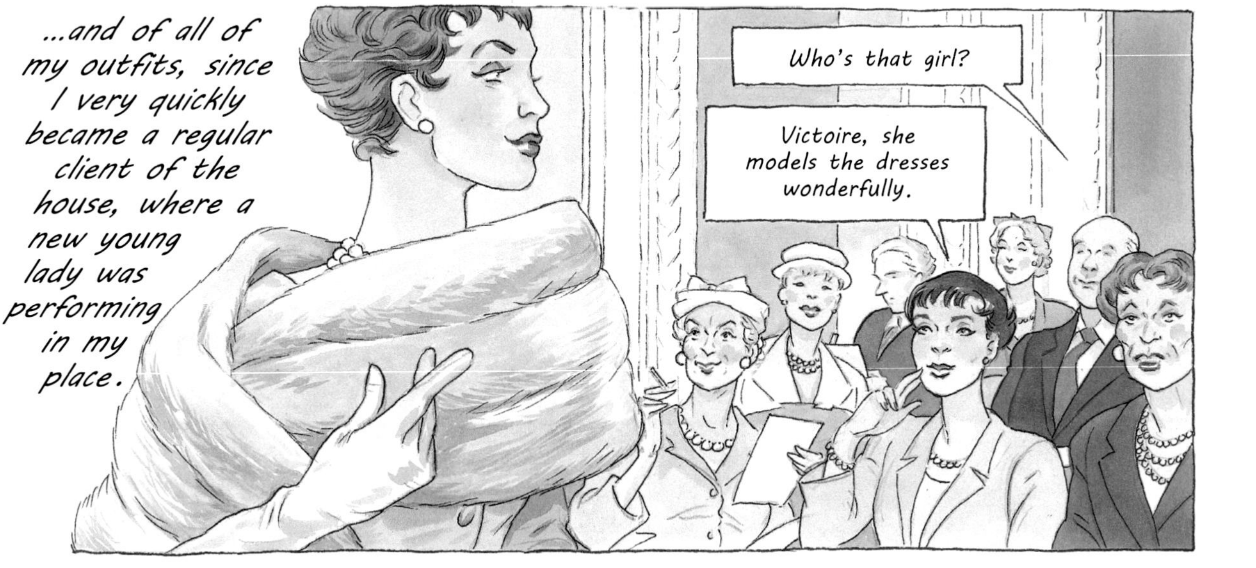

...and of all of my outfits, since I very quickly became a regular client of the house, where a new young lady was performing in my place.
Who's that girl?
Victoire, she models the dresses wonderfully.

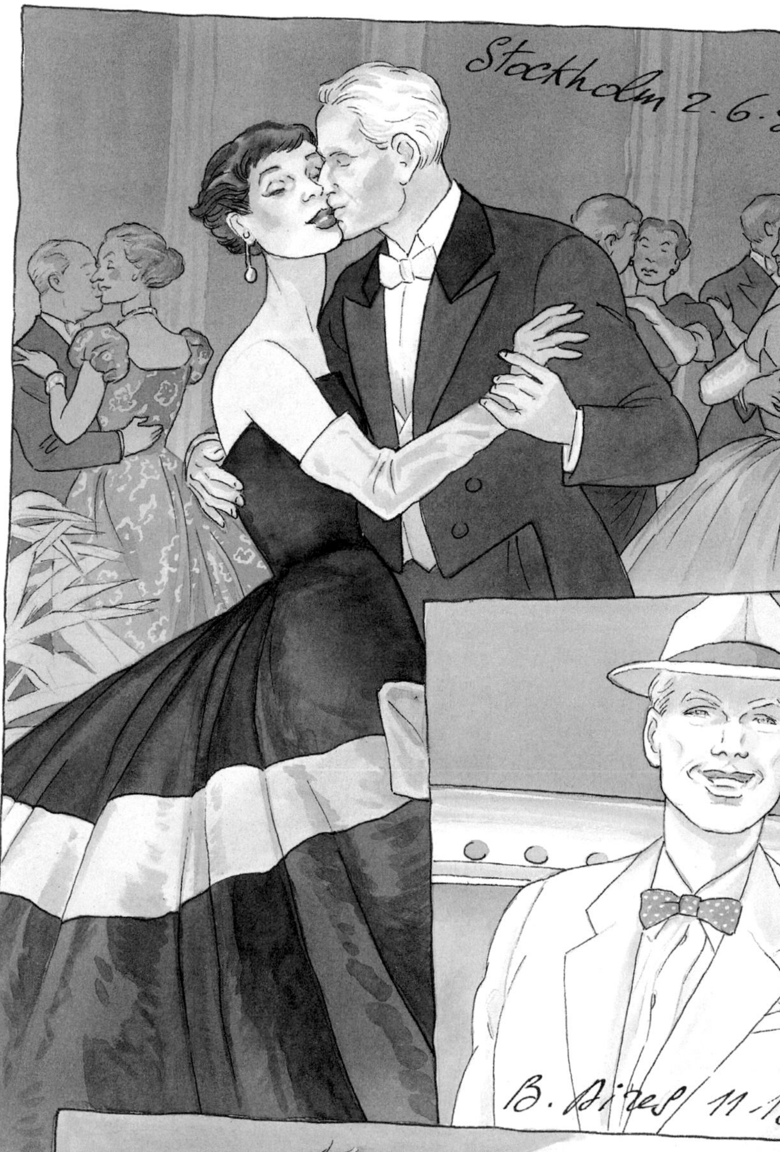
Stockholm 2.6.54

All my years of happiness are associated with that wardrobe of dreams. My attachment to the creation of Avenue MONTAIGNE amused ALBERT SPENCER.

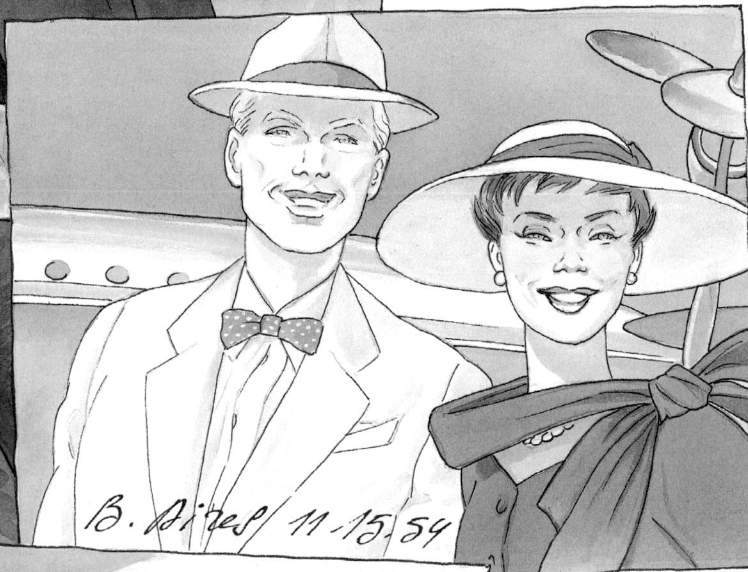
B. Aires 11.15.54

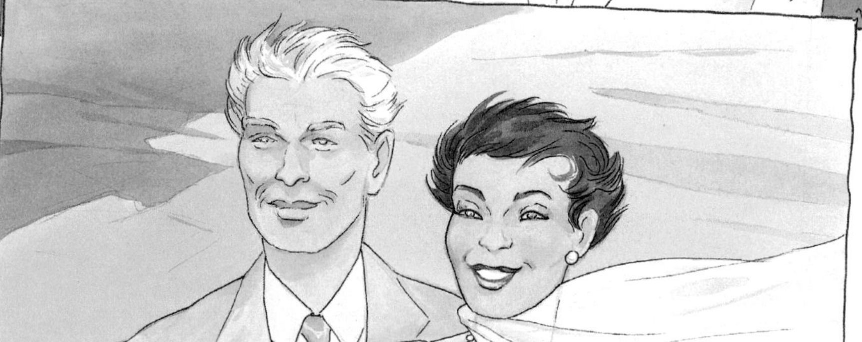
9.23.55

I danced, traveled from one continent to the other on my dear husband's arm, following him in his diplomatic career.

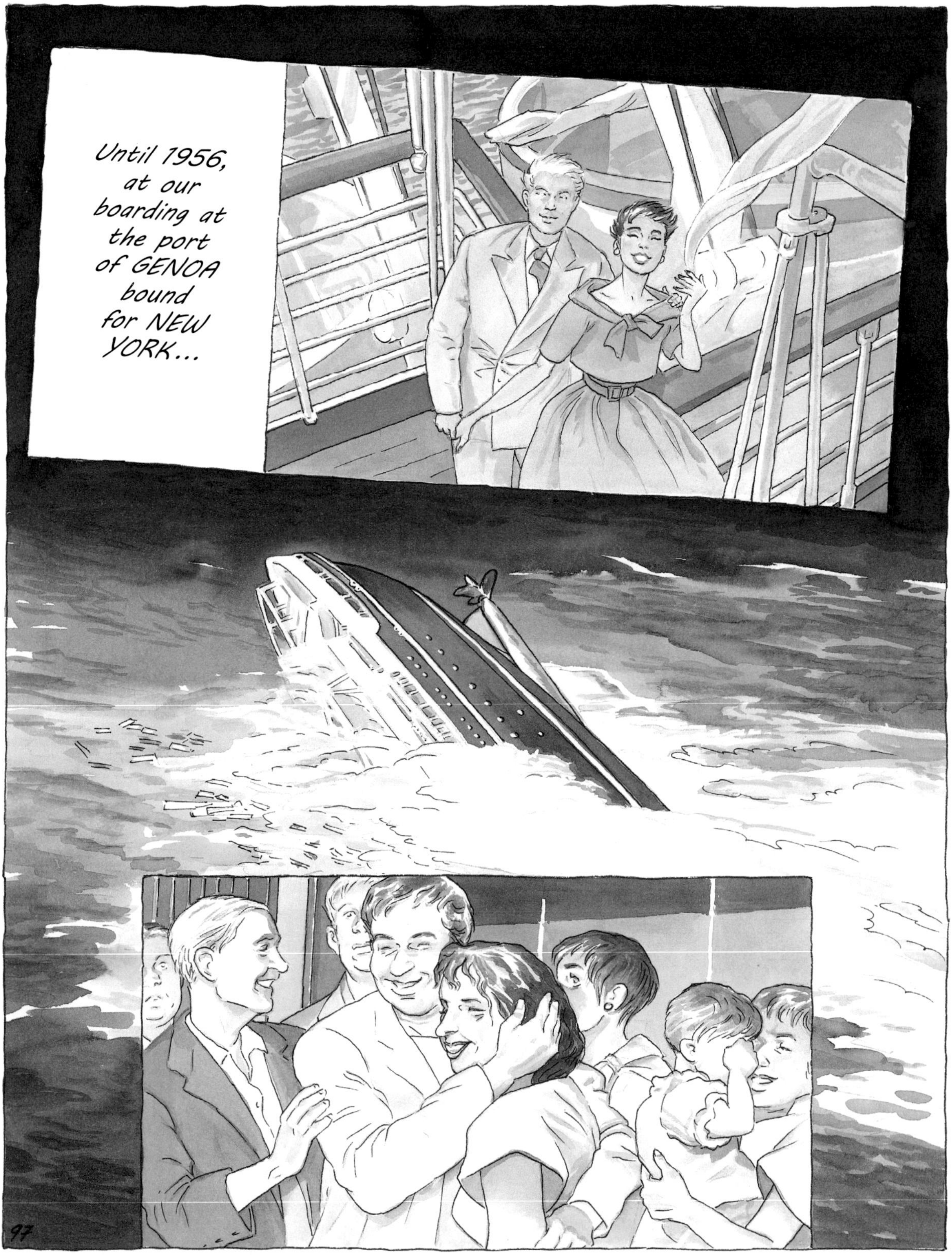
Until 1956, at our boarding at the port of GENOA bound for NEW YORK...
97

On the night of July 26, my husband was one of the 51 victims of the shipwreck of the "ANDREA DORIA," rammed by the "STOCKHOLM," a Swedish ship, in the mid-Atlantic. I was among those rescued.

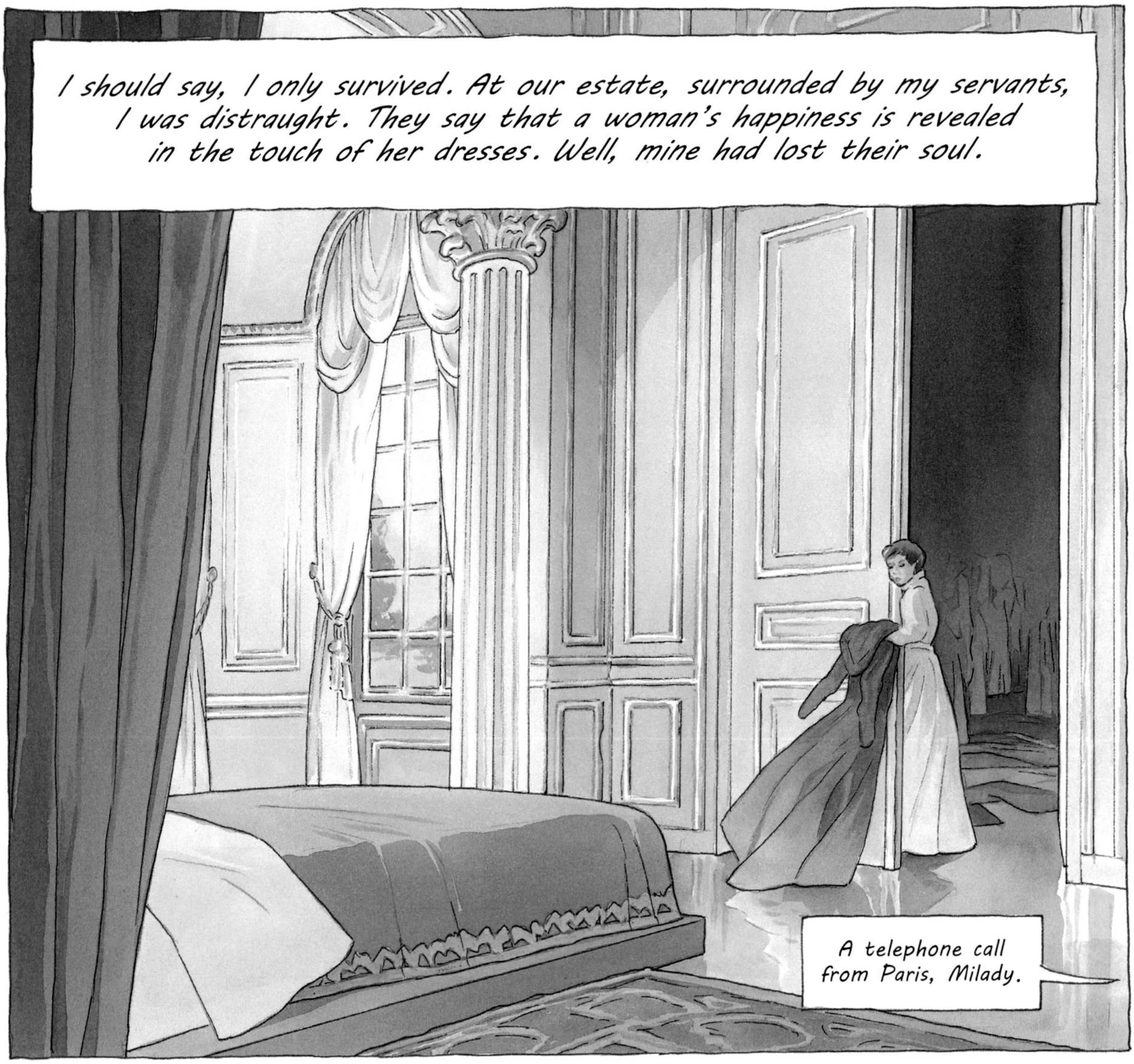
I should say, I only survived. At our estate, surrounded by my servants, I was distraught. They say that a woman's happiness is revealed in the touch of her dresses. Well, mine had lost their soul.
A telephone call from Paris, Milady.
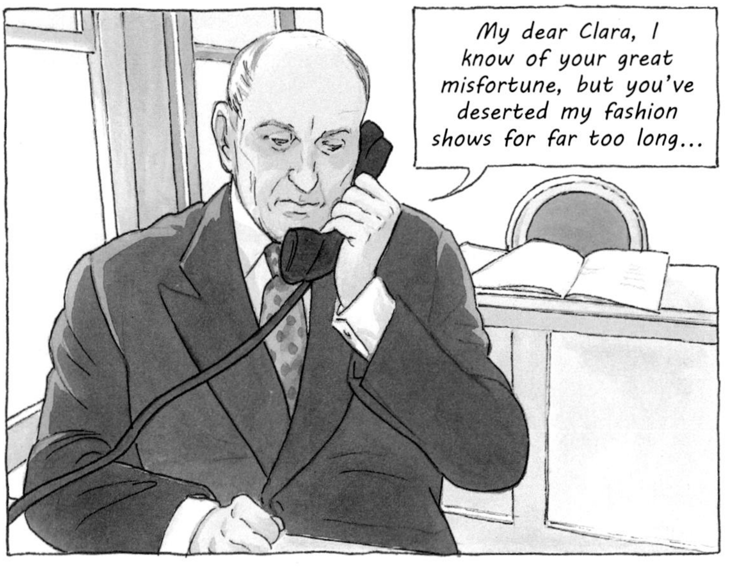
My dear Clara, I know of your great misfortune, but you've deserted my fashion shows for far too long...
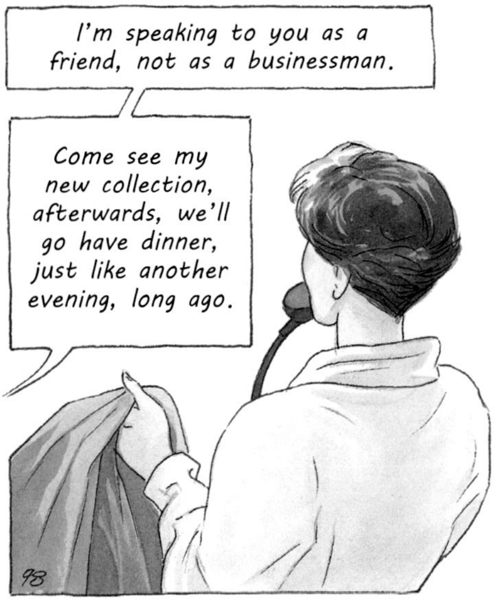
I'm speaking to you as a friend, not as a businessman.
Come see my new collection, afterwards, we'll go have dinner, just like another evening, long ago.

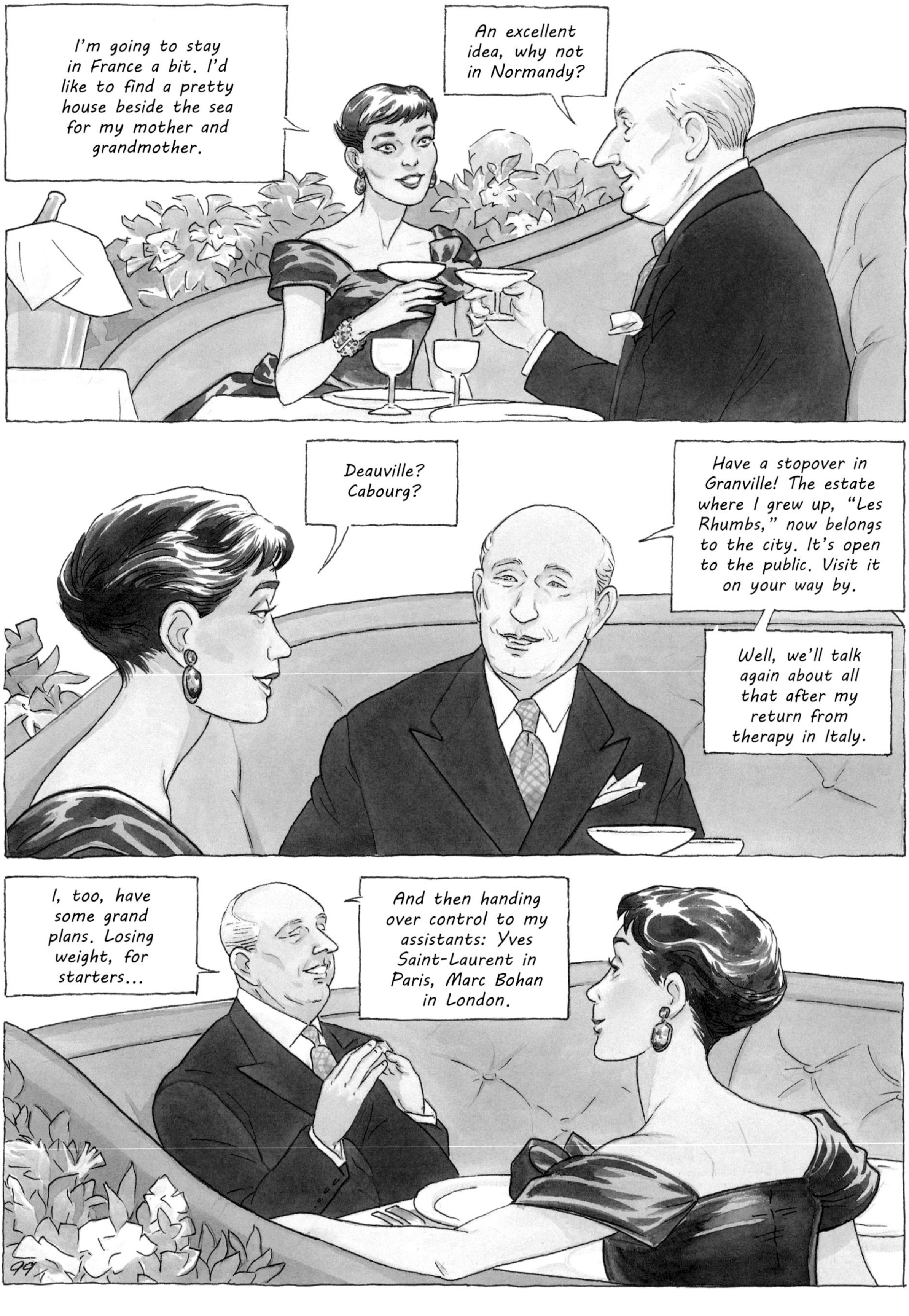

I'm going to stay in France a bit. I'd like to find a pretty house beside the sea for my mother and grandmother.
An excellent idea, why not in Normandy?
Deauville? Cabourg?
Have a stopover in Granville! The estate where I grew up, "Les Rhumbs," now belongs to the city. It's open to the public. Visit it on your way by.
Well, we'll talk again about all that after my return from therapy in Italy.
I, too, have some grand plans. Losing weight, for starters...
And then handing over control to my assistants: Yves Saint-Laurent in Paris, Marc Bohan in London.

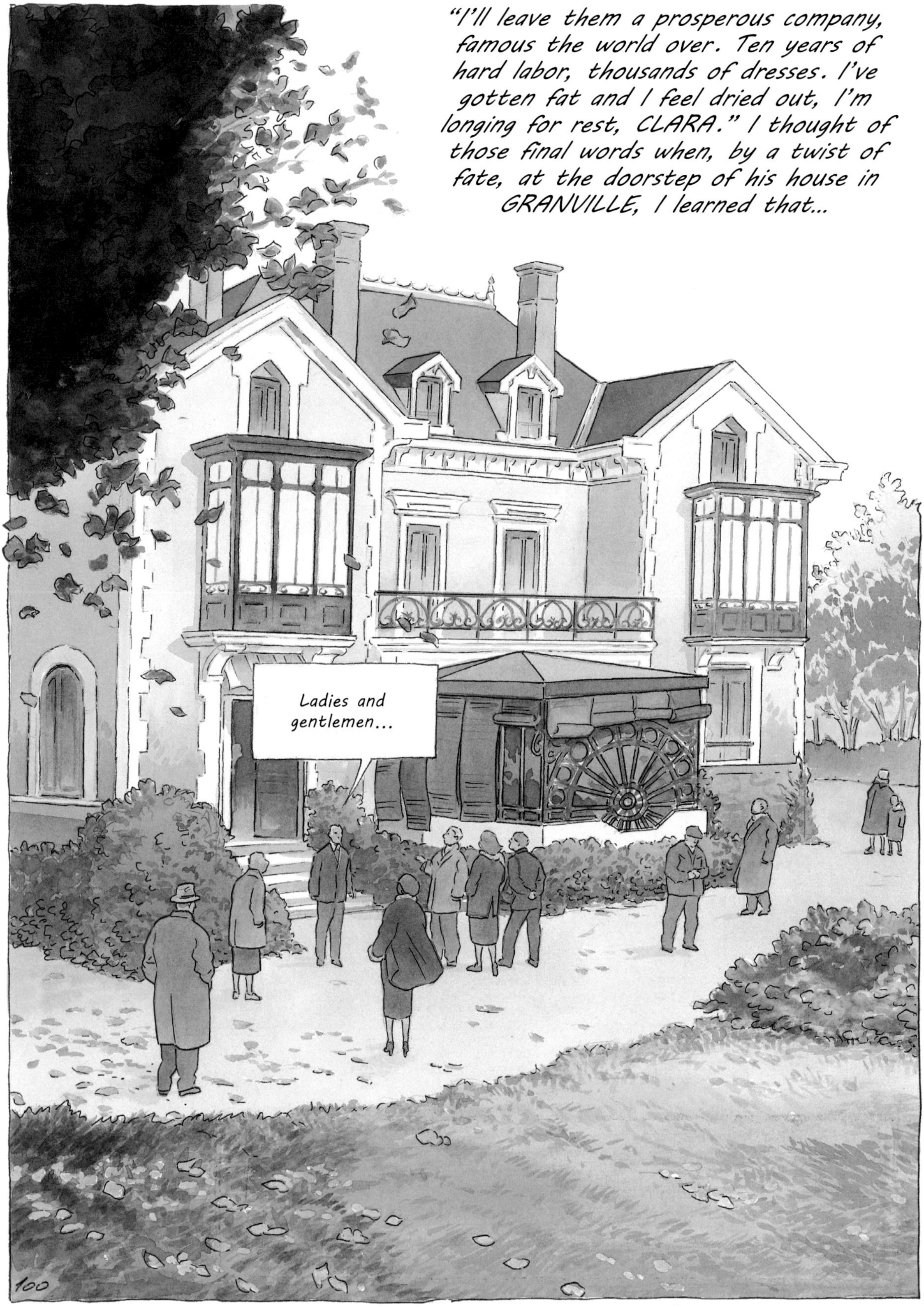
"I'll leave them a prosperous company, famous the world over. Ten years of hard labor, thousands of dresses. I've gotten fat and I feel dried out, I'm longing for rest, CLARA." I thought of those final words when, by a twist of fate, at the doorstep of his house in GRANVILLE, I learned that...
Ladies and gentlemen...
100

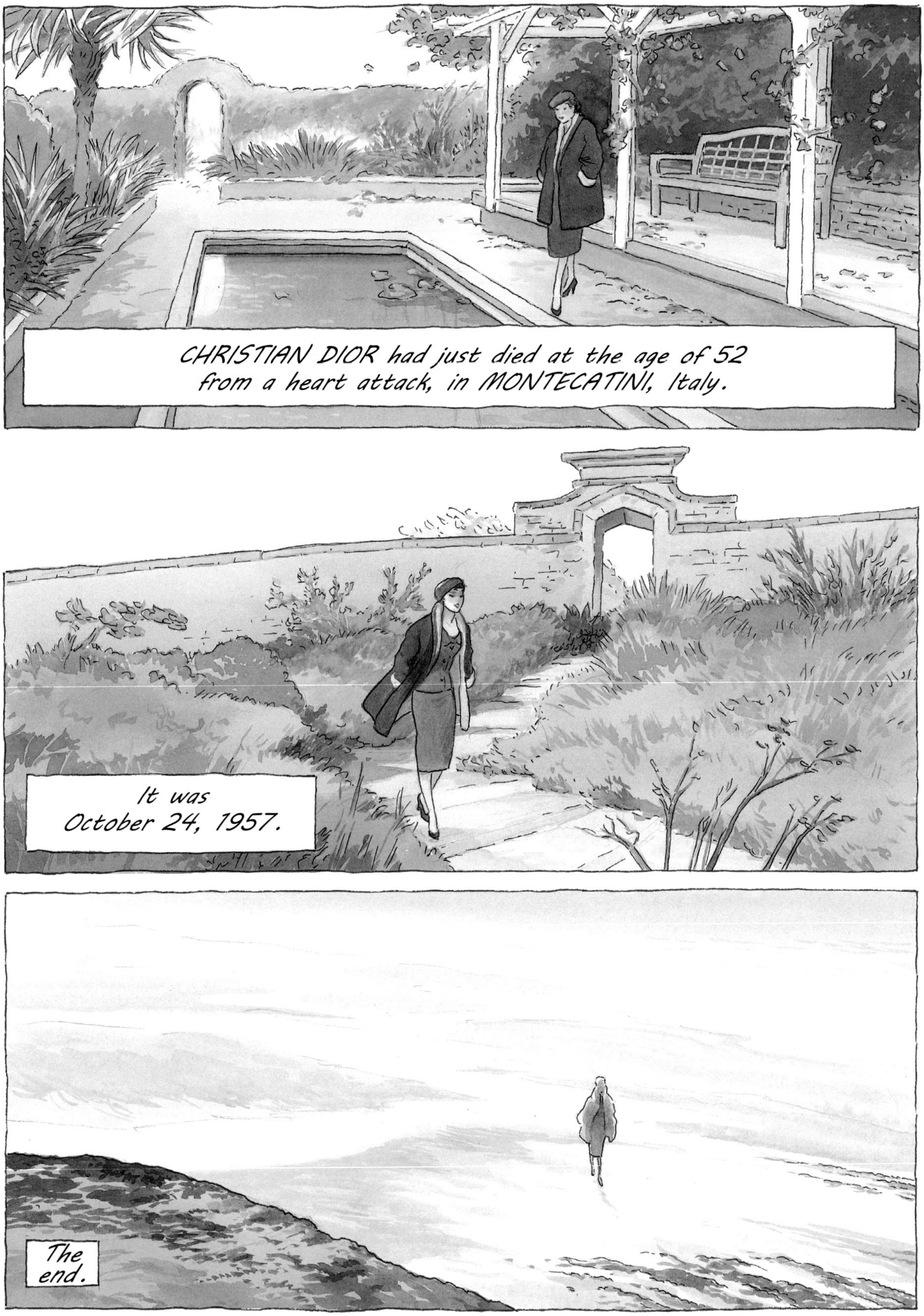

CHRISTIAN DIOR had just died at the age of 52 from a heart attack, in MONTECATINI, Italy.
It was October 24, 1957.
The end.

The elegant and distinguished Clara Nohant, "the girl in Dior" with a little something of Audrey Hepburn, is a fictional character. Her tale is intertwined with that of Monsieur Christian Dior during the final ten years of his life, between 1947, when he created his fashion house, and 1957, the year of his sudden demise.

———

Over the course of ten years, Christian Dior became a legend of the fashion world, a tireless creator, and a boss loved by his employees.

CHRONOLOGICAL REFERENCE POINTS

1905

Birth of Christian Dior on January 21 in Granville.
Parents: Monsieur Alexandre-Louis-Maurice Dior and
Madame Marie-Madeleine Dior, née Martin. He's the
second of five children : Raymond, the eldest, himself,
Jacqueline, Bernard, and Catherine. The Dior
family moves into the villa Les Rhumbs.

1910

The family moves to Paris.

1923-1926

Attends the École des Sciences Politiques.
Makes many friends. Along with Henri Sauguet,
Pierre Gaxotte, and Jean Ozenne, he forms
a little club that regularly meets in a bar, the Tip Top,
on Rue Tronchet, or at the Medrano Circus. Also
makes good friends in painting circles, such as
Christian Bérard and Max Jacob, whose
works he'll display in his gallery.

1927

Military service.

1928

Opens an art gallery with his friend Jacques Bonjean.
Displays paintings by Bérard, Chirico, Tchelitchev,
Braque, Dufy, Laurencin, Léger, Lurçat, Max Jacob,
Picasso, Francis Rose, and sculptures
by Maillol, Zamoyski, Zadkine.

1931

Death of his mother.
Goes on research trips to Russia with a
group of architects. Father goes bankrupt,
a result of the 1929 stock market crash.

1932-34

Closing of the Jacques Bonjean gallery.
Associates himself with Pierre Colle's art gallery,
especially interested in surrealism.
His first exhibition will be dedicated to Salvador Dalí.

1934

February: experiences a bout of tuberculosis
April to November: convalescence in Font-Romeu,
then in the Baleares.

1935

Lives at Jean Ozenne's home, who encourages
him to do fashion design drawings.

1935-1938

Sale of sketches of dresses and hats to
various fashion houses.
He draws for the fashion pages of
Le Figaro and the Jardin des Modes.

1936

Lives at the Hôtel de Bourgogne,
Rue Royale, Paris, 1st Arr.

1937

Lives in an apartment at 10, Rue Royale, Paris, 1st Arr.

1938

Becomes a dress designer at Robert Piguet's. Designs
three collections there. Creates the design "Café anglais,"
with which he makes a nale for himself.

1939

Mobilized, after July, as a private first class in
the engineering corps at Mehun-sur-Yèvre.

1940

Demobilized, he rejoins his father and sister
at Callian, in the Var, where he becomes a farmer.

1941

In December, becomes a dress designer at Lucien Lelong's.

1946

Financed by Marcel Broussac, Christian Dior leaves
Lelong's to establish his own fashion house, which opens
in December at 30, Avenue Montaigne, Paris, 8th arr.
Three sewing rooms (two "multi-purpose" and
one for "suits"); 85 people.
Jacques Rouet is the general manager.
Interior design by Victor Grandpierre.
Christian Bérard does the décor in the
"Boutique des colifichets," the accessories shop

1947

Wednesday, February 12th: presentation of the first
collection, Printemps-Été 1947 ("Spring-Summer 1947")
with two lines, "Corolle" and "En 8," which were the
origin of the expression "New Look" employed by Carmel
Snow, the head editor of Harper's Bazaar.
Opening of two additional sewing rooms.
A movement takes shape in the United States, "The Little
Below the Knee Club," to protest against the length of
skirts. September: awarding to Monsieur Christian Dior
of the "Oscar" of fashion by Mr. Stanley Marcus in Dallas,

in the United States. Christian Dior travels for a market study across the United States (New York, Dallas, Los Angeles, San Francisco, Chicago)

1947

March 4th: creation of the company Christian Dior Parfums, under the management of Monsieur Serge Heftler-Louiche. December 1st: launch of the perfume Miss Dior.

1948

Opening of the department "Fourrures Christian Dior." The management of the hat-making workshop is entrusted to Mitzah Bricard. Creation of the Christian Dior New York Inc. at the corner of 5th Avenue and 57th St. Purchase of the Courdret mill in Milly-la-Forêt.

1949

Launch of a line of stockings in the United States. Launch of the perfume Diorama.

1950

April 26th: private Dior showing for the Queen of England and Princess Margaret, at the French embassy in London. First line of ties "Christian Dior Ties" with Stern, Merritt & Co. in the United States. Creation of the Christian Dior Furs Inc. in New York. Creation of the department "Christian Dior Diffusion" responsible for coordinating the entirety of wholesale operations, exports, and concession licensing. Creation in New York of the company Christian Dior Export, grouping together various departments: hats, gloves, handbags, jewelry, and ties. Contract with the Palacio de Hiero, in Mexico City. Awarding of the Légion d'honneur to Monsieur Christian Dior, in honor of the impetus given to the textile industry and fashion design workers. Creation of the dresses for Marlene Dietrich in the Alfred Hitchcock film *Stage Fright*. Purchase of a townhome at 7, Boulevard Jules-Sandeau, Paris, 6th arr. Purchase of the property "la Colle Noire" in Montauroux.

1951

Creation of the division "stockings and gloves." Contract with Holt Renfrew & Co. in Canada. 900 people comprise the personnel of the Dior fashion house. Creation of the suits for Marlene Dietrich in Henry Koster's film *No Highway in the Sky*. Publication of *Je suis couturier*, the first book by Christian Dior.

1952

Creation of the company Christian Dior Models Ltd in London. Annexation of the entire building at 13, Rue François-Ier.

1953

Opening of the boutique Christian Dior in Caracas, in association with Cartier. Creation of the Dior lipstick inspired by high fashion and composed of 8 base tints. Creation of the first line of custom-made shoes in collaboration with Roger Vivier.

1954

Seven years after the New Look, Christian Dior makes an impression with his "H" line, called the "haricot" or "flat look" line. Fashion show at Blenheim Palace before Princess Margaret and the Duchess of Marlborough. In Paris, the Dior house employs 1,000 people, occupies 28 sewing rooms, and 5 buildings.

1955

Opening of the boutique at the corner of Avenue Montaigne and Rue François-Ier. Opening of a department of ready-to-wear shoes designed by Roger Vivier and produced by Charles Jourdan. Creation of a "girdles and bosom" line in association with the Scandale house. Launch of the first line of costume jewelry with Henkel & Grosse. August 3rd: conference at the Sorbonne by Christian Dior, titled "L'esthétique de la mode" (The Esthetic of Fashion). Yves Saint-Laurent's begins at the studio.

1956

Publication of the designer's memoirs, *Christian Dior et moi*, at Éditions Amiot-Dumont.

1957

Marc Bohan becomes the artistic director at Dior London. March 4th: Christian Dior appears on the cover of Time. On its own, the house produces more than 50% of exports of French haute couture. October 24th: Christian Dior dies of a heart attack in Montecatini, where he was at a health spa. After a ceremony in Paris on October 29th, at the Saint-Honoré-d'Eylau church, he was buried on October 30th in Callian.

DIOR IN 22 COLLECTIONS

1947
Printemps – Été (Spring – Summer)
COROLLE AND EN 8. (Corolla and In 8.)

Automne – Hiver (Fall – Winter)
COROLLE (Corolla)

―――――――

1948
Printemps – Été
ZIG-ZAG AND ENVOL (Takeoff)

Automne – Hiver
AILÉE (Winged)

―――――――

1949
Printemps – Été
TROMPE-L'ŒIL

Automne – Hiver
MILIEU DU SIÈCLE (Mid-Century)

―――――――

1950
Printemps – Été
VERTICALE

Automne – Hiver
OBLIQUE

―――――――

1951
Printemps – Été
NATURELLE (Natural)

Automne – Hiver
LONGUE (Long)

―――――――

1952
Printemps – Été
SINUEUSE (Sinuous)

Automne – Hiver
PROFILÉE (Contoured)

―――――――

1953
Printemps – Été
TULIPE (Tulip)

Automne – Hiver
VIVANTE (Living)

―――――――

1954
Printemps – Été
MUGUET (Lily of the Valley)

Automne – Hiver
H

―――――――

1955
Printemps – Été
A

Automne – Hiver
Y

―――――――

1956
Printemps – Été
FLÈCHE (Arrow)

Automne – Hiver
AIMANT (Magnet)

―――――――

1957
Printemps – Été
LIBRE (Free)

Automne – Hiver
FUSEAU (Spindle)

CHRISTIAN DIOR'S ENTOURAGE

Bacall, Lauren
(1924 – 2014)
Howard Hawks spots her on the cover of Harper's Bazaar in 1943. He hires her to perform in *To Have and Have Not* alongside Humphrey Bogart. She marries him in 1945. They are a model couple until the actor's death in 1957. They perform together in three films after *To Have and Have Not, The Big Sleep, Dark Passage, and Key Largo.*

Ballard, Bettina
(1905 – 1961)
Head editor of Vogue from 1934 to 1961. Just like Carmel Snow, she attends Christian Dior's first fashion show and is witness to the emergence of the *New Look*.

Balmain, Pierre
(1914 – 1982)
French fashion designer. After having worked alongside Lucien Lelong, Pierre Balmain creates his own fashion house in 1945, which he'll direct his entire life.

La Bégum
(1906 – 2000)
By her real name Yvette Labrousse, she becomes Miss France in 1930 and experiences an unusual destiny when she marries the Aga Khan III, in 1944.
She was always very passionate about high fashion, her mother having had a career as a seamstress.

Bérard, Christian
(1902 – 1949)
Also known by the name "Bébé," a nickname used by his friends.
He displays his works in the art gallery run by Jacques Bonjean and Christian Dior. The latter entrusts him with the interior design of the "boutique de colifichets" or accessories shop at the opening of the fashion house.

Bobby
That's the name of Christian Dior's dog. Dior had a habit of naming all of his dogs "Bobby." Beginning in 1950, moreover, he created a "Bobby" suit for each of his collections.

Bogart, Humphrey
(1899 – 1957)
After his beginnings in the era of silent films, he becomes one of the most solid actors in the Thirties, then one of the most mythical characters on American screens between 1942 and 1957.

Bohan, Marc
(1926 -)
The son of a milliner, he learns his trade with Patou, Piguet, and Molyneux.
He joins Dior in 1957.
In 1960, he leads the management of the Dior fashion house, succeeding Yves-Saint Laurent in this position, who'd occupied it since Christian Dior's death.
He will continue there until 1989.

Boussac, Marcel
(1889 – 1980)
The founder of the CIC *(Comptoir de l'industrie cotonnière)* in 1917, horse-breeder, and press magnate (*L'Aurore* and *Paris-Turf*). In 1945, he meets Christian Dior and allows him to create his fashion house by investing large sums of money.
The Boussac empire decays progressively during the Seventies. He goes bankrupt in 1978 and dies ruined two years later.

Bricard, Mitzah

(? – 1983)

Legend has it that she was a kept woman in her younger days. An elegant muse and shrewd counselor, Christian Dior entrusts her with the creation of hats.

Carré, Marguerite

(? – 1998)

Former head-seamstress at Patou's, she is hired at the Dior house along with her entourage of 30 qualified seamstresses around the end of 1946.

The designer creates for her the position of technical manager of the workshops which she will manage devotedly.

Cocteau, Jean

(1889 – 1963)

French writer, author of novels, poems, films, and drawings. Christian Dior's longstanding friend, he defines the designer thus: "That nimble genius unique to our times whose magical name is composed of *Dieu* (God) and *or* (gold)."

Colle, Carmen

(? – 1983)

The wife of the gallery owner Pierre Colle, one of Dior's intimate friends, with whom he associates between 1931 and 1934 to organize exhibitions. She is in charge of the first accessories shop on the ground floor of the designing house.

Dietrich, Marlene

(1901 – 1992)

German actress and singer principally known for her roles in *The Blue Angel* and *Shanghai Express*. Christian Dior's friend, she imposes the designer upon Alfred Hitchcock for her costumes in *Stage Fright* declaring: "No Dior, no Dietrich!"

Doutreleau, Victoire

(1934 -)

Star model in the Dior house beginning in 1953.

A friend of Karl Lagerfeld and Yves Saint Laurent, she rejoins the latter once he creates his own fashion house in 1962. She manages his salons until 1964.

Edward VIII

(1894 – 1972)

King of the United Kingdom of Great Britain, Northern Ireland, the Commonwealth, and Emperor of India, from January to December 1936. He abdicates in favor of his younger brother Albert, in order to marry Wallis Simpson in 1937. He thereupon receives the title of duke of Windsor.

Countess Greffulhe

(1860 – 1952)

Marie Joséphine Anatole Louise Élisabeth de Riquet de Caraman-Chimay, countess Henry Greffulhe.

She was the inspiration for the character of the duchess de Guermantes in Marcel Proust's Remembrance of Things Past. A great admirer of Dior's work.

Hayworth, Rita

(1918 – 1987)

Legendary actess of American cinema, notably for her roles in *Gilda*, *Angels over Broadway*, and *The Lady from Shanghai*.

Marries Orson Welles in 1943, then Ali Khan in 1949. An admirer of Dior's work from the start, she attends his first fashion show.

Lachaume

During his fashion shows, Christian Dior loved for his salons to be adorned with flowers from Lachaume's, a master florist since 1845.

Lazareff, Hélène

(1909 – 1988)

A journalist of *Paris-Soir* and *Marie-Claire*, she exiles herself to New York, along with her husband Pierre Lazareff, during the Second World War.

She discovers American journalism at *Harper's Bazaar* and the *New York Times*.

Returning to France, she founds the magazine *Elle* in 1945, which she will run until 1973.

Lelong, Lucien
(1889 – 1958)

French fashion designer. Considered to
be the savior of French haute couture
during the Occupation, he hires Christian Dior
as a dress designer in 1941. He closes his fashion
house in 1948 and dies of a heart attack during the
night of May 11, 1958, six months after Christian Dior.

Luling, Suzanne
(? – 1988)

Childhood friend of the designer. Christian Dior
entrusts the management of the salons and sales
to her, after the creation of the fashion house.

Marcus, Stanley
(1905 – 2002)

Manager of the American luxury department
chain Neiman Marcus, which he will run until 1975.
He awards a Fashion Oscar to Christian Dior
during a ceremony in Dallas in 1947.

Poiret, Paul
(1879 - 1944)

French fashion designer much admired by Dior.
He begins his career with Jacques Doucet's
fashion house and establishes his own house in 1903.
Known for his daring, he revolutionizes the
female figure by getting rid of the corset.
The Orientalism then in fashion and Diaghilev's Ballets
Russes inspire him with their forms and colors.
He creates the controversial harem-pants and
hobble-skirt. A victim of the 1929 crash,
he's forced to retire. He dies poor and forgotten.

Rouët, Jacques
(1918 – 2002)

The fashion house's administrative and financial manager
after its creation. He becomes the overall manager after
Dior's death in 1957, a role
which he will occupy until 1983.

Saint Laurent, Yves
(1936 – 2008)

French fashion designer who began working
at Dior's in 1955. Art direction is entrusted
to him after the death of Christian Dior. Called
up for his military service in 1960, he won't
rejoin the fashion house, and instead
creates his own house in 1962, in association
with Pierre Bergé. He ends his career in 2002
and dies six years later.

Simpson, Wallis
(1896 – 1986)

An American divorced from E. W. Spencer, remarried to E.
A. Simpson, she begins a relationship with Edward, Prince
of Wales, in 1934.
The latter, having become Edward VIII, abandons his crown
and titles in order to marry her in France in 1937.
She thereupon becomes the Duchess of Windsor.

Snow, Carmel
(1887 – 1961)

Very influential American journalist.
Fashion editor at *Vogue*, then editor-in-chief
of *Harper's Bazaar*.
She's the one who labels Christian Dior's first collection as
the *New Look*, when she attends the February 12, 1947
fashion show.

Windsor, Margaret
(1930 – 2002)

Daughter of the duke of York (the future King George VI)
and of Lady Elizabeth (née Bowes-Lyon). Younger sister of
the present queen of England, Elizabeth II.

Zehnacker, Raymonde
(? – 1989)

A studio manager at Lelong's, she'd said to Christian Dior:
"I'll follow you wherever you go."
And so she becomes, the director of his studio in 1947.
The designer defined her as "my second self."

CAREERS IN THE FASHION WORLD

Aboyeuse
The second sales assistant who's in
charge of announcing the names of
the design patterns and their numbers,
in both French and English.
In English known as the 'emcee'.

Arpète
An entry-level position or apprentice in
a career as a seamstress or dress-maker.
She runs errands between the
workshops and various services.
Nicknamed "hallway rabbit" because
she runs around more than she's seated.

Camériste
A chambermaid.

Coupeuse
A qualified, first seamstress who
cuts the linen of the patterns.

Modéliste
A male or female dress designer
who elaborates a pattern and
constructs a prototype. He or she works the
linen directly on a bust mannequin in the
workshop to establish the garment's
form and volume.

Picoteuse
Workers who hem fabrics on machines.

Premier or première d'atelier
The head tailor or head seamstress.
Responsible for the team of seamstresses in a
workshop: the apprentices and the "qualified"
or "highly qualified" first, second, third
seamstresses. The head's role is to
interpret the designer's sketch to
create a first draft on a mannequin,
then cut it in linen, and assemble it for
the first fitting of the model.

There are four kinds of workshops
Tailleur
(Suit ensembles and coats);
Flou
(Daytime, cocktail, evening,
short and long dresses);
Fourrure
(Fur coats, stoles, collars, facing);
Chapeaux
(hats).

Placeur or placeuse
Ushers who attend to seating the guests
according to their importance and their
affinities, during fashion shows.

FABRICS

Alpaca
A fabric composed of wool fibers, silk or
cotton, and hair from the alpaca
(a cousin of the lama).

Brocade
A method of weaving, which forms designs
spread over the fabric.

Crêpe
Light, cotton or silk material. The most used
varieties: "crêpe de Chine" or "georgette."

Faille
A ribbed, silk fabric.

Flanel
A light wool or cotton material
that's brushed or carded.

Jersey
A knitted material, fashioned from wool,
cotton, silk or synthetic fibers.

Muslin
A flowing, light, supple, transparent material
made of silk, cotton or wool.

Organdy or organza
A sheer cotton or silk material with
a more rigid finish than muslin.

Reps
A very thick fabric made of wool or silk.

Shantung
A coarse silk fabric with a knobbly weave.

Surab
A soft, light twilled silk.

Taffeta
A light-weight silk fabric, woven like linen.

Linen
A fabric made of flax, hemp or
cotton used to fashion the test garment.
Light-weight for dresses; thicker for
suits and coats. Of a white or
light beige color.

Tulle
A very light, transparent fabric of cotton or
silk, with round stiches or spaced polygonals.

Tweed
A wool cloth with a linen or twill weaves,
generally of two colors.

Velvet
A fabric smooth on one side
and covered on the other with a
lustrous, thick, close pile, supported
by the threads of the fabric.
Made of cotton, silk, or wool.

Silk velvet or panne velvet
A lustrous fabric of flattened pile
made of silk or rayon.

ACCESSORIES

Colifichets (Frivolities)
Little objects, accessories,
and small costume jewelry.

Gloves
"In the city, an outfit is incomplete without
gloves and a hat. In the evening, nothing is
more prestigious than very long gloves climbing
to the height of the shoulder or, in a more
conventional fashion, just above the elbow. I
have a preference for natural colors:
black, white, beige or brown."
*Christian Dior's Little Dictionary
of Fashion* (1954).

Bodice
A piece of lingerie that's more supple and
shorter than the corset. Like it, the bodice
shapes the waist and supports the bosom.
It can also function as a garter belt.

Hat
"A hat makes you look merry, solemn,
dignified, happy—sometimes even ugly if
you've chosen badly! A hat is the quintessence
of femininity with all the frivolity that such
a word gives one to imagine. And whether it
be with clothing, handbags or hats: a single
principle: always choose the
most noble materials."
*Christian Dior's Little Dictionary
of Fashion* (1954).

Shoes
"You can never take enough precaution
in the choice of your shoes.

[...] Pumps go with everything.
I don't at all like fancy shoes and,
except at night, I don't appreciate colored
shoes very much. In your choice, it's important
to respect two essential principles: first
of all, quality leather or suede, then a classic
style, simple. What's best is in black, brown,
white, and navy-blue (white shoes nonetheless
have a tendency to elongate the foot).
Heels shouldn't be too flat, or too high,
which lacks elegance. In all cases, comfort
is essential. Uncomfortable shoes will
alter your gait and harm your elegance."
*Christian Dior's Little Dictionary
of Fashion* (1954).

Handbag
"You can wear the best suit from
morning till night, but to be perfect,
don't use the same handbag. In the morning,
it must be simple; for the evening, smaller,
and if you like, a little more fancy.
The most beautiful handbags are
always the most simple and
most classic
ones, of quality leather.
Bargain leather isn't always a good
deal; not having any flair, it can even
turn out to cost very dear. [...] Don't forget,
a handbag isn't a trinket bowl. You can't
simultaneously fill it with a pile of useless
things and hope it'll be pretty and last
a long time. Like all of your clothes, your
handbag deserves your attention."
*Christian Dior's Little Dictionary
of Fashion* (1954).

BIBLIOGRAPHY

Works by Christian Dior

Je suis couturier (I'm a fashion designer)
(Collection "Mon Métier")
Éditions du Conquistador, 1951

Dior by Dior
Victoria and Albert Museum, 2007.

Christian Dior's Little Dictionary of Fashion
Cassell & Co Ltd, 1954.

———

Biographical Works

Christian Dior: The Biography
Marie-France Pochna
Overlook TP, 2009.

Double Dior
Isabelle Rabineau
Denoël, 2012

———

Works on Christian Dior and Fashion

Fashion in the Forties and Fifties
Jane Dorner
Ian Allan Publishing, 1975

Christian Dior
Françoise Giroud and Sacha Van Dorssen
Rizzoli, 1989

Fashion Under the Occupation
Dominique Vallon
Bloomsbury Academic, 2002

*Hidden Underneath:
A History of Lingerie*
Farid Chenoune
Assouline, 2005

The New Look: The Dior Revolution
Nigel Cawthorne
The Wellfleet Press, 1998

Monsieur Dior et nous, 1947-1957
(Mr. Dior and Us, 1947-1957)
Edited collection.
Anthèse, 1999

Christian Dior: Man of the Century
Jean-Luc Defresne
Éditions Artlys, 2011

Christian Dior et le monde
(Christian Dior and the World)
Catalog of the Christian Dior Museum of Granville
Edited collection
Éditions Artlys, 2006

Le Grand Bal Dior (The Great Dior Ball)
Catalog of the Christian Dior Museum of Granville
Éditions Artlys, 2010

Dans les coulisses de la haute couture parisienne,
Souvenirs d'un mannequin-vedette
(Behind the Scenes of Parisian High Fashion,
Memories of a Star Model)
Freddy
Flammarion, 1956

Et Dior créa Victoire
(And Dior Created Victoire)
Victoire Doutreleau
Robert Laffont, 1997

———————

Magazines

Life, March 24, 1947
Paris-Match, November 2, 1957
L'Officiel, "1 000 modèles Dior, 60 ans de creation,"
(1,000 Dior Clothing Models, 60 Years of Creation),
81 (January 2008).

I owe my first memories of making clothes to my grandmothers Marguerite and Suzanne, who fashioned dresses, coats, and blouses for me during my childhood. I remember yards of fabric on the table, chalk markings, the precise bite of the scissors, the pins on the floor that I gathered up with a magnet; the box where I'd find single buttons or similar buttons by the threes, fours or sixes, which I'd thread onto a cotton string. There was a very lovely one, made of a porcelain graced with delicate, hand-painted flowers, and others, of metal, memories of a soldier's uniform.

So, my first acknowledgments go to Madame Paule Boncoure, and to Madame Geneviève Leizour, the marvelous head seamstresses in the workshops of Christian Dior after 1947, as well as Madame Marinella Godefroy, the second seamstress, and to Madame Sylvie Ledoux, of human resources, who introduced them to me.

To Monsieur Sidney Toledano, the CEO of Christian Dior Couture, Monsieur Olivier Bialobos, communications director, thanks to whom I had special access to the private townhouse at 30, Avenue Montaigne.
To Monsieur Jérôme Gautier, editing director, Madame Soizic Pfaff, archivist, Madame Solène Auréal, filing clerk, Monsieur Philippe Le Moult, director of institutional relations, who lavished advice and documents on me, precious for the veracity of the story.

To Madame Pierrette Rosset, Monsieur Pierre Lebedel, faithful journalist friends, who investigated their memories.
To Monsieur Pierre Christin, another faithful friend, who drove me to Granville and to Milly-la-Forêt. He wisely looked over my story, he who writes such beautiful ones for others… and for me.

The elegance of the masculine characters owe much to François Pillu, bookseller, who gave me rare catalogs from the Fifties.

But I dedicate this book to another "Girl in Dior," Léa (1992-2013).
All the while considering Pauline Mermet, editor, as this work's godmother.

ANNIE GOETZINGER

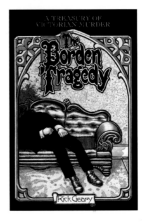